THE CHURCH AND THE
CRISIS OF COMMUNITY

The Church and the Crisis of Community

*A Practical Theology
of Small-Group Ministry*

Theresa F. Latini

WILLIAM B. EERDMANS PUBLISHING COMPANY

GRAND RAPIDS, MICHIGAN / CAMBRIDGE, U.K.

Published 2011 by
Wm. B. Eerdmans Publishing Co.
2140 Oak Industrial Drive N.E., Grand Rapids, Michigan 49505 /
P.O. Box 163, Cambridge CB3 9PU U.K.

Printed in the United States of America

17 16 15 14 13 12 11   7 6 5 4 3 2 1

Library of Congress Cataloging-in-Publication Data

Latini, Theresa F.
The church and the crisis of community:
a practical theology of small-group ministry / Theresa F. Latini.
p.   cm.
Includes bibliographical references (p.   ).
ISBN 978-0-8028-6586-1 (pbk.: alk. paper)
1. Church group work. 2. Small groups — Religious aspects — Christianity.
3. Communities — Religious aspects — Christianity. I. Title.

BV652.2.L37 2011
253'.7 — dc22

2011005873

www.eerdmans.com

Contents

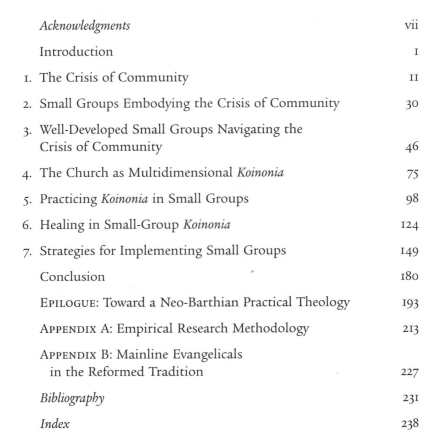

Acknowledgments

＝＝＝＝

I am reminded of the wisdom spoken to me many years ago by one of my mentors: "We are only as good as the people with whom we surround ourselves." If that is true, and I believe it is, then I am indebted to many colleagues, friends, and family members who have surrounded me as I have written this book. And if this book contributes to the church's ministry in today's world, then it does so, in large part, because of their camaraderie, support, and counsel. Among this "great cloud of witnesses" in my life, a few stand out for special mention. Kenda Creasy Dean, Deborah van Deusen Hunsinger, George Hunsinger, and Richard R. Osmer intellectually nurtured the first incarnation of this project during my doctoral program at Princeton Theological Seminary. Their theological acumen, conceptual clarity, and love for the church have shaped not only my thinking but also my vocation. The Lilly Endowment and the practical theology department of Princeton Theological Seminary provided the funding for me to carry out new empirical research of well-developed small-group ministries. Pastors, leaders, and members of six congregations authentically shared their stories of small-group community with me. Their honesty was refreshing, and their practical insights were inspiring. I could not have finished this manuscript without the generous support of Luther Seminary's study leave and research assistance policies. Hilliard Dogbe, a doctoral student in Luther Seminary's Ph.D. program and a first-rate practical theologian in his own right, helped edit the manuscript. Finally, my husband, Tom, has been a faithful companion, listening to my ideas and caring for the details of our life together so I could complete this book. I am amazed again and again by the ways our connection reflects something of that kind of *koinonia* at the heart of this book, which I dedicate to him with love.

Introduction

Small Groups in American Christianity

Small groups were my entrée into my vocation as a pastoral caregiver and practical theologian. In the early 1990s, I joined an interdenominational small group sponsored by a Presbyterian congregation. Like the other young adults in that group, I was sorting through questions about my Christian faith and identity. More fundamentally, I was searching for a place to belong, a group marked by honesty and authenticity. I found that and much more: I found a healing, missional community that reflected life in the kingdom of God.

We were a diverse group: women and men, African-Americans and Euro-Americans, factory workers, teachers, and church musicians. We read Scripture together, ate together, prayed together, confessed our sin together, and shared our sufferings with one another. We encountered each other and God in the midst of poignant questions and pain. We listened to Miriam's stories of growing up in a rigid cult. We helped Sara construct strategies to individuate from her overbearing mother. We wept with Tom in his depression and despair. We confronted Rich when he spoke harshly to others. We supported Cynthia as she navigated through a series of life changes — marriage and graduate school. We persistently prayed that each of us would experience God as trustworthy and kind, that we would find ways to participate more fully in our respective congregations, that we would fulfill both our common and particular vocations.

I

While far from perfect, that small group nurtured my connection to God, my connection to the larger church, and my connection to myself. It launched me into both broader circles of community and participation in God's work in the world. After three years, I joined the congregation and engaged in its life of worship and service. I co-led a support group and taught Sunday school. After a few more years, I headed to seminary to pursue formal training for ministry.

During my years at seminary, I visited my home church and encountered another small group, one whose effects were disheartening at best, divisive at worst, and undeniably tragic. It started off as an intercessory prayer group composed of longtime church members and leaders who gathered together weekly to pray for congregants who were sick and suffering. They prayed for church leadership to follow the leading of God's Spirit. When they heard about a series of "revival" services at a nearby congregation, they attended in order to experience God in new ways, and they encouraged other congregants to join them. Their sense of God's immanent presence and their hope for the healing of the world was contagious. They were tired of being part of the "frozen chosen," that is, mainline Protestants lacking a living faith. So they encouraged change within the congregation. In doing so, however, they dismissed the church's polity and theology. They unwittingly created two factions within the congregation, those who supposedly were open to the Holy Spirit and those who weren't. Spiritual elitism kept them closed to input from outside sources. Within five years, the congregation split up: all of its groups were dismantled, and its members, who had once worshiped and served God together, were dispersed into multiple congregations.

How could this be? How could one congregation establish two groups with such radically different effects? What contributed to authentic communal spirituality in one group and elitism and disconnect from the Christian tradition in the other? Why were lives transformed in one and rent apart in another?

I was still asking these questions when I became a pastor and a doctoral student in practical theology. As a pastor, I witnessed the ambivalence of small groups from a new vantage point. I watched persons immerse themselves in recovery groups and then emerge transformed, carrying both passion and vision for ministry to the downtrodden and oppressed. I watched others participate in Bible study groups and for the first time understand the grace of God and their acceptance in the body of Christ. I led a ministry team that welcomed those on the fringes of the church back into full fellowship, which itself became a community (rather than simply another church committee). But I also discovered small groups meeting without any clear sense of purpose, structure, or spiritual focus. Some veered away from the Christian tradition and unknowingly settled for the shallowness of popular Christianity in America today. I listened to the heart-rending longings of those unable to find a place to grow spiritually with a group of trusted others.

As a practical theologian, I read formal studies of small groups that not only confirmed my own personal and professional experiences but also indicated that such experiences are shared by a significant number of Americans.[1] In the early to mid-1990s, Robert Wuthnow, the director of the Center for the Study of American Religion at Princeton University, studied the proliferation of small groups in North America. After nearly two thousand interviews and direct observation of various kinds of groups, Wuthnow concluded that the small-group movement represents a search for the sacred and a search for community. Small groups provide a social solvent, a means of enduring detachment from traditional forms of community life, and they create space for spiritual growth and exploration. In other words, people gather in small groups to experience or enhance their connection to God, their connection to others, and often, their connection to their truest selves. Thus it is not surprising that congregations provide the strongest support and the resources — that is, leaders, curricula, space, childcare, a common language, and motivation — for small groups.[2]

Wuthnow also discovered that small groups are a mixed bag.[3] (1) *Small groups foster a personal connection to God:* members feel closer to God, and they pray and read their Bibles more. But they neglect the mystery and transcendence of God. Even though they meet together in a group, their faith tends to be individualistic, subjective, and inwardly

---

1. See Robert Wuthnow, *Sharing the Journey: Support Groups and America's New Quest for Community* (New York: Free Press, 1994). In the early 1990s, 40 percent of Americans from all ages, socioeconomic classes, and races regularly participated in some kind of small group, and another 39 percent had belonged to a small group at some point in their lives.

2. At the time of Wuthnow's research, 60 percent (48 million) of all small-group members belonged to church-based groups.

3. Wuthnow, *Sharing the Journey,* pp. 341-66.

focused. (2) *Small groups foster communal connection:* they provide a structured place to belong, yet members do not have a strong commitment to the group. They can (and do) leave at whim. Members provide emotional support for each other, but they also censure particular kinds of sharing. Unspoken rules suppress certain personal and political topics. Small groups stifle conflict and difference and thus inhibit the growth that can emerge when we encounter those different from us. (3) *Small groups foster personal formation:* group members share personal stories, empathize with each other, and give each other feedback on major life decisions. They help each other cope in a fast-paced, ever-changing world. They tolerate each other but avoid challenging each other. (4) *Small groups foster connection to other communities:* they encourage their members to help others in need and to become more connected to their neighborhoods. Yet they can also become disconnected from congregational life. Many fail to engage the theological tradition of the church. In short, the small group movement "mirrors the shortcomings of its host environment." It embodies problematic aspects of American individualism and "secularity."[4]

Wuthnow ended his study of small groups by saying that the small-group movement was at a critical juncture in its history. He expressed hope that small groups would embody a form of community more consistently faithful to the gospel. He proposed numerous strategies by which small groups could achieve this laudable goal. Over a decade has passed since Wuthnow's study, and small groups have continued to flourish in American congregations. Traditional practices of pastoral care and Christian education increasingly occur in small groups. A vast majority (87 percent) of churches have small groups (other than Sunday school classes) that meet at least monthly for so-

---

4. Wuthnow, *Sharing the Journey,* p. 366. Wuthnow writes: "Secularity is misunderstood if it is assumed to be a force that prevents people from being spiritual at all. It is more aptly conceived as an orientation that encourages a safe, domesticated version of the sacred. From a secular perspective, a divine being is one who is there for our own gratification, like a house pet, rather than one who demands obedience from us, is too powerful or mysterious for us to understand, or who challenges us to a life of service. When spirituality has been tamed, it can accommodate the demands of a secular society. People can go about their daily business without having to alter their lives very much because they are interested in spirituality. Secular spirituality can even be put to good use, making people more effective in their careers, better lovers, and more responsible citizens. This is the kind of spirituality being nurtured in many small groups today" (p. 7).

cial, recreational, and/or religious purposes.[5] Small-group resources — books, manuals, leadership guides, and curricula — have been developed to address some of the ambiguities of small groups. Typically, these resources provide practical strategies for effective small-group ministry. They teach leaders how to facilitate meaningful discussion, how to construct group covenants, how to care for group members, how to pray and study the Bible.[6] A few books go beyond the how-to level and try to define community from a scriptural perspective.[7]

At the same time, the nature of community has changed drastically in the last ten years. We are are mobile society. We uproot our families more frequently than former generations did. We connect with friends, family members, and coworkers through electronic communication. Adolescents and young adults form faceless relationships. Congregations try to sustain community in an era of competing truths, distrust of religious authorities and traditions, and widespread conflict about basic Christian beliefs and practices. Small towns and rural areas are marked by racial-ethnic, socioeconomic, and religious diversity. Such widespread changes in our experience of community lead to pervasive feelings of uncertainty and anxiety, because all of us have a basic need for belonging and trust, for a community in which we discover ourselves and God's intention for our lives.

In light of this crisis of community, the nature of small-group life seems as pertinent — if not more pertinent — than ever. We need to know how Wuthnow's suggestions and these small-group resources have impacted small-group ministry in congregations. Are small groups fostering connection to the worshiping life of congregations? Are they grappling with the Christian faith as it has developed throughout history? Are their members supporting each other emotionally and engaging in corporate confession of sin? Are they helping their members figure out what it means to be a Christian while living in a global community?

---

5. Mark Chaves, *National Congregations Study: Data File and Codebook* (Tucson: University of Arizona, Department of Sociology, 1998).

6. See Jeff Arnold, *The Big Book on Small Groups,* rev. ed. (Downers Grove: Inter-Varsity Press, 2004); Bill Donahue and Russ Robinson, *Walking the Tightrope: Meeting the Challenges Every Small Group Faces* (Grand Rapids: Zondervan, 2003); Thomas Kirkpatrick, *Small Groups in the Church: A Handbook for Creating Community* (Herndon, VA: Alban Institute, 2005).

7. See Julie Gorman, *Community That Is Christian,* 2nd ed. (Grand Rapids: Baker, 2002); Richard Meyer, *One Anothering* (Philadelphia: Innisfree Press, 1999).

These questions about "what small groups do" are only the starting place, however, for those of us who are committed to participating in, leading, and developing church-based small groups. We want to know both what small groups "ought to do" in light of God's work of reconciliation in our world and "how to do it." We want to know how small-group community can be shaped less by our cultural ideals, such as individualism, and more by our faith in the triune God. We want to know how small groups can foster authentic spiritual community where lives are formed and transformed by the Spirit of God. These are the questions and issues that propelled me to study small groups and to write this book. To answer these questions, I invite you to join me on a practical theological journey, where our understanding of community, small groups, and the church intersect in creative and illuminating ways. Before we begin, however, I'd like to map the terrain, because we can take this journey whenever questions arise about the faithfulness and effectiveness of ministry.

Toward a Practical Theology of Small-Group Ministry

In the mid-1980s, seminary professors and concerned church leaders began to rethink and reconfigure the study of ministerial arts: preaching, pastoral care, Christian education, and church administration. They wanted to bridge a number of divisions — those between congregations and seminaries, between pastors and professors, between theology and the practice of ministry, between the church and public life — so that seminaries and congregations could work together in participating in God's work in the world. This book flows from and within this stream of reform and seeks to bridge these divides as well. It draws on the wisdom of congregations with well-developed small-group ministries and the wisdom of the theological tradition, particularly ecclesiology (the study of the church). It explores the crisis of community in the United States today and the role of small groups in mitigating this crisis. It constructs guidelines for small-group ministry on the basis of nuanced understandings of (1) the context in which we minister today, (2) the nature of the church, and (3) the nature of God's action in the world. In other words, this book not only presents a practical theology of small-group ministry but also demonstrates *how to do* practical theology.

Practical theology often begins with questions arising from our ev-

6

eryday experience, especially in the church. Conflicts, problems, and concerns about effective and faithful church practices, such as small groups, confront congregations and seminaries every day. Sometimes these questions call for extended analysis. They beseech us to slow down and critically reflect on what is happening in the world, what is happening in the church, and what God is doing in the church and the world. In other words, conundrums in ministry summon us to interpret three forms of action, or practice: societal, ecclesial, and divine. Our goal is to reform current church life and ministry (ecclesial practice) according to the life-act of God (divine practice) for the sake of the world (societal practice).[8] We assess the practice of the church in light of God's practice as revealed to us in the life and death of Jesus Christ. We then seek to conform the church's practice to God's practice. The church's practice must be contextually relevant as well. Just as God in Jesus Christ entered fully into the human predicament, so the church's actions should meet persons, families, and communities in the midst of their deepest need. In other words, the church lives at the intersection of God's action and the world's action (see diagram below).

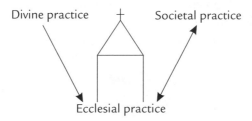

Divine practice   Societal practice

Ecclesial practice

In this book I present a practical theology of small groups (ecclesial practice) that seeks to help the church live more faithfully at this intersection between God's work of reconciliation (divine practice) and the yearning for community in the United States today (societal practice). I explore in depth the crisis of community, and I argue that the church has

8. The phrases "practice," "practices," and "action" are used anything but sparingly — and often in contradictory ways — in the contemporary literature of practical theology. In my usage, "practice" and "action" are synonymous with one another. They refer to an overall gestalt of thinking, speaking, and behaving, or — more colloquially — a way of being in the world. In contrast, "practices" — as in small-group practices — refer to specific communal, tradition-bearing activities that generate knowledge and values intrinsic to the practices themselves. "Action" and "practice" are larger conceptual categories — umbrella categories, so to speak — that influence the development of practices.

responded to this crisis by developing small-group ministries. I examine the strengths and weaknesses of these small groups, particularly the ways that small-group members connect with God, each other, their congregations, and people outside the church. I also study the Word of God and the work of God in Jesus Christ to better understand what God intends to do in the church and in the world. On the basis of all this, I propose guidelines to help small groups become fully integrated into the mission of the church and thus the mission of God in a world that desperately needs authentic, life-transforming spiritual community.

This book constructs these guidelines for small-group ministry by moving through four tasks, or operations, of practical theology. In his book *Practical Theology: An Introduction,* Rick Osmer demonstrates that ministers and professors of practical theology carry out four tasks whenever they encounter challenging situations in the church. These four tasks — the descriptive-empirical, interpretive, normative, and pragmatic — are the four basic moves in our practical theological journey in this book. In each of these moves we focus on understanding one or more of the three forms of practice mentioned above — divine practice, ecclesial practice, and societal practice. It is important to note that these tasks do not proceed in a strict, linear, or stage-like fashion. We move in and out of these tasks because they are all mutually influential (see the diagram below).

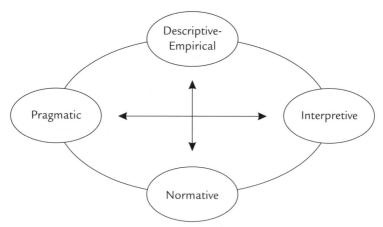

Tasks of Practical Theology[9]

9. Richard R. Osmer, *Practical Theology: An Introduction* (Grand Rapids: Eerdmans, 2008), p. 15.

Descriptive-empirical task. In this task we seek to answer this question: "What is happening in this situation or context?" We gain as much data as possible about a situation or context so that we can describe it from many angles or points of view. We construct what is called a thick description of societal practice or ecclesial practice.

Interpretive task. Here we try to answer this question: "Why is this happening?" We usually draw on theories — sociological, psychological, theological, and so on — to explain our multifaceted depiction of societal practice or ecclesial practice. Though conceptually distinct, the descriptive and interpretive operations of practical theology are not easily divisible. In this book, I begin with the interpretive task. Chapter 1 explains recent changes in community and their impact on interpersonal relationships, religion and spirituality, and personal identity. Chapters 2 and 3 undertake the descriptive-empirical task. Drawing on studies of small-group life, chapter 2 presents the strengths and weaknesses of small groups as both a societal and ecclesial practice. Here we see how groups can foster either life-giving or life-alienating communal spirituality. Chapter 3 presents findings from new research involving six well-developed small-group ministries in mainline Protestant congregations. We will see how these groups overcome many of the ambiguities present in other small groups.

Normative task. This task seeks to answer this question: "What should be happening in this situation or context?" At this point in our practical theological journey, we seek to understand the practice of God in today's world in order to construct a framework for Christian ministry. We indwell an inner dialogue between the resources of the Christian tradition that help us understand the work of God — for example, theology, ethics, church history — and the problems and possibilities of the situation or context. New insights and norms for ministry surface in this conversation. In some sense, the normative operation builds on the previous two; in another sense, however, the normative commitments of the minister and practical theologian influence the project from the very outset. That is, our history, sociocultural location, and training predispose us to ask particular questions and discover particular answers from within a particular framework. For this reason, the epilogue explains in detail how my own theological commitments have shaped this practical theology of small groups.

The bulk of this book (chapters 4, 5, and 6) focuses on the normative move in our practical theology of small groups. Chapter 4 is a dialogue with twentieth-century theologian Karl Barth, whose interpretation of the New Testament and the early church councils suggests that the church exists in *koinonia*. This Greek word, often translated as "fellowship" in the English Bible, refers to a series of intimate relationships in which the church lives, and moves, and has its being. In chapter 5, I describe how small groups can support these *koinonia* relationships and thus help the church become what God has intended it to be. I propose guidelines for small-group practice, which are concrete yet flexible enough to be applied to a wide variety of groups. In chapter 6, I demonstrate how small groups can create space for personal formation and transformation in our context. I argue that small groups grounded in *koinonia* provide opportunities for mending fractured relationships, healing insecurity, and replacing loneliness with belonging to the communion of saints. Chapter 6 ends with guidelines for creating the kind of atmosphere conducive to such personal transformation.

Pragmatic task. The pragmatic task of practical theology answers this question: "How do we make these normative guidelines operational?" This is the most purely strategic move for ministers and practical theologians. We create strategies for implementing practices or for taking certain kinds of action in the church; these strategies are not intended to be followed rigidly or blindly, but adapted aesthetically to the particularities of each congregation. Chapter 7, therefore, discusses how to create and implement small groups that practice transformational *koinonia*. The subjects include: (1) how to construct small-group mission statements that encourage *koinonia;* (2) how to train small-group leaders to practice *koinonia;* (3) how to practice *koinonia* in the congregation by creatively linking small groups to other congregational ministries; and (4) how to assess the growth of small groups in practicing *koinonia*.

By this time we will have completed our practical theological journey (at least for now). I hope that practical theologians, ministers, and seminarians will creatively implement and make nuances in these strategies so that the church might witness to and mediate the reconciling love of God in Christ in and through small-group ministry. I also hope that we will be better equipped to foster a multidimensional life of *koinonia* and thereby participate in God's work of transforming our broken and shallow forms of community into life-giving and life-sustaining relationships.

CHAPTER 1

The Crisis of Community

When I say that Port William suffered a new run of hard times in the 1960s, I don't mean that it had to "weather a storm" and come out safe again in the sunshine. I mean that it began to suffer its own death, which it has not yet completed, from which it may or may not revive. And here, talking against the wind, so to speak, I must enter, along with my lamentation, my objection. You may say that I am just another outdated old man complaining about progress and the change of time. But, you see, I have well considered that possibility myself, and am prepared to submit to correction by anybody who cares about a community, who can show me how the world is improved by that community's dying.

Wendell Berry, *Jayber Crow*

With these words, Jayber Crow, the small-town barber and beloved character in Wendell Berry's novel of the same name, laments the demise of his hometown in rural Kentucky. For an entire chapter, Jayber tells the story of the collapse of a local economy, the conversion of producers into consumers, the replacement of conversation with television, the cessation of intergenerational dependence, and the destruction of the earth's bounty. By way of this and other novels, essays, and poetry, contemporary author and culture critic Wendell Berry jars us into recognizing what we have lost: homegrown businesses and farms, neighborhood schools, quiet roads, and connection to the land and to one another.[1] Berry is far from alone in sounding this alarm.

During the past two and a half decades, the breakdown of community has increasingly become a subject of concern in the United States. Many philosophers, sociologists, and theologians have attributed the loss of community to rampant individualism, narcissism, and myths of heroic self-sufficiency. Some have moved out of the academic ivory tower into the public square by establishing networks that advocate for community-friendly policies in government.[2] Prominent church leaders have created curricula or programs to build community within their congregations.[3] Though some theorists describe our situation as a *change* in communal formation, others, like Berry, suggest that we are in crisis. Consider these words from the recently released third edition of *Habits of the Heart: Individualism and Commitment in American Life,* the watershed work that first alerted scholars and laypeople to fractures in community in the 1980s:

> Much of what has been happening in our society has been undermining our sense of community at every level. We are facing trends that threaten our basic sense of solidarity with others: solidarity with those near to us (loyalty to neighbors, colleagues at work, fellow townsfolk), but also solidarity with those who live far from us, those who are economically in situations very different from our own, those of other nations. Yet this solidarity — this sense of connection, shared fate, mutual responsibility, community — is more critical now than ever.[4]

This crisis is not uniquely American, nor is it limited to local communities, such as cities, towns, and neighborhoods. Instead, it is a thoroughly modern dilemma rooted in the emergence of new forms of social

---

1. See Wendell Berry, *Sex, Economy, Freedom and Community: Eight Essays* (New York: Pantheon, 1993); *The Unsettling of America: Culture and Agriculture* (Berkeley: University of California Press, 1986); *Fidelity: Five Stories* (New York: Pantheon, 1992).

2. For example, see the Communitarian Network: http://www.gwu.edu/ccps/ (accessed July 28, 2008).

3. See Rick Warren, *Better Together: What on Earth Are We Here For?* and *Better Together: 40 Days of Community* (Lake Forest, CA: Purpose Driven Publishing, 2004).

4. Robert Bellah, Richard Madsen, William Sullivan, and Steven Tipton, *Habits of the Heart: Individualism and Commitment in American Life,* updated ed. (Berkeley: University of California Press, 1996), pp. xi-xxx.

life in the eighteenth century. It affects global, communal, interpersonal, and intrapersonal relationships. For this reason, we might call it a crisis of "sociality." While its beginnings roughly coincide with the European discovery of North America and the establishment of the United States, today's crisis of community (or sociality) has been created by the dynamics of modernization and globalization. These dynamics impact the most-developed to the least-developed countries, though the challenges and benefits are not evenly distributed among them.[5]

The Dynamics of Modernity

Sociologist Anthony Giddens has spent the last two decades contrasting life in modern societies with life in traditional societies. According to Giddens, the wheels of modernity were put into motion during the eighteenth century with the standardization of time through the creation of the clock, worldwide calendars, and the exploration of new territories through sea travel. Prior to these technological advances, relationships among people were bound to a particular place, a local community. With increasing travel by sea and a common orientation to time, relationships could be established and sustained across the globe. The customs of faraway places could have an impact on local communities. Economic, political, and personal interactions could be coordinated across large swaths of time and space. Giddens refers to this uniquely modern process as "time-space distantiation."[6]

Advances in communication and the establishment of financial markets have contributed to time-space distantiation throughout modernity. The printing press dispersed information to distant people living in other time zones. Printed mass media fostered the "intrusion of

5. While most theorists agree that Western nations, particularly the United States, benefit inordinately from globalizing economic, political, and cultural trends, they disagree about the extent to which other nations benefit from globalization. Anthony Giddens takes a moderate approach. He argues that the United States dominates but does not control the world economy. It is the only geopolitical superpower left in the world, but there is greater non-Western involvement in global politics today than ever before. See Giddens, *The Runaway World: How Globalization Is Reshaping Our Lives,* 2nd ed. (New York: Routledge, 2003).

6. Anthony Giddens, *The Consequences of Modernity* (Stanford: Stanford University Press, 1992), p. 14.

distant events into everyday occurrence."[7] In recent decades, electronic communication has accelerated this process, creating "face-less" social networks and business associations. Facebook, MySpace, and Twitter have revolutionized friendship, the free flow of information, and the power of the state — as evidenced in the June 2009 Iranian protests. Young people and progressive politicians deftly utilized Twitter to organize themselves and to publicize human rights and other abuses within their country. Reporters have concluded that "totalitarian governments rule by brute force, because they control the consensus worldview of those they rule. Tyranny, in other words, is a monologue. But as long as Twitter is up and running, there's no such thing."[8]

Disembedding mechanisms — money and other expert systems — have also uprooted relationships from particular locales and restructured them across time and space.[9] Global financial markets allow transactions between and among persons widely separated from each other. Whereas traditional or premodern societies had their priests and sages, modernity has its *experts,* in such areas as law, medicine, technology, mechanics, finances, politics, psychology, and so on. None of us can master all of the expert systems that we depend on for our day-to-day functioning. So we are forced to trust people whom we do not know and cannot see and systems that we do not understand. Most of us take this reality for granted until our health and well-being depend on trusting one of many conflicting expert opinions. How should we invest our finances? What should we eat in order to stay healthy? What course of treatment will most likely cure our cancer?

Encountering expert systems and people with different customs and beliefs has created thoroughgoing reflexivity, another uniquely modern dynamic that has also been exacerbated by electronic communication. In explaining reflexivity, Giddens says: "Social practices [in modernity] are constantly examined and reformed in the light of incoming information about those very practices, thus constitutively altering their character." At any given moment, we are aware that any element of our knowledge may be revised. An indefinite range of options

---

7. Anthony Giddens, *Modernity and Self-Identity: Self and Society in the Late Modern Age* (Stanford: Stanford University Press, 1991), p. 24.

8. Lev Grossman, "Iran's Protests: Twitter, the Medium of the Movement," *Time,* June 17, 2009: http://www.time.com/time/world/article/0,8599,1905125,00.html#ixzz0Z1 Pd06Y8 (accessed Nov. 30, 2009).

9. Giddens, *Modernity and Self-Identity,* p. 21.

exists for every sphere of life, causing "routine contemplation of counter-factuals."[10] Consequently, our lives are wedded to doubt and risk. Even the most mundane choices involve incalculable risk.

The inherent insecurity of today's knowledge combined with an awareness of and interaction with global others undermines the authority of tradition. Beliefs and values are no longer knit together in one system. Neither kin nor the local community determines the course of our lives — nor does religion. Giddens refers to this as the "end of tradition." We have traditions (i.e., customs), but we freely choose them, nuance them, and discard them; in this sense, our traditions are antitradition. Tradition as understood throughout the course of human history precludes other options. "What is distinctive about tradition is that it defines a kind of truth. For someone following a traditional practice, questions don't have to be asked about alternatives. However much it may change, tradition provides a framework for action that can go largely unquestioned."[11]

Together these dynamics of modernity — time-space distantiation, expert systems, thoroughgoing reflexivity, and the end of tradition — have transformed our experience of risk and trust (see Table 1 on p. 16). Traditional moorings of trust have come undone. For modern persons, trust is anchored not in kinship and local communal ties, but in a mix of faceless and face-to-face relationships. As I have observed above, we are forced to trust expert systems — or, alternatively, cease to function in society. "Faith is sustained in the workings of knowledge of which the lay person is largely ignorant."[12] No tradition provides secure ground for daily choices or purposeful living. This includes science, for science itself is a tradition. Scientific observations and theories emerge from and are conditioned by a history of fallible scientific interpretations.

Paradoxically, increased individual choice and the attempt to control our own destiny have created a new riskiness in modern life. "Risk presumes a society that actively tries to break away from its past," a society that wants to determine its own future rather than leaving the future to the whims of nature and tradition.[13] Yet our attempts at control — the control of labor through capitalism, the control of nature

---

10. Giddens, *Modernity and Self-Identity*, p. 38.
11. Giddens, *Runaway World*, p. 41.
12. Giddens, *Consequences of Modernity*, p. 88.
13. Giddens, *Runaway World*, p. 40.

Table 1: Trust and risk profiles

	Traditional Societies	Modern Societies
Environment of Trust	1. Kinship relations stabilize social ties. 2. The local community provides a familiar milieu. 3. Religious cosmologies and ritual practices provide providential interpretation of human existence and nature. 4. Tradition connects past and present.	1. Personal relationships of friendship or sexual intimacy stabilize social ties 2. Abstract systems stabilize relations across indefinite spans of time-space 3. Future orientation
Environment of Risk	1. Threats and dangers emanate from nature 2. Threat of human violence from small armies, local bandits, etc. 3. Risk of fall from religious grace or of malicious magical influence	1. Threats and dangers emanate from reflexivity of modernity 2. Threats of human violence from industrialization of war 3. Threat of personal meaninglessness derives from reflexivity of modernity applied to the self

through industrialization, the control of information through surveillance, and the control of violence through military power — have created new uncertainties.[14] There is a new riskiness in modernity that we can neither escape nor control.[15] Whereas traditional societies faced external risks from nature, for instance, modern societies face manufac-

14. Giddens identifies capitalism, industrialism, surveillance, and military power as the four institutional dimensions of modernity. Surveillance refers to the control of information via media and government regulations. See *Consequences of Modernity*, pp. 55-62.

15. Giddens explains: "Moreover, some of the influences that were supposed to make life more certain and predictable for us, including the progress of science and technology, often have quite the opposite effect. Global climate change and its accompanying risks, for example, probably result from our intervention into the environment. They aren't natural phenomena. Science and technology are inevitably involved in our attempts to counter such risks, but they have also contributed to creating them in the first place" (*Runaway World*, p. 3).

tured risk.[16] We worry less about nature per se and more about what we have done to nature. What are the long-term effects of industrial waste on our environment? How will global warming impact future generations? Will international trade agreements help or hurt local economies in the long run? How will genetic modification of crops and animals impact our long-term health? Have attempts to curb violence through military force in one part of the world fanned the flames of terrorism in other parts? Can faceless friendships sustained over the Internet support our moral and psychological development?

In recent decades these dynamics of social life have accelerated exponentially, creating a truly global community, a collective "we." We have entered late modernity, which, as Giddens puts it, is like riding a juggernaut, a runaway train racing into uncharted territory and threatening to destroy everything in its path. We can neither stop nor avoid this juggernaut. And it is likely that few of us would actually choose to revert to a life without choice. But the price we pay is this: radical and unpredictable change yields crises at every level of our common existence. "In modern social conditions . . . crises become more or less endemic, both on an individual and a collective level. . . . A 'crisis' exists whenever activities concerned with important goals in the life of an individual or a collectivity suddenly appear inadequate. Crises in this sense become a 'normal' part of life. . . ."[17] As we will see in the following sections of this chapter, these crises radically alter our relationships to local communities, to friends and family, to religion, and to ourselves.

Disembedded from Community

My father did not grieve alone. He did not need a support group or a therapist. He was surrounded by people who were his friends, who cared about him. Friends and neighbors kept dropping by with food, coming around for visits, or issuing invitations to dinner. They still do — after four years.[18]

---

16. Poorer, less developed countries still face both kinds of risk, which highlights the inequities in our globalized world. See Giddens, *Runaway World,* p. 15.

17. Giddens, *Modernity and Self-Identity,* p. 184.

18. Carl D. Esbjornson, "Does Community Have a Value? — A Reply," in *Rooted in the Land: Essays on Community and Place,* ed. William Vitek and Wes Jackson (New Haven: Yale University Press, 1996), p. 187.

Carl Esbjornson juxtaposes gladness for his father and lament for his own lack of community. In late modernity, relationships among family, friends, and coworkers distend over large tracts of time and space. Persons working for the same company on the same projects live on different continents. Though connected by mysterious digital signals, they may never see, hear, or speak to one another. Those who have shared intimate living quarters for eighteen years suddenly are separated from one another and strain to maintain once-robust but now-thin connections via email, phone calls, and periodic visits. Sharing a common communal history is a rare experience. Deborah Tall's testimony rings true for most of us:

> Given how often I have moved, my community is widely scattered. I have close friends all over the world; none of them know each other. We have only our own brief intensities of common experience to bind us, our telephone calls and letters. Friendship is tethered to loss, dependent on mental reconstruction instead of daily enactment. Sometimes I feel stranded at the center of a fragmented orb, my life divided into a series of experiences and places that can never be brought together — except in the solitude of memory. My family too is deposited all over the continent. Crucial junctures in our lives take place in hospital hallways or over bad coffee in airports.[19]

At the same time, many of our relationships are mediated rather than direct. Distant persons and events enter into local contexts via electronic and satellite communication. We often know — or at least know about — persons on the television more than our next-door neighbors. We share intimate secrets with nameless, faceless, voiceless identities on the World Wide Web. Robert Putnam's research on community and civic life in America, published in his book *Bowling Alone,* reveals that the practices of entertaining friends at home, playing cards, conversing with family members, sending greeting cards, and league sports occur anywhere from 10 to 40 percent less frequently than in previous decades.[20] At the same time, there has been a dramatic increase in "watching" sports, movies, television, and music. We've be-

19. Deborah Tall, "Dwelling: Making Peace with Space and Place," in Vitek and Jackson, *Rooted in the Land,* p. 107.

20. Robert Putnam, *Bowling Alone: The Collapse and Revival of American Community* (New York: Simon and Schuster, 2000), pp. 93-115.

come consumers rather than producers of culture. Group observation has replaced cocreation.

In the United States, one of the most glaring effects of this crisis of community is the steep decline in civic life across the demographic spectrum, that is, without regard to age, race, or socioeconomic status. Consider these statistics. In the past thirty-five years, Americans have become . . .

- 10-15 percent less likely to voice their views publicly by running for office or by writing Congress or the local newspaper;
- 15-20 percent less interested in politics and public affairs;
- 25 percent less likely to vote;
- 35 percent less likely to attend public meetings;
- 40 percent less involved in political and civic organizations in general.[21]

Interestingly, membership numbers have declined at a slower pace, 10-20 percent, than active membership, nearly 50 percent, as membership today often merely requires one's signature on official statements.[22] Thus most of our civic involvement is faceless.

The community's role in our moral formation also has been undermined by the dynamics of modernity. Illness, death, insanity, and deviance are technical matters handled by experts rather than moral issues handled by communities. Institutions hide these moral issues by "sequestering" the persons who suffer from them.[23] Hidden from our daily view, the kinds of existential issues that call for ethical action do not confront us directly. More generally, relationships of trust are disembedded from community. We trust expert systems — transportation systems, banking systems, utility companies, medical establishments, and so forth — to help us function with ease on a daily basis. We depend not on people we know and love but on abstract systems. These systems "deskill."[24] Few of us have friends or neighbors who can help us with our plumbing, electricity, computers, or cars; fewer of us can sustain these basic systems ourselves. So we depend on and trust repre-

21. Putnam, *Bowling Alone,* pp. 48-64.

22. Putnam, *Bowling Alone,* pp. 46, 63.

23. Giddens refers to this as the "sequestration of experience" (*Modernity and Self-Identity,* p. 156).

24. Giddens, *Modernity and Self-Identity,* p. 22.

sentatives of organizations who market their skills to us. Outside of the context of trust that is personal, their sense of obligation to us may be weak, and we may have little incentive to become loyal customers. Our commitment to each other is not based on concern for our mutual well-being; instead, it is based on efficiency and ease.

Transformation of Intimacy

In traditional societies, friendship and marriage were anchored in external social conditions. Friendships were formed as alliances for protection, honor, and war. Marriage and family secured one's economic well-being. Men and women were unequal partners with distinct roles and expectations. The purpose of sexuality was reproduction. Children did not have rights; they were valued primarily for their economic contribution to the family.

Three late-modern dynamics transform these intimate relationships. First, community, religion, and kin no longer determine one's life trajectory. People are not confined by birth to a particular profession, marriage partner, or social status. Second, people's encounters with different beliefs and practices throw their own customs into question. They discover that their way of life is not the only way. Having discovered other practices, they are confronted with choices among many lifestyle options. Third, the needs that community and extended family once fulfilled — trust, dependence, and security — are transferred onto interpersonal relationships, particularly friendship and marriage.

Friendship, marriage, and parent-child relationships have consequently taken on a new form, what Giddens calls the "pure relationship." By "pure" Giddens means unencumbered by external structures. Unlike friendship, marriage, and parenting in traditional societies, the pure relationship form "is entered into for its own sake, for what can be derived by each person from a sustained association with another; and which is continued only in so far as it is thought by both parties to deliver enough satisfactions for each individual to stay within it."[25] Pure relationships are initiated and sustained on the basis of intimacy, self-disclosure, emotional satisfaction, mutual commitment, and choice.

25. Giddens, *Runaway World*, p. 61.

They are characterized by democratic decision-making, equal rights and responsibilities, and freedom from coercion and violence. Couples negotiate sexual practices, domestic practices, parenting styles, and the trajectory of their common history. Dialogue makes the relationship work.

These changes are so radical that Giddens refers to marriage and family as "shell institutions."[26] That is, they have been gutted of their previous structure. Heterosexuality, traditional gender roles, and hierarchical parent-child relations have lost their normative status in society.[27] Sexuality and procreation have been separated from each other. We can sustain active sexual relationships without the fear of pregnancy; and we can conceive and bear children outside of sexual intercourse. When freed from procreation in these ways, sexuality becomes a matter of personal choice. "Sexuality is for the first time something to be discovered, molded, altered. Sexuality, which used to be defined so strictly in relation to marriage and legitimacy, now has little connection to them at all."[28] Heterosexual cohabitation and homosexual relationships can fulfill the criteria of the pure relationship just as easily as heterosexual marriage can. Therefore, they become valid and increasingly accepted lifestyle options.

Like modernity itself, these changes in interpersonal relationships are double-edged. On the one hand, we have freedoms and options previously unimaginable; we can choose whom we love; we can create a shared history; we can even find surrogate parents in adulthood. On the other hand, the pure relationship is inherently unstable: it can be terminated at will, and it lacks external supports.[29] It bears the weight of providing personal meaning and sexual fulfillment for each partner. Therefore, the pure relationship can feel risky: changes in the relationship can create significant anxiety for one or both partners. "In relationships which only exist for their own sake, anything that goes wrong

26. Giddens, *Runaway World*, p. 58.

27. Anthony Giddens, *The Transformation of Intimacy: Sexuality, Love and Eroticism in Modern Societies* (Stanford: Stanford University Press, 1992), p. 154.

28. Giddens, *Runaway World*, p. 57.

29. Giddens writes, "In the pure relationship, trust has no external supports and has to be developed on the basis of intimacy. Trust is a vesting of confidence in the other and also in the capability of the mutual bond to withstand future traumas. . . . To trust the other is also to gamble upon the capability of the individual actually to be able to act with integrity" (*Transformation of Intimacy*, p. 138).

between the partners intrinsically threatens the relationship itself."[30] Separation, divorce, and remarriage create a new set of family relationships that must be negotiated or worked through psychologically. We lack any guiding compass to help us navigate these murky waters of the pure relationship. We turn to expert systems for advice, but they are caught up in the same milieu and present us with conflicting opinions.

Tenuous Self-Connection

The ambiguities of the pure relationship, the fracturing of local communities, the end of tradition, and thoroughgoing reflexivity burrow into the modern psyche. These sociological ground-shifts knock us off balance psychologically, and the forging of self-identity becomes a project that must be worked on continuously. Existential questions often arise with unsettling force and threaten our basic security.

Self-identity becomes problematic in late modernity for the first time in history. Self and society are interrelated globally. Distant others enter and challenge our worldviews and lifestyles regularly. We routinely contemplate an indefinite range of options for all spheres of life — vocational, domestic, economic, political, and so on. We are aware that even the most hypervigilant assessment of counterfactuals cannot guarantee our desired outcomes. Tradition no longer provides a sure guide. Expert systems present us with contradictory information about the most basic of human needs. In response to a bewildering barrage of information, some of us adopt a laissez-faire attitude — "there's no way to know how to care for our bodily needs, so let's eat, drink, and be merry" — while others reify one set of expert advice into a lifestyle — for instance, homeopathy.

Without clear and certain external guidance or rites of passages, we turn inward in order to construct our own identity. We engage in the "reflexive project of the self."[31] We consciously make decisions, from the most mundane to the most existential, in light of who we are and who we want to become. Fueled by our needs for self-actualization and narrative continuity, our reflexivity becomes all-pervasive. We use therapy (an expert system) to reframe past experiences and project new pos-

---

30. Giddens, *Modernity and Self-Identity,* p. 90.
31. Giddens, *Modernity and Self-Identity,* p. 5.

sibilities for our future. As modernity is oriented toward control of the future, so we attempt to control our personal futures. We attempt to break away from constraints of the past, such as our childhood, the socioeconomic and cultural milieu into which we were born, imposed gender roles, and so forth. Sometimes we embrace a particular lifestyle, "a more or less integrated set of practices which an individual embraces, not only because such practices fulfill utilitarian needs, but because they give material form to a particular narrative of self-identity."[32] Yet doubt lingers under the surface of these decisions. We know that our chosen narrative is only one of many stories with which we might interpret our lives.[33]

Likewise, crises and transitions problematize our identity construction. Modern life is structured around defining moments in which we make choices about work, marriage, health, and geographic moves.[34] We wonder, with more or less anxiety, depending on our personal experience and our disposition, Will this job promotion actually bring me fulfillment and growth, or will it deplete my energy? If I move across the country, will I discover meaningful friendships? Do I give up my desire to have children in order to marry this person, or do I wait and hope that I will find someone else to love and create a family with? We weigh options as best we can with the knowledge that there are no guarantees. We are keenly aware that the course of our lives might be altered in unpredictable and undesirable ways. The riskier the choices, the more likely we are to experience an identity crisis.

With freedom comes anxiety. Søren Kierkegaard referred to this as the "dizziness of freedom,"[35] and Jean Paul Sartre spoke of the "condemnation to freedom."[36] What sustains us in the midst of this anxiety, what enables us to maintain our self-connection and connection to others in the midst of identity crises, is ontological security. Drawing on three psychologists, R. D. Laing, D. W. Winnicott, and Erik Erikson,

---

32. Giddens, *Modernity and Self-Identity*, p. 81.

33. Lars Bo Kaspersen, *Anthony Giddens: An Introduction to a Social Theorist*, trans. Steven Sampson (Oxford: Blackwell Publishers, 2000), p. 104.

34. Giddens refers to these moments as "open experience thresholds" (*Modernity and Self-Identity*, p. 15).

35. Søren Kierkegaard, *The Concept of Anxiety*, ed. and trans. Reidar Thomte and Albert B. Anderson (Princeton: Princeton University Press, 1980), p. 61.

36. Jean Paul Sartre, *Being and Nothingness: An Essay on Phenomenological Ontology*, 2nd ed. (New York: Routledge, 2003), p. 550.

Giddens defines ontological security as "confidence in the continuity of one's self-identity and in the constancy of the surrounding environment and persons in the environment."[37] It is a primal sense of trust in the reliability of the world, which keeps us from being overwhelmed to the point of nonfunctioning.

We develop ontological security in the first two years of life in our relationship with our mother or primary caregiver. We experience trust when our mother establishes for us a regular routine of eating, sleeping, and playing, and when she balances time with us and time away from us. As infants, we make the transition from feeling secure when physically held by our mother to feeling secure in her absence. We learn to tolerate separation without disintegration in our sense of self. In Winnicott's words, we gain a sense of "being and going on being."[38] We become ontologically secure. We trust that the world is reliable. This trust, according to Giddens, functions as an "emotional inoculation" against anxieties that arise throughout life. It provides a "protective cocoon" that safeguards us in crises.[39] This early trust also enables us to participate in broader circles of community throughout life. Trusting the world and ourselves, we venture out to connect with the other.

We become ontologically secure as we learn to manage time-space distantiation: that is, separation from our mother, our source of being, in the first few months of life. "At the heart of the psychological development of trust, we rediscover the problematic of time-space distantiation."[40] Yet modernity's dynamism, the instability of the pure relationship, and the sequestration of experience threaten the ontological security of modern people in new ways. (1) Predictable routine remains necessary throughout life for strengthening ontological security, but modernity is rife with perpetual change.[41] Unpredictable,

37. Giddens, *Consequences of Modernity*, p. 97.
38. D. W. Winnicott, "Primary Maternal Preoccupation," in *Collected Papers: Through Paediatrics to Psycho-Analysis* (New York: Basic Books, 1958), p. 303.
39. Giddens, *Modernity and Self-Identity*, pp. 39, 40.
40. Giddens, *Modernity and Self-Identity*, p. 97.
41. Summarizing Giddens, Lars Bo Kaspersen writes: "Several strongly positive and especially predictable routines in relation to the mother create ontological security in the child. The effect of these routines in adult life is that most of our activities — day-to-day routines — provide us with a feeling of security and trust. These activities, says Giddens, are unconsciously motivated routines that reproduce our ontological security. We need this security to avoid those situations in which we are exposed to extreme anxiety and to maintain our self-esteem" (*Anthony Giddens*, p. 39).

high-consequence risks accompany such change. (2) The pure relationship, the primary site in which we develop our life narrative, is inherently fragile. If the pure relationship disintegrates, the self is threatened with annihilation, especially if the trust developed in infancy was tenuous. (3) The sequestration of existential issues is a double-edged sword. On the one hand, we do not have to face the anxieties and questions associated with death, disease, and deviance on a regular basis; on the other hand, none of us can escape these realities for long. Our loved ones suddenly die. Church leaders fall prey to sexual misconduct. We lose some aspect of our physical functioning. Because we have not dealt with these experiences over time in the context of a supportive community, we may be thrown into despair or dread. In the midst of grief and trauma, we cannot suppress our deepest anxieties, and we may become immobilized, unable to function — let alone create meaning in our lives.

New Religious Orientations

In premodern societies, religious tradition provided indisputable guidance for daily living and definitive answers to existential questions. But in a global, cosmopolitan society, religious traditions no longer determine the course of human existence. Religious authorities disagree with one another; we have access to divergent spiritual practices; the abuses of religious leaders become public; we no longer trust religious authorities or religious traditions unequivocally; all beliefs are subject to interpretation because they are fallible interpretations themselves.

These shifts manifest themselves in an emphasis on free will and individual choice in American Christianity.[42] We have a low ecclesiology. We view the church as merely an intentional gathering of individuals, and so we freely leave congregations. Our denominational loyalties are weak at best. We increasingly believe in God without belonging to God's people. "Religious belonging for many is no longer viewed as a presumed outgrowth of belief; it has become a matter of taste."[43] According to the 1998 General Social Survey, the percentage of

---

42. William McKinney and Wade Clark Roof, *American Mainline Religion: Its Changing Shape and Future* (New Brunswick: Rutgers University Press, 1987), p. 43.

43. McKinney and Roof, *American Mainline Religion*, p. 52.

Americans who hold basic beliefs about God has remained constant over recent decades; however, church membership has declined by 10 percent and active participation by 25-50 percent. It is important to note that membership in evangelical Christian congregations has increased in recent decades. While mainline Protestant denominations have lost 15-20 percent of their members, evangelical and fundamentalist churches have gained 33 percent.[44]

This represents a significant change in the religious ecology in the United States. As Putnam explains, evangelical and fundamentalist churches, though distinct from one another, strengthen bonding social capital but not bridging social capital.[45] Briefly, social capital refers to social networks and the reciprocity, trustworthiness, and mutual assistance provided by them.[46] These networks are the essence of community in late modernity. Bonding social capital strengthens ties among members of homogeneous groups, while bridging social capital strengthens ties between different groups. Both types of social capital are necessary for the sustaining of community in a pluralistic world. Bonding social capital without bridging social capital may contribute to exclusivity and antagonism toward "out-groups." Bridging social capital without bonding social capital may contribute to a diffuse self-identity. In American Christianity there seems to be an imbalance in bonding and bridging social capital. Putnam writes: "[T]he fact that evangelical Christianity is rising and mainline Christianity is falling means that religion is less effective now as a foundation for civic engagement and 'bridging' social capital."[47]

44. Putnam, *Bowling Alone*, pp. 72, 76.

45. See Christian Smith with Michael Emerson, *American Evangelicalism: Embattled and Thriving* (Chicago: University of Chicago Press, 1998). This study indicates that evangelicals amass bonding social capital in a variety of ways. First, evangelicalism provides "meaning and belonging by establishing group boundaries and social solidarity" (p. 142). By identifying out-groups, such as mainline Protestants, Roman Catholics, fundamentalists, and non-Christians, evangelicalism reinforces in-group identity. We can assume that this bonding social capital also supports ontological security. Second, evangelicals' emphasis on a personal relationship with Christ gets transposed to other personal relationships, such as family and friends. Maintaining and honoring these relationships is an ethical imperative. Third, evangelicals cross socially constructed barriers on an interpersonal level but largely fail to confront the systems and structures that maintain these barriers. They do not bridge difference at the institutional level.

46. Putnam, *Bowling Alone*, p. 19.

47. Putnam, *Bowling Alone*, p. 78.

Not only have patterns of religious belonging changed, but we also hold our beliefs differently in late modernity. Many mainline and evangelical church leaders alike tend to defend their traditions in nontraditional ways. They accept doubt. They strive to be self-critical. They dialogue with other religious perspectives and other academic disciplines, such as ethics and the social sciences.

At the same time, American Christianity has become less focused on confession (right belief) and more focused on practice (right action). This seems partly attributable to intractable conflict about our beliefs. For instance, after two decades of vitriolic debates about sexuality, some Presbyterians proclaim that mission unites but theology divides. It also seems attributable to the fragility of the pure relationship and our experience of ontological insecurity. Congregations market themselves as serving the psychic needs of their members. They regularly provide recovery groups, grief counseling, and educational forums on marriage and childrearing. In short, congregations support our quest for wholeness and a coherent life narrative.[48]

Yet this isn't the only religious response to the end of tradition. According to Giddens, there are two general religious orientations in late modernity: cosmopolitanism and fundamentalism. Cosmopolitan religion defends tradition in nontraditional ways. It is open to dialogue and critique from within and without. Fundamentalism, as Giddens puts it, "is beleaguered tradition. It is tradition defended in the traditional way — by reference to ritual truth — in a globalizing world that asks for reasons."[49] Like cosmopolitan orientations to faith, fundamentalism seeks to bolster ontological security. But it does so by rejecting ambiguity and doubt. It provides clear-cut answers in an era riddled with distrust of authority. It creates a closed system that cannot consider the possibility, let alone the likelihood, of its own fallibility. It is as if the acceptance of other valid lifestyles and worldviews threatens to overwhelm the fundamentalist believer with unthinkable anxieties. In other words, holding onto a particular set of religious beliefs while simultaneously engaging in dialogue with others requires significant

---

48. It is not surprising, then, that narrative theology and narrative pastoral care have become predominant in recent decades. In narrative theologies, we interpret our lives in light of God's narrative of salvation. We reframe our experiences in light of this larger story, which gives us meaning and coherence. See Charles Gerkin, *Introduction to Pastoral Care* (Nashville: Abingdon, 1997).

49. Giddens, *Runaway World,* p. 49.

ontological security. At the same time, it threatens to undo ontological security. For if we discover that our lives have been based on a falsehood, chaos and despair may overtake us.

In conclusion, modernity is characterized by a crisis of community that impacts life at every level, from the global to the intrapersonal. While late-modern persons have extraordinary opportunities in many domains of life (work, marriage and family, religion), they also lack the external structures and supports (extended family, local community, tradition) that provide security in a risky world. Our connections to family, friends, community, religion, and self have changed so radically that we experience the threat of fundamentalist violence on the global level and the threat of debilitating anxiety on the personal level. We are disembedded from our extended families and local communities, deluged with conflicting expert information, and shaken by global events over which we have little or no control. We expect intimate relationships to bear the weight of our needs for trust, meaning, and the creation of a coherent life narrative. When these relationships buckle under this weight, our self-connection becomes tenuous. We face the daunting task of rewriting our own life narratives.

The dynamics of modernity challenge our basic sense of security and thus make it all the more necessary. Nevertheless, this security can be strengthened and maintained throughout the lifespan by participation in social practices. The routine nature of social practices strengthens the protective cocoon by enabling us to bracket out unthinkable anxieties. Therefore, the dynamics of modernity heighten awareness of the significance of social practices and impel us to establish them with intentionality.

For Giddens, social practices constitute social life, and clusters of social practices constitute society.[50] Social practices consist of trust rela-

---

50. Giddens's treatment of social practices is central to his social ontology, called "structuration theory." While an assessment of this theory remains outside the bounds of this project, the following core aspects of his argument have been summarized by Lars Bo Kaspersen: (1) social practices, when reproduced, become social systems, which in turn yield patterns of social relations; (2) there is a dialectical, reflexive relationship between human agency and social structures; (3) human action is structured by and yet structures society; (4) thus social structures both constrain and enable human action; (5) disciplines such as sociology, political science, history, and so on, must study social practices given their impact on society. See Anthony Giddens, *The Constitution of Society: Outline of the Theory of Structuration* (Berkeley: University of California Press, 1986).

tionships and patterns of action. "The many actions and interactions that constitute social practice are bound together by relations of trust."[51] These trust relationships facilitate decision-making in the midst of multiple competing options and expert systems. "When insecurity and many choices exist, trust in a person or a system is decisive for the choice being made. Relations of trust are therefore absolutely critical for a person's developmental and action potential."[52] As I will illustrate in the next chapter, small-group practice clusters activities and trust relationships in a new form in an attempt to bolster ontological security, foster spiritual connection, and establish life-giving community.

51. Kaspersen, *Anthony Giddens*, p. 98.
52. Kaspersen, *Anthony Giddens*, p. 102.

CHAPTER 2

Small Groups Embodying the Crisis of Community

In the past three decades, new forms of community have cropped up all over the American landscape: constellations of persons united around their common needs for emotional connection, identity formation, and spiritual exploration. By the mid-1990s, 79 percent of Americans (205 million), representing all ages, races, religions, and social classes, had participated in a small group at some point in their lives. Nearly forty million Americans had belonged to two or more groups simultaneously.[1] The variety and quantity of these groups seems endless, including book clubs, discussion groups, political advocacy groups, Sunday school classes, self-help groups, twelve-step groups, prayer groups, affinity groups, and mission groups. Add to that all the variations within basic types of groups created by market forces, for example, Alcoholics Anonymous, which alone has 63,000 groups and two million participants worldwide,[2] and which has spawned a school of similar groups, including ACOA, Al-Anon, Ala-teen, NA, SA, EHA, ISA, to name just a few.[3]

The American church, particularly the Protestant church, has pro-

1. Robert Wuthnow, *Sharing the Journey: Support Groups and America's New Quest for Community* (New York: Free Press, 1994).

2. Sara Wuthnow, "Working the ACOA Program: A Spiritual Journey," in *I Come Away Stronger: How Small Groups Are Shaping American Religion,* ed. Robert Wuthnow (Grand Rapids: Eerdmans, 1994), p. 184.

3. Adult Children of Alcoholics (ACOA), Family Members of Alcoholics (Al-Anon and Ala-teen), Narcotics Anonymous (NA), Sexaholics Anonymous (SA), Emotional Health Anonymous (EHA), Incest Survivors Anonymous (ISA).

Typology of Small Groups

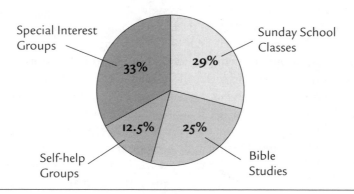

vided the strongest institutional support — resources such as leaders, participants, space, childcare, common language, and motivating ideals — for the small-group movement.[4] Of those participating in small groups in the mid-1990s, 60 percent (48 million) belonged to church-based groups.[5] More specifically, 29 percent were members of Sunday school classes; 25 percent were members of Bible studies, prayer fellowships, and covenant groups; 12.5 percent were members of self-help groups, some of which had a religious orientation; and 33 percent were members of special-interest groups, that is, political, advocacy, hobby, and book-discussion groups.[6]

Conversely, the small-group movement has altered the structure — and, to some extent, the meaning — of American ecclesial practice. Christian education and pastoral care, which during the early twentieth century occurred in the classroom and the pastor's office, respectively, have been relocated to small groups. Thus have laypeople assumed a greater role in the ministry of the church, a positive gain in light of the Reformation emphasis on the priesthood of all believers. While small groups are not new to ecclesial practice, today's groups cluster a repertoire of traditional Christian activities (prayer, meditation, Bible study, confession, and table fellowship) in a new form or arrangement. Sociologist Mark Chaves says: "Repertoires of ideas and actions do not stay constant over time; new elements become legitimated and thereby enter the repertoire,

4. Wuthnow, *Sharing the Journey*, pp. 89-115.
5. Robert Wuthnow, *I Come Away Stronger*, p. 370.
6. Robert Wuthnow, *I Come Away Stronger*, pp. 65-76.

old elements become irrelevant and thereby drop out of the repertoire."[7] Confession is a prime example. Throughout church history, in different cultures and different religious traditions, confession has been practiced (1) silently in worship, (2) privately to an ordained minister, (3) publicly to a congregation, and (4) semipublicly in a small group of confidantes. In today's small groups, however, the perceived meaning and content of confession has changed. Group members talk about their weaknesses, anxieties, and emotional needs more than they talk about sin against God and neighbor. Confession in today's small groups intermingles and often conflates psychological and theological interpretations of the human predicament. Even in instances where these distinctions remain clear, many ecclesial small groups — either intentionally or unintentionally — have incorporated the objectives and practices of the self-help and twelve-step movements.[8] In short, the quest for healing often trumps the quest for sanctification.

The proliferation of small groups, whether inside or outside the church, is fueled by acute psychosocial and spiritual yearnings of people living in the United States in late modernity. People gather in small groups to experience or enhance a connection to God, a connection to others, and often a connection to their truest selves. The vast majority of participants report significant positive changes in their experience of God, of themselves, and of others. (See Table 2 for self-reported positive changes in various levels and types of relationships among small-group participants.[9])

More recent research suggests the same. Sociologist Robert Put-

---

7. Mark Chaves, *Congregations in America* (Cambridge, MA: Harvard University Press, 2004), p. 130.

8. For example, see Keith Miller, *Hunger for Healing: The Twelve Steps as a Classic Model for Christian Spiritual Growth* (San Francisco: Harper, 1997); James B. Nelson, *Thirst: God and the Alcoholic Experience* (Louisville: Westminster John Knox, 2004); Saul Selby, *Twelve Step Christianity: The Christian Roots and Application of the Twelve Steps* (Center City, MN: Hazelden, 2000); David L. Thompson, *Holiness for Hurting People: Discipleship as Recovery* (Indianapolis: Wesleyan Publishing House, 1998); Bill Morris, *Complete Handbook for Recovery Ministry in the Church: A Practical Guide to Establishing Recovery Support Groups within Your Church* (Nashville: Oliver Nelson, 1993).

9. By "level" I mean that the circle of community, or sociality, expands outward to include more distant others. As Robert Bellah writes, community is "a cultural theme that calls us to wider and wider circles of loyalty, ultimately embracing that universal community of all beings" (*Habits of the Heart: Individualism and Commitment in American Life,* updated ed. with new intro. [Berkeley: University of California Press, 1998], p. xxx).

Table 2: Self-reported changes among small-group participants

Percentage that Experienced Change in Relationship to God

Feel closer to God	90%
Bible is more meaningful	84%
Experienced answered prayer	75%
Prayer is much more important now	60%
Sensed God's presence in the group	59%

Percentage that Experienced Change in Interpersonal Relationships

Deeper love toward others	87%
Better ability to forgive others	85%
More open and honest with others	83%
Helped someone inside the group	80%
Healing of relationships	53%

Percentage that Experienced Change in Relationship to Persons Outside the Group

Shared faith with those outside the group	75%
Helped others outside the group	72%
More interested in peace and social justice	61%
Donated $$ to another charitable organization	46%
Involved in volunteer work in community	42%

Percentage that Experienced Change in Relationship to Self

Ability to forgive self	82%
Feel better about self	87%
More open and honest with self	84%

nam identifies small groups as one of four countertrends to the depletion of social capital in the United States. In *Better Together: Restoring the American Community,* Putnam and coauthor Lewis Feldstein describe two small-group ministries as "exceptional cases in which creative social entrepreneurs [are] moving against the nationwide tide and creating vibrant new forms of social connectedness."[10] In her ethnographic

10. Robert Putnam and Lewis Feldstein, *Better Together: Restoring the American Community* (New York: Simon and Schuster, 2003), p. x.

study, Anne Marie Minnick concludes that twelve-step groups facilitate moral reconstruction and spiritual renewal in a time of cultural upheaval, that is, primarily since the 1960s. She writes: "The crisis . . . stems from a disorientation in people's value frameworks, in their ways of viewing, understanding, and being in the world."[11]

Yet Wuthnow, Putnam, and Minnick do not praise small groups without reserve. Putnam notes that many groups foster *bonding* social capital to the neglect of *bridging* social capital. Minnick warns that self-help groups cannot cure our cultural fragmentation. And Wuthnow vividly illustrates that small groups simultaneously mitigate and accommodate individualism: "Small groups are colored by the same shades of individualism that pervade the rest of our society," he says. "Just because people are joining support groups, we should not conclude that they have made the needs of others a priority in their lives. They may be seeking community but only finding themselves."[12]

The rest of this chapter summarizes the strengths and weaknesses of small groups as reported by Wuthnow and others. In doing so, we move into the descriptive-empirical task of our practical theological journey. As we shall see, small groups are a societal and ecclesial practice that embodies our current crisis of community. Small groups simultaneously enhance and undermine connections to God, others, and self. Because description and interpretation are deeply entwined, in this chapter I will analyze these findings in light of the crisis of community. Thus the chapter does more than simply report the findings of sociologists; it places these findings within a new framework of meaning.

Connection to God: Personal, not Ecclesial

I do not believe that such groups as these which I found my way to . . . are perfect any more than anything human is perfect, but I believe that the church has an enormous amount to learn from them. I also believe that what goes on in them is far closer to what Christ meant his church to be, and what it originally was, than much of what goes on in most churches I know. These groups have no buildings or official leadership or money. They have no rummage sales, no altar guilds, no

11. Anne Marie Minnick, *Twelve Step Programs: A Contemporary American Quest for Meaning and Spiritual Renewal* (Westport, CT: Praeger, 1997), p. 4.

12. Wuthnow, *Sharing the Journey*, pp. 194, 215.

every-member canvasses. They have no preachers, no choirs, no liturgy, no real estate. They have no creeds. They have no program. They make you wonder if the best thing that could happen to many a church might not be to have its building burn down and to lose all its money. Then all the people would have left would be God and each other.[13]

These words from Frederick Buechner's memoir mirror the sentiments and longings of small-group members throughout the United States. Small groups quench a profound thirst for connection to God. They provide space for persons, especially those who distrust religious authorities and institutional religion, to search for the sacred. In this setting, people learn to trust God, grow closer to God, and experience God's love. They learn to know God as friend, healer, provider, and helper. God becomes more accessible and faith more personal as small-group participants pray and read the Bible together.

While small groups help people connect to God through Scripture, prayer, and personal sharing, their faith may become highly subjective in the process. For example, they may often read Scripture through the filter of personal experience. Group members' God-concepts get domesticated. "In the telling and retelling of their stories . . . God also becomes more like them. They are worried about termites and cakes. So they assume God is, too."[14] Gone are the reverent fear of God and the acknowledgment of God's majesty, mystery, and irreducible otherness. In this unmistakable anthropological turn, God exists for the sake of humanity, rather than the reverse; or even worse, God exists solely to make life easier and more enjoyable. Wuthnow writes: "The signs of the sacred [in small groups] are all pragmatic. They reveal themselves in feelings of peace, happiness, and a good self-image. The sacred, above all, *works*. It helps people get along better on the job, behave better with their families, and feel better about themselves."[15] In other words, God is reduced to an instrumental value. Psychological health replaces spiritual growth. Spiritual maturity becomes equated with emotional stability and healing from childhood wounds.

Church-based small groups may also disconnect from the communion of saints, the beliefs and practices of our theological forebears, the

13. Frederick Buechner, *Telling Secrets: A Memoir* (New York: HarperCollins, 1991), p. 93.
14. Wuthnow, *Sharing the Journey*, p. 303.
15. Wuthnow, *Sharing the Journey*, p. 18.

historic creeds and confessions of the church, and the current pastoral and teaching authority of the congregations to which they belong. In Wuthnow's study, 49 percent of group members chose the statement "my religious beliefs are very personal and private," and 47 percent chose "my spirituality does not depend on being involved in a religious organization."[16] The faith demonstrated by small-group members "needs little knowledge of the traditional attributes of God [and] indeed, theology tends to be relatively unimportant."[17] Personal sharing, singing, table fellowship, and common projects consume more time than the study of Scripture does, even in those groups that explicitly focus on Bible study.[18] In fact, 40 percent agreed that "it doesn't matter what you believe, as long as you are a good person."[19]

Small-group members' subjective faith and disconnection from congregations and the larger communion of saints mirrors the trust profile of late-modern persons. Premoderns placed their trust in religious cosmologies and religious leaders. They were oriented toward the past, specifically the tradition of their ancestors. Trustworthy traditions provided answers to existential questions and spiritual guidance for daily living. Late-modern persons are oriented toward the future. They trust neither tradition nor religious authorities; or if they do, that trust is provisional and situational and hence radically different from that of premodern humans. Even though persons today are exploring their faith with others in a communal structure (a small group), their faith is subjective and self-reflexive rather than ecclesial in its orientation.

Connection within the Group: Reembedded Social Ties

Traditional forms of community in America have fractured. The hectic pace, transience, and technological advances of modernity have displaced at least two generations. Disembedded from extended family, neighborhoods, and their own ethnic groups, people are left to estab-

---

16. Robert Wuthnow, *I Come Away Stronger,* p. 387.

17. Robert Wuthnow, *I Come Away Stronger,* p. 233.

18. Robert Wuthnow says: "Bible studies are thus accommodating more traditional religious patterns to the needs and interests of contemporary society. They are a new format that allows people to gain some exposure to religion while pursuing their need for community" (*Sharing the Journey,* p. 148).

19. Robert Wuthnow, *I Come Away Stronger,* p. 387.

lish and reestablish their own communities. Friendship is "tethered to loss."[20] In this context of perpetual homelessness, small groups provide a social solvent, a way of enduring the fragmentation of traditional ties. Members give mutual empathy, affirmation, and feedback on decision-making. They nurture self-esteem. During times of personal upheaval, those open experience thresholds that shape our life narratives, small groups rally around their members, even providing financial and other practical kinds of care.

In essence, small groups foster supportive and caring interpersonal relationships as a form of reembedding in response to time-space distantiation in late modernity. Reembedding mechanisms, according to Giddens, enable people to establish new connections in local contexts. They enable us to establish face-to-face relationships in community. Many small groups, especially twelve-step groups and support groups, function as primary groups: they provide a source of personal identity, emotional support, accountability, and moral exemplars. These groups become substitute families, places of "shared vulnerability."[21] In many small groups, people come home and discover family as that discovery could only be made in late modernity. For this family is chosen, not given. Consider again Frederick Buechner's testimony:

> These groups I speak of, on the other hand, are more like what families at their best can be than what most families are, certainly more than what the family I grew up in ever was. They are more like families because in them something which is often extraordinarily like truth is spoken in something that is extraordinarily like love. They are more like families because if ever the members of AA or Alanon or Adult Children of Alcoholics or the rest of them would find themselves in trouble almost anywhere in the world, they know that they will find people who are less like strangers than like sisters and brothers and who will offer them a degree of human understanding and practical help which I am afraid most church goers would rarely be apt to go to a church to find and which I'm afraid most churches would rarely know how to give them in the event they did.[22]

20. Deborah Tall, "Dwelling: Making Peace with Space and Place," in *Rooted in the Land: Essays on Community and Place,* ed. William Vitek and Wes Jackson (New Haven: Yale University Press, 1996), p. 107.

21. Sara Wuthnow, "Working the ACOA Program," pp. 168-69.

22. Buechner, *Telling Secrets,* p. 94.

Interestingly, Putnam's research demonstrates a similar phenomenon. Small groups are significant reembedding mechanisms for those who have experienced the dismantling of the pure relationship. "[T]he rate of participation in such groups is two to four times higher among divorced and single people than among married people."[23]

While small groups provide support for those experiencing the disintegration of the pure relationship, they also embody the structural weaknesses of the pure relationship. Group members' relationships with one another become subject to advanced planning, require little personal sacrifice, and are easily broken. The social contract binding people to each other in small groups is weak. Many persons group-hop as much as they church-hop. "[T]he group is not a people with a history. It is a transient gathering, a place where nomads meet to share temporary insights."[24] Members do not exist for the sake of the group, but rather the inverse: the group exists solely for the sake of its members. Wuthnow says: "It is striking that most group members feel they compromise nothing to be part of their group; they do not even feel that the group nudges them in one direction or another. They like being in the group because it allows them to express their individuality."[25]

Connection within the Group: Homogeneity and Privatism

As I mentioned in the preceding chapter, late-modern community is sustained by both bonding social capital and bridging social capital. Small groups provide community. But is this community strengthening both forms of social capital? On the one hand, some groups contribute to bridging social capital. All Saints Episcopal Church, a 3500-member congregation in Pasadena, "intentionally gathers [in small groups] people as unlike as possible, to reflect its belief in inclusiveness and the essential oneness of all people."[26] In other settings, groups contribute to bridging social capital by bringing formerly privatized or sequestered issues into the public realm. Groups that address alcoholism, developmental disabilities, incest, sexual addiction, and discrimination against

---

23. Robert Putnam, *Bowling Alone: The Collapse and Revival of American Community* (New York: Simon and Schuster, 2000), p. 151.

24. Wuthnow, *Sharing the Journey*, p. 313.

25. Wuthnow, *Sharing the Journey*, p. 190.

26. Putnam and Feldstein, *Better Together*, p. 136.

homosexuals reframe personal struggles as social maladies requiring so-cial remedies. Others, such as Mothers Against Drunk Driving (MADD) and Association for Retarded Citizens (ARC), by definition pursue civic goals.

On the other hand, most small groups strengthen ties among like-minded people. Consider Saddleback Church, a ten-thousand-member megachurch in Southern California: eight thousand of its members participate in small groups. One of Saddleback's associate pastors re-ports that "the biggest factor in keeping a group together is affinity: people whose concerns, ages, and backgrounds are similar tend to con-nect and stay together."[27] This is not surprising. Wuthnow's research in-dicates that, overall, small groups tend to be theologically, politically, ra-cially, and socioeconomically homogeneous. Yet with little diversity comes little challenge to current thinking and ways of relating. Such in-sularity creates "intentional groups of like-minded persons," or, to use another metaphor, "a hall of mirrors."[28] The push for bonding capital is so strong that even inherently diverse groups, such as Alcoholics Anony-mous, emphasize members' commonalities and downplay differences.

Insularity plagues small groups in other ways as well. Overall, they do not mediate between individuals and the legal, economic, and governmental structures of our society. Neither do they embed per-sons in multilayered social networks. Therefore, their contributions to social capital are significantly less than large-scale religious bodies, such as denominations and civic organizations — certainly in the first half of the twentieth century. Putnam writes: "Self-help groups are not nearly so closely associated with regular community involvement such as voting, volunteering, giving to charity, working on commu-nity problems, or talking with neighbors, as are more traditional civic associations."[29]

Similarly, small groups may avoid social issues that beg for pro-phetic ecclesial response. Daniel Olson, a member of Wuthnow's team, observed a "Disciple Bible Study," which was sponsored by a United Methodist congregation. Even though the curriculum called for the discussion of sociopolitical issues from the standpoint of the gospel, certain group members thwarted this aspect of discussion on a weekly

27. Putnam and Feldstein, *Better Together,* p. 130.
28. Wuthnow, *Sharing the Journey,* p. 366.
29. Putnam, *Bowling Alone,* p. 151.

basis.[30] Other ethnographers have witnessed the same dynamic. "Relationships [with others, such as spouses, children, extended family, coworkers] dominated members' prayers and concerns."[31] The group rarely, if ever, discussed social, economic, or political issues. Instead, the group engaged the world through the lives of its individual members. Even their one social-action project, collecting books for incarcerated boys, stayed at the interpersonal level. The group never considered large-scale advocacy as a form of care. For this same reason, many sociologists and critical theorists criticize twelve-step groups for ignoring the social, political, and economic contributors to psychological distress and disorder.[32]

In light of these observations, we might say that small groups tend toward privatism rather than active engagement with the world. Distant and often alarming events that threaten to undo global and personal well-being intrude into our everyday lives in late modernity and create crises for which there are neither easy nor uncontested solutions. Many of these events are moral in nature: they call for thoughtful theological responses grounded in an ethic of mutual regard. Yet small groups shy away from a discussion of such issues. They embody a posture of pragmatic acceptance instead of radical engagement with large-scale political and economic risks and injustices.[33] In this regard, small groups function analogously to institutions that sequester existential issues in late modernity. They support personal ontological security by creating a protective cocoon where small-group members can bracket out the anxieties created by complex and alarming events in the larger world. However, the protection offered by this cocoon is limited, for "no amount of bracketing out is likely altogether to overcome the background anxieties produced by a world which could literally destroy itself."[34]

<hr />

30. Daniel V. A. Olson, "Making Disciples in a Liberal Protestant Church," in Wuthnow, *I Come Away Stronger,* p. 141.

31. George M. Thomas and Douglas S. Jardine, "Jesus and Self in Everyday Life," in Wuthnow, *I Come Away Stronger,* p. 195.

32. Minnick, *Twelve Step Programs,* p. 7.

33. Giddens describes four responses to the riskiness of life in late modernity: pragmatic acceptance, sustained optimism, cynical pessimism, and radical engagement (*The Consequences of Modernity* [Stanford: Stanford University Press, 1990], pp. 134-37).

34. Anthony Giddens, *Modernity and Self-Identity: Self and Society in the Late Modern Age* (Stanford: Stanford University Press, 1991), p. 183.

Connection to Self: Reflexivity unto Authenticity

Modern life is risky; it produces new anxieties and insecurities. Neither kin nor religion provides a sure source for decision-making. Due to extreme time-space distantiation, people encounter competing moralities, worldviews, and cultural others. No one sphere of life anchors identity. The end of tradition, unprecedented reflexivity, the fragility of the pure relationship, and the barrage of contradictory expert advice in nearly every sphere of life disorient and destabilize self-identity.

Small groups lay secure ground for those adrift in this sea of unprecedented change. They emphasize personal experience and self-discovery in their quest for self-actualization. Self-help groups support and contribute to the reflexive project of the self, often through a prescribed set of lifestyle guidelines. Thus twelve-step groups are less about addiction than moral and spiritual reconstruction. Minnick observes:

> Al-Anon was a cultural response developed in the 1950s by women who were trying to cope with the discontinuity between cultural ideals and their own lives. Unable to attain what they considered to be normal, happy marriages and families, these women devised a means of coping that involved a complex process of self-discovery, faith in God, and relations with others which did not compromise their new-found sense of self.[35]

Some support groups connect and empower disenfranchised and marginalized persons in American society, for example, gays and lesbians and persons with developmental disabilities. In *The Strength in Us: Self-Help Groups in the Modern World*, Alfred Katz and Eugene Bender say: "We see self-help groups as vehicles through which these outcast persons can claim and grow toward new identities, redefining themselves and society; can overcome solitariness through identification with a reference group; and sometimes can work toward social ends or social change that they see as important."[36]

Self-actualization in late modernity occurs through the control of time, that is, through reconstructing one's past in order to project a

---

35. Minnick, *Twelve-Step Programs*, p. 8.

36. Alfred H. Katz and Eugene I. Bender, eds., *The Strength in Us: Self-Help Groups in the Modern World* (New York: Franklin Watts, 1976), p. 6, quoted in Putnam, *Bowling Alone*, p. 151.

better future for oneself. Small-group members tell and retell, interpret and reinterpret their experiences in order to construct a coherent and authentic life narrative. In Wuthnow's research, over 60 percent of small-group members discussed their childhood experiences. Of those who reported that their faith had been strengthened in small groups, 80 percent discussed stories from the Bible (or another book), told stories about their own life experiences, and compared their personal stories with those of other group members.[37] This multistranded storytelling helps group members weave together the otherwise disparate threads of their lives. In describing a Presbyterian Bible study group, one of Wuthnow's researchers observes: "The [scriptural] texts generated stories, conversations, interpretations, and connections to life experiences. The group was a kind of living Midrash, an ongoing commentary upon these texts. The Word, it could be said, generated more words."[38] Another researcher, Daniel Olson, reports the same phenomenon in a Methodist group: "Hearing others use religious language and religious analogies to describe their life experience makes it easier for members to interpret their own lives in a religious framework."[39]

While small groups support the reflexive project of the self, it is unclear whether or not this self is formed on anything sturdier than "being true to oneself." Small groups homogenize ideas and censor expression. The deep code of these groups is "avoid judgmentalism."[40] This chokes out potentially constructive conflict. Even in evangelical Bible studies, doctrinal discussion may be eschewed in favor of personal application in order to prevent potential disagreement. Advice-giving is taboo. Some twelve-step groups have a "no cross-talk" rule: members are prohibited from addressing what others have shared unless they are explicitly invited to do so. Moreover, certain emotions, such as anger, may be censored by unspoken group rules. Out of fear of vulnerability, some participants avoid sharing prayer concerns of any emotional depth, let alone any personal confession of sin.[41] This leaves us wondering: What kind of self-connection do small groups foster? To what degree do small groups support a distinctly Christian formation?

37. Wuthnow, *Sharing the Journey*, p. 297.

38. J. Bradley Wigger, "Gracious Words: A Presbyterian Bible Study," in *I Come Away Stronger*, p. 46.

39. Olson, "Making Disciples," p. 146.

40. Wuthnow, *Sharing the Journey*, p. 206.

41. Thomas and Jardine, "Jesus and Self in Everyday Life," p. 193.

To what degree do they simply legitimate their members' actions and attitudes?

In summary, research indicates that small groups represent an ecclesial and societal practice that both facilitates and undermines spiritual, communal, and personal formation. As Giddens suggests about social practices in general, small groups simultaneously free persons for new action and hem them within prior action. In Wuthnow's words, the small-group movement "mirrors the shortcomings of its host environment."[42] In the context of the end of tradition, small groups enhance a personal connection to God, though they tend to disconnect from the church and its heritage. They are a creative form of reembedding in response to disembedding from local communities, kin, and religion. Group members build trust with one another through emotional communication and democratic decision-making processes. Yet their relationships remain tenuous, subject to change because anyone can choose to leave the group at any time. While small groups strengthen bonding social capital, they also embody the structural weaknesses of the pure relationship. As in modernity overall, anxiety follows on the heels of freedom in small groups. The pragmatic acceptance — or privatism — of small groups creates a protective cocoon in a milieu of pervasive, high-risk change that confounds the experts, let alone the rest of us. Besides emotionally inoculating their members against anxiety, small groups strengthen ontological security by creating space for beleaguered souls to foster trust relationships by which they can create a coherent life narrative. The double edge is that one's life narrative may rest solely on the thin moral thread of authenticity.

Conclusion: Beyond Current Research

At the conclusion of his research, Robert Wuthnow declared that the small-group movement was at a critical juncture in its history. He expressed hope that small groups could move Americans toward a more communal culture and the church toward a form of community more faithful to the gospel. Both he and Robert Putnam have set forth suggestions for achieving this laudable goal: (1) engage in common projects; (2) be guided by specific objectives; (3) function as groups rather

42. Wuthnow, *Sharing the Journey,* p. 366.

than simply aggregates of individuals; (4) participate in preserving the faith and practices of the Christian tradition; (5) integrate small groups into a multifaceted ministry program; (6) allow leadership of small groups to come from many directions — clergy, mental-health specialists, therapists, educators, and so forth; (7) contribute to the common, public good; (8) nest smaller groups within larger groups;[43] (9) encourage healthy debate and disagreement within groups.[44]

More than a decade has passed, and small groups continue to populate the landscape of American congregations. According to the 1998 National Congregations Study, 87 percent of churches have small groups (other than Sunday school classes) that meet at least monthly for social, recreational, and/or religious purposes. Of these churches, 48 percent have one to five monthly groups; 20 percent have six to ten monthly groups; and 11 percent have more than ten monthly groups.[45]

At the same time, the juggernaut of modernity has lunged forward in unexpected and devastating ways. The world seems more and more out of control. The inevitability of risk and the overall riskiness of life have become undeniable. In his most recent book, Giddens says:

> The idea of risk has always been involved in modernity, but I want to argue that in the current period risk assumes a new and peculiar importance. Risk was supposed to be a way of regulating the future, of normalizing it and bringing it under our dominion. Things haven't turned out that way. Our very attempts to control the future tend to rebound upon us, forcing us to look for different ways of relating to uncertainty.[46]

As I write this chapter, the U.S. government is mired in a debate about the potential benefits and risks of bailing out banks and automobile

43. Putnam and Lewistein write: "One clear solution is federation: nesting small groups within larger groups. Small groups within larger organizations can foster the personal relationships that would not be so easily formed within the larger organization alone . . . This 'nested', federal strategy is especially effective when (as in Saddleback and All Saints) members can participate in more than one small group, thus weaving personal ties among the small groups and reinforcing a sense of identity with the larger whole" (*Better Together*, p. 278).

44. Wuthnow, *Sharing the Journey*, pp. 341-66.

45. Chaves, *National Congregations Study*.

46. Anthony Giddens, *Runaway World: How Globalization Is Reshaping Our Lives*, 2nd ed. (New York: Routledge, 2003), pp. 43-44.

makers. Meanwhile, the stock market fluctuates erratically, unemployment is the highest in two decades, the housing market flounders, and millions of Americans have lost significant portions of their retirement savings. And that is not to mention the impact on Asia and Europe! No one has definitive answers to this complex global crisis. The best anyone can do is make educated guesses on the basis of recent history and a vision for a secure future.

As community has expanded to include distant others, worldwide crises like the above pierce the protective cocoons of late-modern humans. The riskiness of global connections creates widespread anxiety. Thus Wuthnow's questions — "Will the small group movement encourage serious commitment to others in the wider community? Will it deepen its understanding of spirituality?" — are all the more pertinent today. Yet they remain unanswered. Likewise, we do not know what impact Wuthnow's suggestions for reforming small groups have had. Has the implementation of these guidelines enabled small groups to acculturate persons into a communal faith? What is the quality of group members' connection to God, the communion of saints, and persons in other communities? These empirical-descriptive questions, combined with the continued presence of small groups in American churches, call for further inquiry into small groups.

CHAPTER 3

Well-Developed Small Groups
Navigating the Crisis of Community

As partners together in Christ, small group members enjoy mutual prayer and personal sharing of the joys and sorrows of life, find opportunities to demonstrate the love of Christ to one another, grow in Christian discipleship, and mature in faith. In addition, some specialized groups invest in mutual support, healing, recovery, and mission ventures.

E. Stanley Ott, "Small Group Ministries:
Vital for Christian Living"

Small groups remain a distinctive marker of the religious landscape in twenty-first-century America. In 2002, 25 percent of all Protestants — and 53 percent of evangelicals — attended a weekly small group.[1] Discipleship, pastoral care, and community formation often occur in these settings. Yet the most recent research indicates that small groups are an ambiguous response to the multilayered crisis of community in late modernity. What about small groups that incorporate sociologists' suggestions for reform, such as leadership training, purpose statements, and intentional organization? Do these groups overcome the tendencies toward individualistic spirituality, insularity, and homogeneity? If so, what can other congregations learn from them? How can our practical theology of small-group ministry be shaped by the wisdom embedded in these groups?

1. George Barna, *The State of the Church 2002* (Ventura, CA: Issachar, 2002), p. 31.

To answer these questions, I summarize in this chapter new research on well-developed small groups in six congregations.[2] By "well-developed" I mean small groups (1) guided by mission statements, (2) supported through regular leadership training, and (3) embedded within the congregation's overall ministry design. The well-developed small groups in these congregations are identified by other churches and pastors as "best practices," that is, models of faithful small-group ministry. Four of the congregations belong to the Presbyterian Church (USA), and two belong to the Reformed Church in America (RCA).[3] They can be characterized as "mainline evangelical" in their theological orientation.[4] The congregations exhibit a wide range of active membership (from 250 to 1200 persons), and they are situated in different socioeconomic contexts (ranging from an upper-middle-class suburban community to an urban, predominantly blue-collar community).

The well-developed small-group ministries in these six congregations have divergent levels of leadership training, organizational structure, and mission development. Some congregations provide group-

2. Specifically, I investigated how well-developed small groups in these six congregations understand and connect to God, how they relate to one another, and how their life together extends beyond their small group to include broader circles of community. Information from thirteen focus interviews with group members and leaders, individual interviews with pastors and other staff members, brief surveys, participant observation and review of small-group curricula and leadership-training material created a multidimensional portrait of small groups navigating the crisis of community in these six congregations. See Appendix A for a fuller description of the mixed-methods research that I used in this project. See the Epilogue for an interpretation of this research as an aspect of neo-Barthian practical theology.

3. I expected to discover an affinity between the practices of these groups and Wuthnow's guidelines, given his current affiliation with a Presbyterian congregation. Groups embedded in other theological traditions — Eastern Orthodoxy or Roman Catholicism, for example — likely would conceptualize and practice community in other ways. Second, I wanted to explore whether or not any aspects of Reformed ecclesiology filter down into the practice of well-developed small groups. Third, from an empirical standpoint, studying congregations within the same tradition limited the number of dependent variables.

4. These six congregations do not fit neatly into any of the common sociological categories used to depict congregations — fundamentalist, evangelical, mainline, liberal, independent, and so on. Instead, they seem to be "mainline evangelical" congregations, embedded within a denomination yet simultaneously differentiated from it by the subidentity "evangelical." For further discussion of these six congregations as mainline evangelical, see Appendix B.

specific training, while others provide the same training for all group leaders. For instance, small-group leaders at one congregation attend a yearly "vision day" for all lay and ordained leaders. They then attend periodic seminars focused on the needs of specific groups, and they receive coaching from a small-group coordinator on staff at the church. At another congregation, the leaders of one group receive outside training on a particular curriculum with loose oversight from the pastors, and the leaders of another group, a prayer-and-visitation ministry team, receive monthly training from one of the pastors.

Some congregations have a mission statement for their small-group ministry, an umbrella kind of vision that guides all groups. Others develop mission statements for each individual group. Nearly all groups have a covenant statement, a mutually agreed-on set of guidelines and expectations for group participation. Some intentionally connect the mission of their small-group ministry to the mission of the congregation. For instance, one congregation's mission centers on "discipleship," of which there are six marks: a heart for Christ alone; a mind transformed by the Word; arms of love; knees for prayer; a voice to speak the good news; and a spirit of servanthood and stewardship.[5] The mission of the small-group ministry is the same. In fact, small-group members and leaders complete a yearly assessment to determine their growth in these six marks and to discern areas for future study. Similarly, another congregation's mission is "to know Christ and to make Him known." This entails spiritual formation through "core activities: prayer, worship, teaching, encouragement/support/service, and witness." It involves "living balanced relational lives — with God, family, brothers and sisters in Christ, and seekers." Five different kinds of small groups — home groups, study groups, ministry teams, seeker groups, and recovery groups — help the congregation reach this mission. Each of the small groups uses an assessment tool to discern whether and how it is achieving this overall mission of spiritual formation.

At another congregation, the connection between the mission of the small groups and the mission of the congregation is more implicit. The third bullet point of the congregation's mission is "to provide a Christ-centered home and family for all of God's children." The exposition of this goal declares: "We are committed to making this church a

5. See Glenn McDonald, *The Disciple-Making Church: From Dry Bones to Spiritual Vitality* (Grand Haven, MI: Faith Walk Publishers, 2004).

safe haven for all of God's wounded, frightened, and stressed-out children." The men's group, prayer groups, and prayer-and-visitation ministry team all seek to facilitate personal healing and transformation.

These well-developed groups are not only related to the mission of the congregation, but are also integrated into the ministry design of the congregation. They are viewed as an essential component of the ministry of the congregation, though they are not viewed as a panacea. They are not expected to be the primary site of catechesis, for instance; nor are they expected to be the means of numerical growth. They embody a variety of the core practices of the congregation, and they are integrated with the other practices of the congregation. For instance, one congregation has a four-dimensional ministry design — a mission statement, core practices, defining practices, and small groups/ministry teams. The congregation's stated mission is "to glorify God by making disciples and meeting human needs." Its defining practices are "reach, grow, and send": reaching those uninvolved in the church or uncommitted to Jesus Christ; helping one another grow as disciples of Jesus Christ; and sending one another to serve in the church and the world. According to their senior pastor, "We expand reach-grow-send with six defining practices, what you may call a 'missional lifestyle': witness, prayer, care, Word, with-me, and send." The fourth component of the ministry design is small groups and ministry teams. The latter combine the devotion and fellowship of small groups with the task-orientation of committees.[6] Small groups and ministry-team meetings follow the same overall format: Word (20 minutes reflection on Scripture), Share (50 minutes addressing common tasks or discussing personal experiences, depending on the group), and Prayer (20 minutes).

More generally, all six congregations seem to have what a few of them explicitly identify as a balance among large-group, small-group, and individual mentoring. In large-group settings, pastors take the lead in teaching the faith and leading worship. In small-group settings, congregants have fellowship, pray, listen, and, as one pastor put it, "have conversation over Scripture." In individual mentoring, pastors and congregants provide more specific spiritual, emotional, and relational support for those with particular needs.

While the small-group ministries within these six congregations

---

6. For more information, see E. Stanley Ott, *Transform Your Church with Ministry Teams* (Grand Rapids: Eerdmans, 2005).

have various mission statements, group covenants, forms of leadership training and congregational-ministry design, they fulfill a common set of human needs and ecclesial purposes. As I explain in more detail below, these well-developed small groups

- practice communion with a personal God;
- support wider involvement in the congregation;
- enhance the congregation's ministry of care;
- provide intimacy, friendship, and family;
- strengthen bonding social capital;
- prop up the pure relationship (particularly marriage);
- witness in word and deed; and
- facilitate healing and the strengthening of ontological security.

They overcome many (not all) of the ambiguities of small groups in general, that is, those studied by Wuthnow. They especially help persons establish a connection to God, the church, one another, family, and friends in the context of the crisis of community. Though there are theological weaknesses in these groups, they nevertheless support the church's participation in the mission of God in the context of late modernity.

Practicing Communion with a Personal God

Previous research suggested that small groups, while creating a much-needed venue for spiritual exploration, embody an inward, privatized, and domesticated spirituality. Our well-developed small groups resemble this assessment in their highly interpersonal conception of God. Small-group members and leaders overwhelmingly describe their connection to God in interpersonal terms. Nearly all,[7] 95 percent, report "feeling closer" to God as a result of group participation (see Table 3 on p. 51).[8] Group members consistently use the phrase "grow in my/our re-

7. Though slightly higher, this percentage, compared to general church-based groups, is statistically insignificant. Only a 10 percent or higher variation is enough to suggest the need for further research.

8. Note that the tables in this chapter distinguish three categories of small groups: general small groups, church-based small groups, and well-developed church-based small groups. The former two categories I have extrapolated from Wuthnow's data; the latter comes from my research of well-developed small groups in six congregations.

Table 3: Small-group participants' relationships to God

Percentage Who Experienced Change in Relationship to God	General	Church-based	Well-Developed
Feel closer to God	36%	90%	95%
Bible is more meaningful	23%	84%	90%
Experienced answered prayer	25%	75%	95%

lationship with God." Such growth seems to be defined as feelings of personal closeness and companionship with God. As one group member exclaimed, "I want to talk to [God] more. He's my other conversation partner. Even though I can't necessarily hear his answers physically, I know that God is listening. I love that!" In other words, God becomes part of everyday life for small-group participants. "Experiencing God" in daily life is the core curriculum in a number of groups. For example, some groups followed *Experiencing God,* a twelve-unit Sunday school curriculum, and the 2005 Lenten groups at one church studied *Practicing the Presence of God* by Brother Lawrence.[9]

These well-developed groups seem to propagate or at least bolster a domesticated faith. To what degree is this problematic? On the one hand, Nancy Ammerman, in direct challenge to Wuthnow, interprets this aspect of the small-group movement as a commendable reclamation of a lost spiritual practice. She asserts that women and non-Western religious practitioners historically have integrated the exigencies of daily life into their spirituality. Lives are not neatly divided into completely separate spheres; overlap occurs within the person. Daily concerns expressed in small groups "reflect the sorts of integration (diffuseness) of lives not neatly divided into institutional roles."[10]

On the other hand, the well-developed small groups in these six congregations put God's immanence in the foreground to such a degree that God's transcendence nearly disappears from the landscape altogether. Of the approximately hundred small group members and leaders, none emphasized God's holiness, majesty, or otherness. Fewer

9. See Henry Blackaby, *Experiencing God: Knowing and Doing God's Will* (Nashville: Lifeway Press, 1990); see also Brother Lawrence, *The Practice of the Presence of God* (New Kensington, UK: Whitaker House, 1982).

10. Nancy Ammerman, *Congregations and Community* (New Brunswick, NJ: Rutgers University Press, 1997), p. 354.

than 8 percent mentioned the word "sin." Well-developed or not, small groups seem to transpose the "pure relationship" onto the Almighty. Connection to God is interpersonal — "me and Jesus" — and anchored in emotional intimacy and open communication. Subjective experience of one's connection to God becomes the source of ontological security. As Giddens writes, in modernity "the individual feels bereft and alone in a world in which she or he lacks the psychological supports and the sense of security provided by more traditional settings."[11] Theologically, we have no being outside of Jesus Christ, and thus God is the source of our ontological security. Many passages of Scripture portray God as working in and through very human, seemingly mundane activities: eating, sleeping, parenting, family fighting, and making love. These texts also portray God as personal, for example, Abraham's friend and the one who hears the psalmists' laments, exultation, loneliness, and fear. However, if believers overemphasize the affective dimension of their relationship with God, then this existential connection is prone to the fragilities of the pure relationship. God may seem to stop communicating; God may seem to deny the presence of the Holy Spirit. Security vested in human experience rather than the promises of God is inherently insecure. It neglects the decisive fact that the divine-human relationship is upheld on both sides by God, a knowledge that can sustain us during dark nights of the soul.

Small groups commune with God through two devotional practices: prayer and Bible study. Not surprisingly, given groups' interpersonal slant on the connection with God, their studies are predominantly application-oriented. Unless specifically designed as in-depth Bible studies, groups move quickly from "encountering the text" to "appropriating the text," with little or no time spent on literary context, historical background, or theological analysis.[12] In contrast to Wuthnow's assessment, however, such thin encounters with Scripture may not be spiritually detrimental. As the pastors of all six congregations express it, small groups are not the primary site for Christian education. They provide opportunity to "have conversation" over the written Word; but in-depth study of Scripture and the Christian tradi-

11. Anthony Giddens, *Modernity and Self-Identity: Self and Society in the Late Modern Age* (Stanford: Stanford University Press, 1991), pp. 33-34.

12. According to Richard R. Osmer, Bible-study lessons should include three moments: preunderstanding, encountering the text, and appropriating the text (see Osmer, *The Teaching Ministry of Congregations* [Louisville: Westminster John Knox, 2005]).

tion occurs in other contexts, such as churchwide retreats, large-group teaching sessions, and parachurch programs.

Perhaps most significantly, practicing their faith inside these well-developed small groups enables participants to practice their faith outside the group. Groups create a safe space to learn the basic practices of Christian faith. Interviewees overwhelmingly reported that groups teach them how to read and study Scripture, pray, and talk about their faith with friends, family, and coworkers. In small groups, novices take risks by asking questions that they fear reveal their supposed spiritual ignorance. Many pray out loud for the first time ever, slowly gaining confidence, until they surprise themselves by praying at home or at work on a regular basis.

Quantitative data further indicate the significance of practicing the faith in our well-developed groups. A slightly higher percentage of persons in well-developed groups report that the Bible has become more meaningful to them as a result of group participation (see Table 3). A significantly greater number — 20 percent — have experienced answered prayer as a result of their group participation. Leadership training — through which small-group leaders learn to pray and meditate on Scripture — and intentional incorporation of spiritual practices in these groups may create this wide variance between well-developed and general groups. Though not listed in the table above, 100 percent of members in well-developed small groups study the Bible as compared to 85 percent in Wuthnow's church-based groups.

To summarize, well-developed small groups emphasize connection with a personal God. This is not, in and of itself, theologically problematic, particularly if other aspects of congregational ministry focus on God's otherness. What is problematic on both sociological and theological grounds is the transposing of the pure relationship onto group members' understanding of God.[13] This transposition makes one's existential connection to God dependent on mutual communication and emotional intimacy. In all fairness, this may not be a consequence of small groups per se; rather, it may be characteristic of evangelicalism in general.[14] Positively speaking, well-developed small groups in these six

13. Note that here my interpretation of well-developed small groups is influenced directly by my normative commitments, which will be spelled out in upcoming chapters. This points to the fact that the four movements in the practical theological spiral are not linear; rather, they interpenetrate each other.

14. See Andrew Root, *Revisiting Relational Youth Ministry: From a Strategy of Influence to*

mainline evangelical congregations facilitate spiritual integration. They help persons practice their faith in other spheres of life. In this sense, they illustrate the turn toward orthopraxy (right action) and away from orthodoxy (right belief) in late-modern Christianity.

Connecting to the Congregation and Enhancing the Ministry of Care

The well-developed groups in our six congregations stand in stark contrast to Wuthnow's finding that small groups disconnect from local congregations and from the pastoral/teaching authority of the church. These well-developed groups form the connective tissue of the congregation. As their lives are knit together in small groups, members reach out and support others in the congregation, particularly those in crisis, bereavement, or loss. Sometimes these groups function as ministry teams commissioned to participate in the congregation's ministry of care. More often than that, they simply care for one another and other church members as a natural outflow of their life together. They describe themselves as going all the way with people, even to the end of life, as depicted in the following remarks from one of the focus groups (M = male; F = female).

> M1: We had, in our group, a couple. The man had stomach cancer. Fred lived a little over a year, which was a miracle. We went through all of that with them, every level of it.
>
> F1: We did that with Joanie, too. She had cancer. She went from being fine to where she couldn't speak, but she continued to come Wednesday morning and occasionally you would see a tear. We took her to communion on occasion. We went right through that to the end with her, too.
>
> F2: When we started in October with Forty Days of Community, one of the ladies in our group had three major surgeries . . . and we've gone through that with her and been very supportive of her. When she couldn't come to the group in between, we'd take

a *Theology of Incarnation* (Downers Grove: InterVarsity Press, 2007). Root persuasively argues that evangelicalism in the U.S. is a response to the emergence of the pure relationship in the early-to-mid-twentieth century.

meals to her. You try to be there for [each other], driving [people places] and that kind of thing.

F3: We had a fellow in the church, not in our life group, who had something on his brain. He had to go to a teaching hospital. When he got there, the life group was there. It's about 160, 180 miles away, and we stayed with him.

The pastors in all six congregations understand the ministry of care of their small groups to be an essential part of the congregation's service to its members. One pastor remarked: "Usually when someone's fallen ill and I visit them at home or the hospital, their small-group members have already been there, praying with them, listening to them, and bringing food for their family. Small groups are the first responders. They excel at caring for each other in Christ's name." Pastors and group members and leaders alike recognize that such *diakonia* is not the sole responsibility of the pastor(s) or staff. In fact, they admit that compassionate service depends on active participation of lay leaders and the work of small groups. One group leader expressed it like this:

Pastor Jerry can't get around to everyone. He can't go and visit people who are shut in and do all the things that a lot of [small group members] do. The only way that the tentacles can spread out and we can build upon what we started is through the small group thing. We can minister to each other, primarily listening to each other about our problems, our concerns, our desires, and our praying together. . . . Without that, [with just] a minister on Sunday standing up there on the pedestal and preaching out to "all of us sinners" out there, there is not going to be an awful lot happening.

Besides formally and informally leading in the congregation's ministry of care, members and leaders of these well-developed groups are highly involved in their congregations. More than 50 percent participate in more than one group, and 50 percent are ordained elders or deacons. They remain in dialogue with — and in some cases overtly seek oversight from — the pastor(s). Pastors frequently prepare or approve group study materials at all six congregations. At one congregation, group participants internalized the pastor's defining vision and core practices of small groups, even if they struggled to implement them. Of those interviewed, 67 percent referred to their pastor's training materials and 100 percent specifically mentioned the core practices of either "word-share-prayer" or "reach-grow-send."

Group leaders intentionally promote respect for their pastoral staff as well. In spite of a year-long conflict with a member of the pastoral staff, one set of group leaders reportedly never disparaged this person. In another group, two leaders challenged group members to avoid triangulation (at least within the group) when frustrated with the pastoral staff. "In our group, we said, 'We can't make this a church-bashing session. If there are true concerns, then let's pray about them at the end of our time together. But we can't spend an hour talking about problems with persons or leaders in the church, because that's not growing in our relationship with the Lord.'"

While these well-developed small groups support participation in congregational ministry and respect the authority of the pastoral/teaching office, their connections to the faith tradition and to the communion of saints remain weak. All of the small-group ministries seem far less connected to their ecclesial heritage, the Reformed tradition, than to their local congregations. Fewer than 20 percent of interviewees indicated that their groups discuss Reformed theology, and fewer than 15 percent experienced a new understanding of Reformed theology as a result of their group participation. Given the fact that focus groups included many ordained elders and deacons and other highly committed members, these numbers are quite low, especially when compared to the 90 percent who indicated that the Bible had become more meaningful to them because of small-group participation. When completing the survey, many interviewees even asked, "What is Reformed theology?" One Presbyterian man sheepishly said, "Then let me ask the embarrassing question. So are we a Reformed church?"

More generally, theological language was absent among small-group members and leaders in five of the six congregations. Any mention of explicitly theological concepts — for example, justification, sanctification, confession, grace, sin, forgiveness, body of Christ, kingdom of God — was exceedingly rare. The presence (not abundance) of theological concepts in the focus-group interviews at one congregation is likely a consequence of the senior pastor's long-term goal to form the congregation in a Reformed identity. One group reported that their associate pastor taught a year-long educational series entitled "Being Reformed." With the exception of this and another group that reported a study of Luther, Calvin, and Zwingli, small-group curricula in these congregations did not engage the theological tradition. Instead, most groups used popular Christian books, which might be characterized as a generic American Christianity.[15] In this we see evidence of the end of tradition and the late-modern orientation away from the past, away from church history and the development of theology in the communion of saints. Even so, this manifestation of the end of tradition in well-developed small groups is not synonymous with what Wuthnow's groups exhibited. Whereas those groups also turn away from trust in religious authorities and communities of faith, these well-developed small groups intentionally invest trust in their congregations and in their ministers.

Intimacy and Reembedded Friendship and Family

Like groups in general, the well-developed small groups in our six congregations overwhelmingly indicated needs for belonging, trust, acceptance, and intimacy. What was different is that these groups seem to function as communities, not merely as gatherings of rugged individualists. Members were committed to one another. When one was absent repeatedly, others renewed contact with him or her via phone, email, or other communications. When one was ill, distraught, or incapacitated in some way, group members rallied around him or her to provide emotional, spiritual, or financial support.

Members belonged to their small group, which in turn enhanced their sense of belonging to the congregation. Group members were at ease in church, especially in larger congregations, when they were known by at least a few others. As their need for intimacy on the human plane was met, they experienced intimacy with God. Intimacy with God may be woven together with and even contingent on intimacy with others. As one group member reported, "[As a result of being in a small group], you just feel like you know the people you're worshiping with, and you can just be intimate as well. You become more intimate with God, I think, as well. . . . I can't be intimate and open with God unless I know who's next to me [in the church]."

15. See J. Todd Billings, "The Problem with Mere Christianity," *Christianity Today,* February 2007, pp. 46-47.

Intimacy in small groups entails the capacity to be vulnerable, to speak openly and authentically about struggles with regard to one's spouse, children, parents, or coworkers. Intimacy involves risk, and it is contingent on active trust. Consequently, intimacy needs to be worked at. Sometimes it takes new practices that encourage openness. Members of one couples' group, tired of their lack of intimacy, decided to alter their group structure for a season. They created a "hot seat," where one person would sit each week and answer this question: What do you want Jesus to do for you today? This is what they reported: "We listened to each person individually, not as a couple . . . and each person individually said this is what I'm struggling with and I need prayer. Then we individually prayed for that person. And it took hours, but after that week it changed our small group."

What is striking about this practice is that it created a democracy of emotional disclosure in a mutually agreed-on and constructed sacred space. Like the pure relationship form, intimacy in these small groups is equivalent to mutuality, autonomy (the free choice to participate or not), emotional communication, and self-disclosure. When these characteristics are present, the need for acceptance is satisfied. When group members experience acceptance from one another, they believe that God accepts them as well. One group member put it this way:

> Groups of people can come together and offer the heart of God [to each other], and the safest place on earth can be God's heart in another person. And that's the wonder of people being able to be intimate, to show the stuff that's in their hearts and really be accepted. . . . And Christ's love is there, and he doesn't condemn you and neither do I.

Perhaps not surprisingly, small-group members and leaders at all six congregations repeatedly framed their relationships with one another in terms of friendship and family. As Giddens describes it, family and friendship in late modernity are founded on needs for intimacy, emotional communication, and creating a shared history. Small-group participants fondly labeled their groups as "closer than family," "my true family," or "extended family." Many spend time together outside of group and church activities. As two focus group members put it, "[Our group] misses each other, so we're all going to get together and go out to dinner because we just miss each other," and "We need a fix.

We need our life-group fix." Sometimes these friendships are sustained in spite of ongoing time-space distantiation. As one couple said, "We're still in touch with all the small groups that we've ever been a part of. It's amazing. They come and visit up here, even from California. Small groups really make good friends."

Bonding Social Capital with Ecumenical Longings

Tom and Anne have attended their Presbyterian congregation for over twenty years. They have been ordained as elders and deacons. They have participated in a number of men's groups, women's groups, Bible studies, Sunday school classes, and ministry teams. Their positive experience in small groups has impelled them to join an ecumenical group, which in turn has created a new excitement about their own faith.

> My wife and I attend a neighborhood Bible study, fourteen to sixteen people from different traditions and cultures. We have Catholics, Presbyterians, Baptists, and people from Germany and Scotland. We're all from different faith traditions, countries, and cultures, and we study the Bible and associate with each other knowing that each has a different way of worshiping the Lord. Yet we click. When we come out of that Bible study, we're just on fire for the Lord. That small group of different people loving the Lord together invigorates me. It's easy to study in a small group with other Presbyterians, but here are people doing it differently and we're still together.
>
> Small groups lead out to larger groups and out to people of different denominations worshiping the Lord, men and women, fathers and sons, mothers and daughters — all worshiping the Lord. There's nothing more exciting. And what unites us is that we all love Jesus and we have a good prayer time together.

This passion and appreciation for ecumenical connections expressed by Tom and Anne surfaced in interviews in each of the congregations. Those who experience diversity in their small groups highly value it, because they are challenged to think about and practice their faith in new ways. They are also encouraged by the presence of other Christians who surround them at work and in their neighborhoods and who join them in the often dispiriting task of faithfulness to the gospel.

In this sense, these well-developed small-group ministries are not as insular as those studied by Wuthnow. Some group participants long for and seek out diversity, at least ecumenical diversity. As Putnam discovered, groups can strengthen bridging social capital if they are intentionally structured to do so. While members and leaders of these well-developed groups seemed interested in ecumenical prayer groups, Bible studies, and mission groups, their congregations did not intentionally nurture this longing. None of the pastoral staff from any of the congregations mentioned the presence or value of ecumenical small groups. Only one of the six congregations actually sponsors an ecumenical Bible study. Interviewees from the other churches who are interested in connecting with Christians from other faith backgrounds do so outside of congregational programming.

While these well-developed small groups potentially could contribute to bridging social capital, they excel at enhancing bonding social capital. As I have mentioned above, group members care for one another holistically. In fact, every focus group interview included one or more poignant stories of congregational care: a group of retired men supporting a member in the midst of his painstaking decision to admit his wife of fifty years to a nursing-care facility; a group that prayed for and informally advised a couple considering divorce; another group that provided meals, transportation, and visitation for a group member's family as he slowly wasted away from cancer.

Group activities and conflict resolution (or lack thereof) also suggest that these well-developed groups contribute far more to bonding social capital than bridging social capital. Bonding activities occur more frequently in our well-developed groups than in those studied by Wuthnow. A significantly higher proportion of these groups let people share their problems, provide emotional support, hold members accountable, and socialize with one another (see Table 4 on p. 61). None of the focus-group participants reported conflict within their group(s) during the interviews. Wondering if the term "conflict" evoked negative connotations, I then asked about generic differences between and among group members. Typical responses included personality types and different interpretations of particular biblical texts. Most notably, five group leaders at one congregation were silent about the protracted conflict (perhaps best described as a standoff) between two of them and one of the pastors. However, 24 percent of all interviewees reported on the survey that conflict exists within their groups, suggesting that,

Table 4: Small-group participants' relationships to each other

Relationship within the group	*General*	*Church-based*	*Well-developed*
Let people share their problems	75%	83%	100%
Provide emotional support	78%	91%	100%
Focus on a specific need/problem	71%	65%	58%
Hold members accountable	39%	37%	58%
Have parties	61%	60%	74%
Eat together	71%	77%	100%

similar to Wuthnow's findings, these well-developed groups suppress or avoid dealing with conflict.

A final indicator of bonding and bridging social capital is diversity, based on age, race, gender, and socioeconomic status. Well-developed groups at these six congregations are equally or slightly less diverse than Wuthnow's church-based and general groups, with the exception of racial diversity, which they woefully lack (see Table 5 on p. 62). All three categories exhibit equivalent age diversity, while church-based and well-developed groups exhibit somewhat greater gender diversity. This disparity may reflect the presence of "men's groups" in congregations. A comparison of socioeconomic diversity is not possible, since it was not obtainable from Wuthnow's survey. Yet even with these data, it is difficult to assess the extent of age and socioeconomic diversity within well-developed small groups. Surveys were not administered to all group members, and staff members were not asked for demographic information on *all* group members. Furthermore, when age diversity was mentioned in the focus-group interviews, the relativity of the phrase became apparent. For instance, one interviewee measured diversity as an age range of 40-65, while another expanded the range to 25-80 years.

These well-developed small groups are homogeneous and resist certain forms of diversity when it threatens the stability of group relations. Members and leaders in all six congregations shun discussion of public moral issues, including those cast in explicitly religious terms, such as prayer in local schools and the withholding of medical or life support on religious grounds. Group leaders in two congregations reported that they were admonished to avoid any discussion of politics as part of their training. Though not explicitly acknowledged, fear

Table 5: Diversity in small groups

Diversity in small groups as reported by interviewees	*General*	*Church-based*	*Well-developed*
Race (percentage of nonwhite group members)	13%	10%	3%
Socioeconomic (all different statuses)	N/A	N/A	44%
Gender (evenly mixed)	39%	51%	48%
Age (all different ages)	57%	52%	53%

that difference and disagreement would shatter group bonds was quite palpable.

The fact that well-developed small groups enhance bonding social capital means that they are an "antidote to social disconnectedness."[16] They function like sociological superglue. Negatively, long-term affinity groups — those meeting for over ten years with the same core members — often fall prey to "inertia" and "complacency," which may even mitigate against their contribution to bonding social capital. Four pastors reported that, over time, groups challenge their members less frequently. Members and leaders reported that their groups became less diligent over time in planning outreach activities. New members stopped joining. For some groups, length of existence is inversely proportional to the influx of new people. While they recognize the importance of hospitality, they long to maintain the close bonds that tie them together. Hence they are highly ambivalent toward new members. These long-term groups may resist further leadership training as well. In this sense, Wuthnow's interpretation provides an apt warning: the danger of stagnation lurks in long-term affinity groups. Such groups may slowly become characterized by a stagnant homogeneity. Not only do they lack socioeconomic and racial diversity, but they also maintain the same sameness, so to speak. As a result of their ambivalence toward new members, their avoidance of conflict, and their demographic homogeneity, they miss opportunities for new vitality that can be created by changing group dynamics.

16. Robert Putnam, *Bowling Alone: The Collapse and Revival of American Community* (New York: Simon and Schuster, 2000), p. 178.

To summarize, well-developed small groups embedded in these six congregations strengthen bonding social capital. The trust relationships in these groups compensate for the loss of local ties with family, neighborhood, and town. Moreover, they cannot be defined merely as pure relationships. While these trust relationships emphasize emotional intimacy, communication, and authenticity, the relationships are not dyadic but communal. Members are committed to the group, and the group to its members. Some even consider their participation in the group a matter of vocation (even if not clearly defined as such), placing their commitment in a theological context. Numerous group members and leaders sensed God calling them to participate in particular small-group communities. As one man said, "The group changes you in the way you interface with them, and I think God assembles a group for a specific reason."

Propping up the Pure Relationship

Jared, Gary, and Kyle, elders and leaders of well-developed men's groups and couple's groups, have never met each other. They do not follow the same group curriculum. Yet their stories complement each other so much that they could be woven together in one tapestry.

Jared's small group of twelve men, which emerged from a short-term "ministry to fathers," has been meeting and supporting members in their roles as father, husband, and disciple of Christ for nearly twenty years. Jared explains:

> The number-one purpose of our small group is to try to grow in relationship with the Lord. In order to grow in relationship with the Lord, there's a need for a small group and accountability. We try, and we all have our faults, but our purpose is to grow in relationships, to become better husbands and fathers.
>
> The group's had a big impact on wives and children as [we try] to be better persons, fathers, and husbands. We all have downsides as well as upsides. It might be an accident, but I'd like to think that it's not. It's not the social norm to have twelve people who haven't been divorced. In fifteen years, there have been a lot of close calls. We've tried to stay biblically based and work through [our marriage difficulties].

Gary's enthusiasm electrified the entire leaders' focus-group interview at his congregation. He belongs to three small groups, though his stories focused on the couples' group that he spearheaded.

> We formed our couples' group because I was sitting in a men's ministry meeting and leaned over to a friend and said, "I'd really like to be in a couples' group. . . ." We felt that there was something missing. Men were off doing their groups and women were doing theirs and never the twain shall meet! That's not what we wanted.
>
> One of the themes that runs through couples' groups is balance. We're interested in but not necessarily attaining balance in our relationships with each other, our children, our work, and the Lord. We are all working on this.

Five years ago, Kyle returned from a Promise Keepers conference determined to start a men's ministry in his congregation. Today, nearly thirty-five men attend their yearly men's retreats, and approximately fifteen participate regularly in two small groups. They study books on sexuality, marriage, communication, and parenting. In stark contrast to the overall lack of accountability in most small groups, Kyle and two other leaders honestly confess to one another "failures" in their marriages and "sins" against God, specifically their tendencies toward self-centeredness, misdirected anger, or use of pornography. Besides praying for each other, they phone each other during moments of crisis. For instance, Tim and his wife were arguing about money once again. In utter frustration, Tim stormed out of the house and went for a drive. He called Kyle, who was familiar with the history of this marital conflict. Kyle listened, prayed with Tim, and admonished him to return home and talk with his wife. Feeling "heard" and acknowledging that Kyle was "right," Tim returned home to reconcile with his wife.

These stories suggest that small groups at all six congregations help persons living in late modernity navigate through the murky waters created by transformations of intimacy. They help bear the burdens of the pure relationship in its marital and parental forms. With regard to the latter, one group for couples with young children has been studying a book on raising kids from a Christian perspective. This group "wants to learn what it means to be godly parents." One man shared how his group listened to him and offered him advice as he became a foster parent. Similarly, group members and leaders mentioned that they also support each other in figuring out how to respond to aging, to the physical decline and death of their parents. On occasion, older group members mentor younger group members in sorting through the multiple layers (emotional, social, and financial) of change in their simultaneous status as parent and child.

Men's groups and couples' groups function like adolescents who are traveling together through the uncharted journey into adulthood. Together, these small groups learn how to relate to each other and their loved ones in a world without clear social roles. In so doing, they seem to avoid the extreme yet complementary paths followed by evangelicals, on the one hand, and liberal Protestants, on the other. In recent decades, evangelicals have reacted against the transformations of intimacy by reasserting the "traditional" family form at the ecclesial and political levels.[17] Consider the public presence, popularity, and publishing history of organizations such as Focus on the Family, the Family Research Council, and the American Family Association. On the other side, consider the failure of mainline Protestants — with the exception of Don S. Browning and his research team — to offer a proactive response to deleterious effects of family breakdown, such as poverty, emotional instability, educational difficulty experienced by children of divorce.[18] In contrast, these six mainline evangelical congregations provide, by means of their small groups, a space to explore the implications of the changing roles of gender, marriage, and parenting. Group participants value family and consider their relationships — and hence obligations — to their children and spouses as a spiritual matter without adopting either of the above extremes.

Well-developed small groups not only help couples manage the burdens created by the pure relationship, but they also emotionally support those experiencing the loss and disequilibrium of divorce and widowhood. Terri openly shared her pain and anger with her small group following her divorce, as well as the stresses of single parenting and eventually her questions about reentering the dating scene. Others

17. The supposed "traditional" family form is, in a sense, a myth. It does not represent the organization of families throughout history, but rather the 1950s family form and perhaps some forms of Victorian families.

18. See Don S. Browning, *From Culture Wars to Common Ground: Religion and the American Family Debate* (Louisville: Westminster John Knox, 1997); see also Browning, *Marriage and Modernization: How Globalization Threatens Marriage and What to Do About It* (Grand Rapids: Eerdmans, 2003).

reported similar experiences. Even parents whose adult children experienced divorce found their small groups to be a place to share their perplexity and grief openly.

These small groups also aid couples in establishing a joint devotional life. In the safe presence of other couples, they learn to pray, read Scripture, and talk about their faith together. As a result, they discover new freedom to practice their faith in the domestic sphere. Alexis said:

> Our small group has given my husband and me a chance to talk about the Bible study afterward. We don't always talk about the Bible and what God wants us to do every day, even though this was the basis for us getting together (we met each other at a Bible study). [Now] we're focused on the kids and everyday life. But this group gives us a chance to be together as a couple and go together before God.

Other groups encourage their members to inquire about the presence of God in the midst of challenges within their marriage relationships. Mary and Ted, leaders of a couples' group, said that each week a different couple seems to bring a marital difficulty to discuss in the group. While helping the couple work at communicating with each other in new ways might be a laudable goal, it is not enough. Mary and Ted believe the group has a "responsibility" to encourage the couple to seek God's presence and wisdom in the midst of their impasse. They ask questions like, "What is your attitude toward each other and how can God enter into all of this?" and "What does Scripture even have to say about all of this?"

Witnessing in Word and Deed

Chip has been participating in his current small group since its inception. Prior to that, he participated in *Experiencing God.* Chip, his new wife, and their small-group leaders testify to his dramatic spiritual growth, which moves forward from inner healing to prayerful, evangelistic outreach. "My life has expanded," Chip declares exuberantly. "I look at someone and try to discern if they need prayer."

> The Holy Spirit gives me an immediate sense, an urgency to be attentive to others' needs. The Holy Spirit talks to me audibly (in my

head) and says, "Do this now." At Creation [a Christian music festival], a teenager sat down and God told me, "No one stood up to pray with her and I want you to go pray with her." I took J with me to pray for her, and the girl said, "Yeah, I was praying that God would send somebody to go up with me [for the altar call]." . . . God is intertwining everybody's lives together. If a stranger comes in [to church], it's a window of opportunity. I'm more willing to take a step of faith and pray for that person as a result of the small group.

Chip exemplifies one of the most predominant threads woven throughout this research project: the impact of groups on participants' willingness and ability to witness in word and deed. In this sense, the well-developed groups at our six congregations are not insular; rather, they propel their members into encounters with the other, particularly the non-Christian, the marginalized, and the lonely.

Groups at each of the six congregations incorporate regular mission projects into their schedule. Some groups include outreach or service in their covenant statements in order to hold themselves accountable to this aspect of their life together. Their mission activities include: serving meals at homeless shelters; purchasing and delivering Christmas gifts to families within their communities; hosting a community day; and visiting hospitals and nursing homes. While such activities do not confront social structures that contradict the kingdom of God, they still enable members to "proclaim release to the captives, recovery of sight to the blind, and freedom to the oppressed" (Luke 4:18).

Interviewees overwhelmingly experience an increased ability and freedom to share their faith in word and deed. Like Chip, their witness emerges from new sensitivity to human need and a discernment of God's ministry to persons outside the church. In the midst of their busy lives, they stop and express care for others. One man said, "The Holy Spirit has led me to do things that I normally wouldn't do. [At a former job], I knew a gentleman who had cancer. He walked by me one day and I just felt that I had to talk to him. I stopped him and starting talking to him about his relationship with God." Group participants also answer the questions and challenges posed by non-Christians, especially extended family members. In the words of the New Testament writer, they are prepared to give an answer, with gentleness and respect, to those who ask them to give a reason for their hope (1 Pet. 3:15, 16). One man said: "I have more knowledge to [answer] my brother when he challenges my faith. Now I can respond to him. All the classes and groups have made me grow in my faith so that I can understand it better and so that, when the time comes, I can [communicate] what I know."

Members and leaders also reported that participation in a small group has helped them relate better to people in general. In the small-group community, they discover the value of interdependence and expose the myth of self-sufficiency. They learn friendship; they learn to listen; they learn to love. Larry said:

> We've had training about listening and being empathic with people. I think I've improved somewhat because a lot of times you have a conversation with a person and you're thinking about how you're going to react to what they're saying. Instead, I'm learning to just let them talk and concentrate on what they're saying. . . . [W]ith outside work and here in the church, these skills have been helpful.

Participants seek to understand others compassionately rather than judgmentally. One woman stated it starkly: "I've learned not to be prejudiced or think I am superior to others." More generally, small-group members and leaders reported that they are more attentive to others' needs. After risking rejection and experiencing acceptance in their small groups, they gain confidence in their abilities to contribute to conversations and decision-making in other settings. They feel empowered and freed to practice vulnerability. Lilly described a new openness about feelings and needs: "I think we all have learned to be a little more open on the outside. I'm finding that I'll go up and give somebody a hug. Or I'll say, 'I need a hug.' You become more personal with people you are with on a daily basis."

To summarize, well-developed small groups nurture social connections outside the congregation in ways that resemble the profiles provided by Wuthnow and Putnam. They do not link individuals to larger social structures. By and large, they do not enhance bridging social capital, and they are not civic-oriented. They seem to embody what Giddens calls "pragmatic acceptance" when it comes to addressing societal ills. However, they may contribute indirectly to the public good by propping up the pure relationship and by practicing mission. They value family and recognize the challenges created by the transformation of intimacy without retreating into patriarchy. By carving out space to discuss marital and parenting concerns and confusions, they mitigate the burden placed on couples by the pure relationship. These groups also hold together social justice and personal evangelism, emphasizing the former more than conservative evangelicals do and the latter more than liberal-moderate mainliners do. However, their social ministry remains episodic, and it avoids dealing with large-scale structures and practices that undermine the flourishing of human life. To put it bluntly, none of the interviewees showed any awareness of political, socioeconomic, or racial injustices and the church's call to participate in the humanization of humanity by confronting those injustices.

Healing the Self and Strengthening Ontological Security

The individual and group interviews focused predominantly on well-developed small groups' connection with God, their own community life, their relationship to the congregation, and the connections they foster to persons and groups outside of the congregation. Yet another category of sociality emerged in this research: self-connection. In all six congregations, groups enhance participants' self-relatedness. They give much-needed psychological and spiritual support during open threshold experiences, such as transition, crisis, and trauma.

During my visit at one congregation, Karen stood behind the pulpit anxiously, yet certain of her "call" to proclaim the grace of God by means of her own story. Through tears and frequent references to biblical texts, Karen recounted her addiction to alcohol and her struggle to be free from crippling guilt and shame. She and her fiancé (now husband) had aborted their pregnancy twelve years ago. Though they were still mourning the loss of their twins, she talked of God's forgiveness and her consequent ability to forgive herself (over and over again). Not one of the two hundred persons attending that morning worship service stirred during her presentation. Few eyes were dry. At the end, Karen and the pastor invited congregants forward to light a candle in remembrance of any child lost through abortion, illness, or miscarriage. Fifteen minutes later, over two hundred tea light candles burned brightly on the Lord's table.

Karen reported that she had "collapsed" under the tangible presence of the Holy Spirit during prayer time in her small-group meeting a few months earlier. Surrounded by her "sisters- and brothers-in-Christ," as she put it, she wept as she was overwhelmed physically, mentally, and emotionally with the knowledge of God's forgiveness. Other group members did not know her story, but they recognized that she was experiencing, in their words, some sort of "inner healing." At the next group meeting, Karen openly shared her story of sorrow and shame. After being embraced both physically and emotionally by her fellow group members, she asked the senior pastor for an opportunity to share her experience with the congregation "so that other women and men might be healed."

At another congregation, Emma told a similar story. Her women's group participated in a prayer session for her under the associate pastor's direction. During the prayer she "saw" Jesus opening his arms to her, covering her with his robe, and walking her out of the room in which she had been molested by her older brother. Like Karen, Emma not only achieved peace with her own history; she also reinterpreted the meaning of her life. Understanding herself as one healed by God (from breast cancer and childhood abuse), Emma now co-leads a small group and joyfully heralds Jesus' love for and desire to heal others. "I'll share my story with anybody," she says. "I don't care. I'll just talk about it [because] everybody has pain." Likewise, Karen started a local outreach to those who have lost children through miscarriage, abortion, and illness. In other words, their small groups facilitated a creative reworking of the reflexive narrative of the self. The groups wove together spiritual practices (prayer and confession) and psychological interpretations of childhood trauma. In this sense, the groups "reskilled" parishioners to care for one another. Significant healing occurred without the presence of experts, that is, without therapists.

While not all stories are this dramatic, other small-group participants in all six congregations reported meaningful changes with respect to themselves. Numerous group members experienced healing of memories as a result of their group participation. As Chip said, "I can't keep those things suppressed anymore." Some interviewees claimed that by observing the suffering of others, they have become more grateful and complain less about their lives. Others report the group's discerning role in their decision-making. For some, the small group bolsters their self-esteem. One person attributed the following to her group's support and the content of their Bible study: "I'm no longer afraid to make mistakes, for instance, at work. I know I can work

Table 6: Small-group participants' relationships to self

Percentage Who Experienced			*Well-*
Change in Relationship to Self	*General*	*Church-based*	*developed*
Ability to forgive self	52%	82%	79%
Feel better about self	85%	87%	90%
More open and honest with self	72%	85%	92%

through it, and I didn't make that mistake because I'm stupid." Overall, these changes in group members' self-connection cut across church-based and well-developed small groups (see Table 6 above).

To interpret these changes in self-relatedness, we might say that well-developed small groups bolster ontological security. As I have defined it above, ontological security is a primal, embodied, even cosmic sense of trust in oneself, others, and the world. It enables us to maintain meaningful connections to ourselves and to others in the midst of time-space distantiation, transitions and crises, and competing advice about how we should live. Ontological security is sustained throughout life by (a) balancing autonomy and belonging; (b) affirming face-to-face encounters with others (i.e., mirroring); (c) continuity of routine (often provided by social practices); and (d) bracketing out unbearable anxieties. In late modernity, our disconnection from moral structures, lack of routine, pervasive reflexivity — in short, the constant upheaval of life — create anxiety and insecurity. The trauma, shame, and guilt experienced by Karen, Emma, and others further erode ontological security. Participation in these well-developed small groups counters this erosion. The face-to-face encounters in small groups are a source of mirroring for group members. This may partially explain the lack of challenge and confrontation in most groups. They focus on mutual affirmation and enjoyment. It may also explain the homogeneity of groups, because mirroring comes from "those similar to me, those from whom I come — historically and socioculturally."

These small groups strengthen ontological security in two other ways. They prop up the pure relationship and provide a forum for sorting through the meanings of family, gender, and parenting. They provide space for persons to weave together a consistent personal narrative grounded in a larger theological narrative in a milieu of constant change and the loss of tradition.

On the other hand, the well-developed small groups in these congregations fail to provide a context for dealing with aggression and, in this sense, undermine ontological security. Conflict is stifled rather than received. Groups suppress not only the potential negative effects of conflict, such as breach in relationships, but also the potential for forgiveness and reconciliation. If aggression is the underside of love, then the suppression of conflict dulls the love that might grow within the group. Similarly, group members and leaders at three of the congregations expressed a desire for deeper intimacy and more transparency and accountability. There was strong consensus that groups want accountability, but they don't know exactly what that means or how to implement it.

Conclusion

Well-developed small groups in these six congregations overcome numerous ambiguities of small groups in general. (1) The spirituality embodied in these well-developed groups is not disconnected from local faith communities. Instead, these groups support and enhance participants' connection to and involvement in their local congregations. They uphold the pastoral and teaching authority of the local church. And they enhance the congregation's ministry of fellowship and care. (2) These groups strengthen bonding social capital, and thereby potentially empower group members to contribute to the broader social good. (3) Though homogeneous, these groups are not insular: they propel their members to witness in word and deed outside their church buildings. (4) They also provide much-needed external support for the inherently insecure pure relationship. Members help one another navigate through the murky waters created by transformations of intimacy. While they do not provide definitive answers to questions about relationships, gender roles, and parenting, they do comfort one another in the midst of common confusion. (5) These groups mitigate the pure relationship in another sense: they are not expressions of the dyadic trust relationship. Groups relate to one another as groups; they are not mere gatherings of individualists. They provide communal connections and, for some members, a surrogate family. (6) The small-group community sometimes functions as a safe, supportive space for grief work, growth in self-acceptance, acknowledgment of God's forgiveness, and confession of sin. In other words, group members assist one another in their quest for personal integrity and continuity in their own stories. (7) Finally, these groups provide a space for modern persons to practice their Christian faith. They learn to read the Bible and pray. They then transpose these skills to other spheres of life.

The well-developed small groups certainly have some resemblance to the ambivalences of general small groups. They do not strengthen connection to the larger Reformed tradition. Group members exhibit a loss of theological language, including the most basic concepts of sin, grace, and justification. Though there is evidence of ecumenical interest, small groups do not enhance connection to other congregations or faith traditions. Group members' conception of God remains almost exclusively at the interpersonal level: God is companion and friend but not almighty, transcendent, holy, or other. Even more problematic, group members and leaders seemingly have transposed the pure relationship onto their subjective connection to God.

The small groups may not be to blame for these weaknesses. Instead, these shortcomings may suggest deficiencies in congregational-ministry designs as well as in American Protestantism in general.[19] Small groups are not "little churches." They cannot fulfill all the tasks of the teaching ministry of congregations, let alone all the core ecclesial practices. As pastors in all six congregations concluded, small groups are not the primary site for Christian education. Likewise, it seems unrealistic to expect small groups to contribute to bridging social capital on their own, given their significant role in filling the relational void traditionally occupied by kin, neighbors, and towns.

Mission statements, leadership training, and congregational-ministry design seem to contribute significantly to the emergence of authentic, life-giving community in small groups. Clear and realistic expectations of such well-developed small groups are also very important. Small groups do not remedy all the church's ills. Yet they foster community characterized by hospitality and nurture, exhortation and

19. In regard to the latter, the latest research suggests that most Protestants lack robust theological language and a connection to the larger Christian tradition. In their national study of youth and spirituality, Christian Smith and Melinda Lundquist Denton concluded that, with few exceptions, most teenagers, including evangelical Protestants, embrace a "moralistic therapeutic deism" (teenagers reflect the larger ecclesial culture). See Smith and Denton, *Soul Searching: The Religious and Spiritual Lives of American Teenagers,* reprint ed. (New York: Oxford University Press, 2009).

discernment, service and witness. Primarily, they excel at building relational connections around the practices of prayer and Scripture reading, and at caring for and serving one another. Many groups engage in periodic outreach activities beyond the walls of the church, though they seem to equip persons for practices of witness more than actually engaging in such practices themselves.

At this point in our practical theological journey, we have engaged the descriptive-empirical and interpretive tasks by asking and answering these questions: What is happening in small groups generally? What is happening in well-developed small groups by comparison to these other small groups? Why is this happening? This last question pushes us toward the next leg of our journey, seeking to understand what should be happening in well-developed small groups. I will turn to Karl Barth's ecclesiology, particularly the ontological reality of *koinonia* that is embedded within his understanding of the church. While ecclesial practices can be studied and analyzed from sociological and psychological frameworks, the inner essence of the church, its *koinonia,* is recognized and known by faith and interpreted by theology. For ecclesial practices must be shaped by the church's mission and its inner reality of *koinonia.*

CHAPTER 4

The Church as Multidimensional Koinonia

My prayer is not for them alone. I pray also for those who will believe in me through their message, that all of them may be one, Father, just as you are in me and I am in you. May they also be in us so that the world may believe that you have sent me. I have given them the glory that you gave me, that they may be one as we are one: I in them and you in me. May they be brought to complete unity to let the world know that you sent me and have loved them even as you have loved me.

Righteous Father, though the world does not know you, I know you, and they know that you have sent me. I have made you known to them, and will continue to make you known in order that the love you have for me may be in them and that I myself may be in them.

John 17:20-23, 25-26

On the eve of his arrest, Jesus prayed for the unity of all believers with God and each other for the sake of the world. In so doing, he pointed toward the ontological reality of *koinonia* — a multidimensional union and communion of the greatest possible intimacy and integrity. This *koinonia* constitutes the being of God, the church, all humanity, even the cosmos. It defines the identity of the church and orders all its practices. Yet it is visible only to faith, known only through God's self-revelation in Jesus Christ. For this reason, Wuthnow, Putnam, and

Giddens have taken us as far as they can in our practical theological journey. The social sciences can assist in describing the church as an empirical reality, but they cannot reveal the church's identity in Christ through the power of the Holy Spirit. They can interpret ecclesial practices from within their own framework, but on their own they cannot tell us what such practices should look like, how they should be implemented, or their ultimate aim.

Therefore, in order to assess how small groups can faithfully participate in God's ministry in the midst of the crisis of community, we must discern — prayerfully and to the best of our human ability — the essence of the church, its divinely determined *telos,* and its role in the ministry of the triune God. In other words, we begin the normative task of practical theology. As part of this task, we will turn to the ecclesiology of the Swiss Reformed theologian Karl Barth (1886-1968). On the basis of his later work (volumes 3 and 4 of the *Church Dogmatics*), I will define the church as multidimensional *koinonia,* a profoundly social reality that mirrors the triune life of God. I will then note how *koinonia* distinguishes the church from other communities, organizations, and institutions. Finally, I will compare and contrast *koinonia* with sociality in late modernity. It will become clear that *koinonia* is the solution to the crisis of community. For the *koinonia*-creating work of God seeks to transform this crisis and those of us caught up in it.

Koinonia Relationships

God, the church, and the world all live and move and have their being in a series of constitutive relationships. The essence of all these relationships is *koinonia,* typically translated as "fellowship" in English; however, the term "fellowship" fails to grasp the complexity, mystery, and beauty of *koinonia.* The infinitely lavish reality of *koinonia* exceeds the limits of human language and cognition. In awareness of this limitation, George Hunsinger suggests that *koinonia* means "mutual indwelling," "participation," "coinherence," and "coexistence."

> *Koinonia* in Barth's sense, as in the New Testament, means that we are not related to God or to one another like ball bearings in a bucket, through a system of external relations. We are, rather, something like relational fields that interpenetrate, form, and participate

in each other in countless real though often elusive ways. *Koinonia,* both as a term and as a reality, is remarkable for its range and flexibility and inexhaustible depth. In Barth's theology I think it may fairly be said that *koinonia* is the ground of all being. *Koinonia* stands for the final reconciliation and interconnection of all things through a living, luminous system of internal yet diverse relations.[1]

To say that the church exists in *koinonia,* therefore, is to say that it is caught up in union and communion with God and all of creation. The church exists in a series of intimate relationships, all of which have their origin in the Trinity.

Koinonia is multidimensional: it is comprised of five interlocking relationships: (1) the *koinonia* of the Trinity; (2) the *koinonia* of the incarnate Son, Jesus Christ; (3) the *koinonia* between Christ and the church; (4) the *koinonia* among church members; and, (5) the *koinonia* between the church and the world. In all of these *koinonia* relationships, the Holy Spirit is the "mediator of communion."[2] The Spirit binds the Father to the Son, Jesus to the church, the members of the church to one another, and the church to the world. Jesus is the center or hub of all the relationships between God and humanity and within humanity. As Jesus' high priestly prayer illuminates, we exist in him; through him we are united to the Father; through him we exist in one another. All of these *koinonia* relationships are marked by intimacy and integrity; some of them are also marked by order. Intimacy means that both acting subjects are inseparably united to each other. They coinhere or indwell each other. Jesus indwells the Father; the church indwells Jesus; the members of the church indwell one another and the world. This multistranded union cannot be severed. Integrity means that both acting subjects are differentiated from one another. Their unity does not lead to a loss of identity. In fact, mutual indwelling actually enhances

---

1. George Hunsinger, *Disruptive Grace: Studies in the Theology of Karl Barth* (Grand Rapids: Eerdmans, 2000), p. 257. While Barth does not explicitly designate *koinonia* as central to his ecclesiology, Hunsinger persuasively argues that *koinonia* is implicit throughout Barth's work. My definition of the church as multidimensional *koinonia* builds on Hunsinger's interpretation, as well as my own reading of Barth. At points, I nuance or depart from Hunsinger's delineation of the *koinonia* relationship, particularly when I suggest that the church and the world exist in a *koinonia* relationship, whereas Hunsinger suggests that the church and the world exist in a relationship of solidarity.

2. Hunsinger, *Disruptive Grace,* pp. 148-85.

their individual particularity. Order means that when God and humanity are joined in a *koinonia* relationship, God takes precedence and initiative. It is only through God's action that the church exists, let alone joins God in ministry in the world.[3]

Koinonia *of the Trinity*

> In Himself [God] does not will to exist for Himself, to exist alone. On the contrary, He is Father, Son and Holy Spirit and therefore alive in His unique being with and for and in another. . . . He does not exist in solitude but in fellowship.[4]

Here Barth points to the sociality in the being of God. God is triune and therefore relational. But God is more than relational as understood from a human perspective. God exists in a *perichoretic koinonia:* that is, the three persons of the Trinity — Father, Son, and Holy Spirit — interpenetrate each other at all points without loss of distinction. This *perichoretic* sociality, or intra-Trinitarian *koinonia,* is characterized by self-giving, loving, knowing, communicating, glorifying, and creating.[5] It is superabundant and thus overflows, moving outward beyond itself like an ever-widening dance of joy. The *koinonia* of the Trinity cre-

3. In his exegesis of Barth's theology, Hunsinger explains that the *koinonia* relationship adheres to the Chalcedonian pattern. Following the Council of Chalcedon's (451) description of the relationship between the divine and human natures of Jesus Christ, this pattern has three terms: intimacy (inseparable unity), integrity (indissoluble differentiation), and order (asymmetry). See George Hunsinger, *How to Read Karl Barth: The Shape of His Theology* (New York: Oxford University Press, 1991), pp. 185-224.

4. Karl Barth, *Church Dogmatics,* 4 vols. in 13 pts., ed. G. W. Bromiley and T. F. Torrance, trans. G. W. Bromiley (Edinburgh: T. & T. Clark, 1956-1975), II/1, p. 275 (hereafter, volume, part, and page references to the *CD* appear in parentheses in the text).

5. The "Farewell Discourses" in John 14-17 repeatedly point to this mystery: Father and Son abide in one another (14:10, 19); the Son freely gives himself to the Father, surrendering to his will and ways, and the Father freely gives his authority to the Son through the Holy Spirit (17:2). The Father speaks to and works in and through the Son, and the Son reciprocally does and says what he sees and hears the Father doing in the world (14:31; 15:15). The Holy Spirit bears witness to Jesus Christ in the world (15:26; 16:8-11) and guides the church into truth (16:13). The Holy Spirit glorifies — reveals, illumines, makes known the majesty of — Jesus, who glorifies the Father by finishing the work of reconciliation. And the Father, through the work of the Spirit, glorifies the Son in his resurrection, ascension, and heavenly reign (16:14, 15).

ates new, completely other life for the sake of a qualitatively distinct form of *koinonia,* a relationship of loving, communicating, and knowing that crosses the ontological divide. Humanity — indeed, all of creation — emerges from *koinonia* for the sake of living in *koinonia* with God and each other. In other words, *koinonia* is the origin and *telos* of human existence.

Tragically, we choose the "impossible possibility" (*CD* IV/3.1, p. 463), to use Barth's phrase, and we live in negation of this *koinonia.* We attempt to exalt ourselves above our creaturely status and hence our dependence on the mercy of God. We are presumptuous and ungrateful, frivolous and despairing. We persist in falsehood, denying our created intent. We contradict our created goodness. Bending inward, we declare that we know better than God; we deceive ourselves. We defiantly shout "no" to the gracious "yes" of God, thereby spurning our determination for multidimensional *koinonia.*

Mercifully, God's communion-creating *koinonia* is not thwarted. Though we absurdly resist and reject *koinonia,* God is long-suffering. God's love does not retaliate with self-protective inviolability; though rejected, it does not abandon; though ignored, it does not become forever silent. "The love of God always throws a bridge over a crevasse. It is always the light shining out of darkness. . . . That He throws a bridge out from Himself to this abandoned one, that He is light in the darkness, is the miracle of the almighty love of God" (*CD* II/1, p. 278). This bridge is Jesus Christ, in whom humanity and divinity exist in perfect *koinonia.*

The Koinonia *of the Incarnation*

The incarnation of the second person of the Trinity is, on the one hand, a *koinonia* of divinity and humanity, and on the other hand, it establishes *koinonia* with God and humanity. Because Jesus is fully divine and fully human, he is internally a *koinonia* of God and humankind. Because he persists in this *koinonia* in life and death, he establishes communion between God and the entire created order. In other words, the incarnation is a *koinonia* relationship that establishes *koinonia* with those who are not incarnate but who nevertheless are called to participate in the life of the Trinity.

To begin with, the *koinonia* internal to Jesus Christ is a hypostatic union of human nature and divine nature. Like the *koinonia* of the Trinity, the *koinonia* of the incarnation is unique in kind and cannot be replicated. In it, the divinity and humanity of Jesus Christ cannot be separated or confused. They maintain their ontological distinctions with the divine nature preceding and the human nature following. The human nature of Jesus Christ has no existence apart from the Word of God. Jesus of Nazareth exists only in union with the eternal Son of God. But it is a real, fully human existence. As such, Jesus' humanity corresponds perfectly to his deity. In life and death, Jesus lives in perfect correspondence to the Father. His words and deeds mimetically reflect the *koinonia* of the Trinity. He is the image of the invisible God. He loves God in gratitude, obedience, humility, and self-giving. Thus "Jesus is the one truly spiritual human being."[6]

Jesus Christ establishes *koinonia* between God and sinful humanity. In and through Christ, God opens blind eyes and brings the prodigals home. Jesus Christ is God's self-revelation to humanity and humanity's reconciliation to God. Jesus reveals the nature of God; he reveals God's intent for creation; and thus he reveals what it means to be truly and fully human. He reveals the reality of multidimensional *koinonia*, and he accomplishes it through his life, death, and resurrection. He reconciles us to God and each other for the sake of *koinonia*.

Reconciliation, and hence the creation of *koinonia*, is a single event in three modes or tenses — the past tense, the present tense, and the future tense.[7] Barth writes:

> [Reconciliation] is not, therefore, an event which has merely happened and is now a past fact of history. God's revelation is, of course, this as well. But it is also an event, a happening in the present, here and now. Again, it is not this in such a way that it exhausts itself in the momentary movement from the past to the present once for all, that is, in our today. But it is also an event that took place once for all, and an accomplished fact. And it is also future — the event which lies completely and wholly in front of us, which has not yet happened, but which simply comes upon us. Again, this happens with-

---

6. Hunsinger, *Disruptive Grace*, p. 160.

7. For the conceptual framework of differentiating salvation history according to perfect, present, and future tenses, see George Hunsinger, "A Tale of Two Simultaneities: Justification and Sanctification in Calvin and Barth," in *Conversing with Barth*, Barth Studies, ed. John McDowell and Mike Highton (Aldershot, UK: Ashgate, 2004).

out detriment to its historical completeness and its full contemporaneity. On the contrary, it is in its historical completeness and its full contemporaneity that it is truly future. "Jesus Christ the same yesterday and today and forever" (Heb. 13:8) (*CD* II/1, p. 262).

In other words, *koinonia* between God and humanity (and within humanity) has occurred objectively in Christ. Divine and human action have been brought together perfectly in the history of Jesus Christ. By the power of the Spirit, all humanity has participated in the death and resurrection of Jesus Christ. The justification and sanctification of the ungodly have taken place in Christ: "It is finished!" However, multidimensional *koinonia* is not yet fully manifest to, nor realized in, all. Creation waits, whether consciously or not, for the "consummation of all things." In this sense *koinonia* is a future event; it will take its final and ultimate form in the *eschaton*, when "God will be all in all." Then all human action will correspond to Jesus Christ. Though remaining qualitatively distinct from the *koinonia* of the Trinity, our *koinonia* with God and each other will be experienced in all its creativity, glory, joy, knowledge, communication, and self-giving. In the present tense, the time between the resurrection and consummation, Christ exists on earth in and through his body. As such, the church is a provisional representation of *koinonia*, witnessing to the long-suffering Love that reconciles us to God and each other.

Koinonia *between Christ and the Church*

Two concepts — the *totus Christus* and the body of Christ — explain the *koinonia* between Jesus Christ and the community of faith. Jesus exists as the *totus Christus:* "Christ including all those who are elected and justified and sanctified and called in Him; Christ as the Head with His body and therefore with His community" (*CD* IV/2, p. 624). By means of the Holy Spirit, Jesus Christ and his community are inseparable: "together they comprise salvation history."[8] Jesus and the church are inseparably united. Christ has chosen to exist in the world with the church and not without it. Though united in the greatest possible intimacy, Christ and

---

8. Kimlyn Bender, "The Living Congregation of the Lord Jesus Christ: Karl Barth's Christological Ecclesiology" (PhD diss., Princeton Theological Seminary, 2002), p. 312.

the church retain their ontological distinctions. The church is not a second incarnation. The church does not replace Christ in the world. "Because Christ is present in the power of the Holy Spirit, the church does not stand as a surrogate for Christ on earth."[9] Christ has logical and irreversible priority over the church. The church has no being, no existence, outside of Christ. In contrast, Christ is both immanent in and transcendent of the church — within and above it, present and absent in it, united to but not bound by it. His work of reconciliation continues outside of, in spite of, and often in opposition to the church.

Jesus is the head of his body, the church. As Barth points out, Christ is first and foremost a body: Christ is not merely embodied in the church, but Christ is the body. In the here and now, Christ exists as "one in many," a unified plurality (*CD* IV/1, pp. 663, 664). He is the originator and Lord of all those who acknowledge, recognize, and confess their *koinonia* with him. By means of the Spirit, he imparts gifts to his body so that it can fulfill its vocation. By means of the Spirit, he encounters his body and conforms it to his likeness, making it the crucified, dead, and risen body of Christ in the present mode of reconciliation. Therefore, as Christ's body, the church is not a social grouping, a bureaucracy, or institution. It is not formed on the basis of kinship patterns or any other socialization process.

This *koinonia* between Christ and the church springs from the fount of grace. Human beings not only lack any inherent capacity to commune with God, but they also contradict and oppose this relationship. Nevertheless, Jesus Christ encounters the church by means of the Holy Spirit, who binds them together in a relationship of mutual presence, belonging, and self-impartation.[10] Just as the Holy Spirit incorporates all humanity into the death and resurrection of Christ, so the Holy Spirit awakens and gathers persons into the body of Christ in the here and now. And because the church belongs to Christ so intimately, it also participates in the life of the Trinity. It exists in *koinonia* with the triune God by virtue of its incorporation into Christ through the power of the Holy Spirit.

9. Bender, "The Living Congregation," p. 224. Bender also writes: "The church is not a second incarnation, and its correspondence to God is imperfect. The relationship between Christology and ecclesiology is thus one of radical dissimilarity *and* real similarity. The relationship is therefore one of analogy and correspondence established as a divine gift" (p. 273).

10. Hunsinger, *Disruptive Grace*, p. 161.

Koinonia *among Christ's Members*

Koinonia with Christ entails simultaneous *koinonia* with the communion of saints. To be united to Christ is to be united to believers in all times and places. The church's *koinonia* with Christ and the *koinonia* among its members cannot be severed from each other. Participation in both is the twofold vocation of every Christian. There is no such thing as a "lone-ranger" Christian. Private Christianity is a contradiction in terms. The disciple believes and grows "only in and with the community, only in the sphere and context of it, only in the limitation and determination set by its basis and goal. The royal freedom of his faith is the freedom to stand in it as a brother, with other brothers and sisters in the possession granted to it and the service laid upon it" (*CD* IV/1, p. 688).

Christian life, by definition, is communal life. It is also an active life. Members of Christ's body are united to Christ and one another in their corporate worship, baptism, and eucharistic feast. This common worship nourishes them and shapes their entire lives. Their communal prayer grounds and generates any and all individual and group prayer (*CD* IV/1, pp. 615, 627, 705); together, they fulfill their common vocation. Their service certainly is differentiated, but no member is more important than any other. Moreover, they all stand on common ground at the foot of the cross, as sinners equally in need of redemption and saints equally called to service. In their differentiation and equality, their *koinonia* reflects that of the Trinity.

Threefold Koinonia *between the Church and the World*

The *koinonia* between the church and the world derives from (1) their common objective existence with Christ, (2) their common creaturely status, and (3) the vocation of the church. In other words, the church is in the world (dialectically included in the world by means of their coexistence in Christ) — with the world (creaturely and sinful) and for the world (commissioned by God to serve the world).

First, the church is in the world, caught up in *koinonia* with the world by virtue of their mutual connection to Christ. All humanity has been incorporated into the life, death, and resurrection of Jesus Christ by the power of the Holy Spirit. Christ is the Creator and Reconciler of all. "In him *all* things in heaven and on earth were created . . . *all* things have been created through him and for him . . . in him *all* things hold together . . . and through him God was pleased to reconcile to himself *all* things" (Col. 1:16, 17, 20, emphasis added).[11] Therefore, the church and the world indwell Christ. Church and world — indeed, all things — coexist and coinhere in Christ. As Hunsinger illuminates, coexistence and coinherence are patterns of relationality that govern Barth's later theology. "Nothing is to be conceived . . . as existing except as together with [Jesus Christ]. . . . Nothing is to be conceived in which Jesus Christ is not somehow coinherent and which, in turn, is not somehow coinherent in him."[12]

Second, the *koinonia* between church and world derives from their common creaturely status. Together, the church and the world stand on the opposite side of the ontological divide from God. The church and its members share with the world in an inheritance of sin, suffering, and death. Though awakened to faith, quickened to love, and enlightened to hope, the church nevertheless remains *simul justus et peccator,* the communion of saints and the communion of sinners. Therefore, the distinction between the church and world is noetic rather than ontic. In contrast to the world, the community of believers acknowledges and accepts what Christ has accomplished for it and the world. It lives eschatologically, based on the promise of the full actualization of reconciliation in all creation; therefore, its decisions and actions (when properly ordered) spring from the power of the Holy Spirit (*CD* IV/1, pp. 661-62).

Third, Jesus Christ binds the church to the world by means of its vocation. The church "has the meaning and purpose of being, on behalf of God and in the service and discipleship of His existence, an existence for the world and for men" (*CD* IV/3.2, p. 762). The church exists for God and thus necessarily for all humanity; in this way the church exists for itself as well. Barth writes: "Even within the world to which it belongs, it does not exist ecstatically or eccentrically with reference to itself, but wholly with reference to them, to the world around. It saves and maintains its own life as it interposes and gives itself for all other human creatures" (*CD* IV/3.2, p. 762). In correspondence to Jesus

11. Barth writes: "The work of atonement, the conversion of man to God, was done for all. The Word of God is spoken to all. God's verdict [justification] and direction [sanctification] and promise [vocation] have been pronounced over all. To that extent, objectively, all are justified, sanctified and called" (*CD* IV/1, p. 148).

12. Hunsinger, *How to Read Karl Barth,* p. 273.

Christ, the church exists in solidarity with the world. Its ministry is incarnational, though it never replaces nor functions on the same level as the ministry of the incarnate Son.

Formally, the church exists with the world in a double-asymmetrical, bipolar unity. The church and the world cannot be separated, yet they remain distinct: priority is given to the church, on the one hand, and to the world, on the other. Their unity exists in the church's solidarity with and genuine attachment to the world. Their distinction exists in the church's knowledge of Christ and its knowledge of its own and the world's true identity. The church precedes the world in its awakening to the self-revelation of God in Jesus Christ. This precedence is not superiority; rather, it is nothing more or less than its call to serve the world in conformity to the gracious, self-giving love of Jesus Christ. Yet the church's existence is temporal. It provisionally (penultimately) represents the justification and sanctification of all humanity in Christ. It will cease to exist in the *eschaton*. Thus the world has teleological priority over the church.

In summary, the church exists objectively in a complex, interpenetrating set of *koinonia* relationships. The essence of God, the church, and the world is multidimensional *koinonia*. *Koinonia* characterizes, or constitutes, both God's being *ad intra* (within the Trinity) and *ad extra* (with regard to the church and world), and consequently the church's being *ad intra* (in relationship to Christ and among its members) and *ad extra* (in relationship to Christ, to God the Father, and to the world). As we will explore in the next chapter, these *koinonia* relationships shape the life of the church and its practices, including small groups.

The Church in Contrast to Other Communities

By now it should be apparent that the church, by virtue of its determination for multidimensional *koinonia,* is distinct from other social institutions and communal formations. It is not equivalent to a business, even if it adopts business practices. It is not equivalent to an institution of higher education, even though it teaches. It is not equivalent to a support group, even though its members live in the most intimate of relationships. The church has an inner life, a spiritual life that distinguishes it from other social organizations. Yet this distinction is not one of superiority or isolation from other communities.

First, the church is distinct from other communities because it is simultaneously invisible and visible. To use Barth's language, the church is three-dimensional. It consists of its members, their activity in the world, and divine activity. The first two dimensions of the church — its practices, polity, leaders, art, and media — are visible. Its third dimension — its *koinonia* — is invisible. Consequently, these dimensions of the church are perceived and studied differently. Its visible dimensions can be observed by the human senses and studied accurately by the social sciences. "It is a phenomenon of world history which can be grasped in historical and psychological and sociological terms like any other" (*CD* IV/1, p. 652). In contrast, its invisible dimension eludes all but the sight of faith given by the self-revealing God.[13]

Though the essence of the church is invisible, it presses for visibility. The appearance of *koinonia* is fleeting and always tainted by human error, but it does show up in multiple, and often unexpected, ways. It comes to expression in and through a community of faith, a local congregation. Thus the *koinonia* and its communal form are inseparable. For this reason we cannot live in *koinonia* separate from a gathered group of believers. We cannot faithfully retreat from the church's gathering in worship, its upbuilding in love, or its sending into the world. Further, *koinonia* is the transformational factor in the church. In the present mode of reconciliation, *koinonia* seeks expression in, under, and even against ecclesial practices. Jesus Christ, through the power of the Holy Spirit, aligns the church's ministry, governance, and theology according to its inner life of *koinonia*. The church becomes what it is when its visible form, that is, its practices, attests its third dimension. The practices themselves are not *koinonia*. Rather, they are signs (witnesses)

---

13. Any practical theology that ignores any of these dimensions is incomplete, risking Docetism on the one side and Ebionitism on the other. Failure to account for its first two dimensions is a form of Docetism, which in its christological form denies the reality of Jesus Christ's humanity. Failure to account for its inner reality is a form of Ebionitism, which reduces Jesus Christ to humanity. Those practical theologies that treat the church as merely a religious society analogous to other sociological groups are two-dimensional, or Ebionite. They ignore the determinative dimension, interpreting its activity and suggesting norms and rules of art based solely on sociological and historical analysis. Practical theologies that ignore the human dimensions of the church are Docetic. Any practical theology that neglects either the first or the second dimension might be analogous to the theological error (from Barth's perspective) of disconnecting the person and the work of Christ, i.e., separating the being from the act of the triune God.

of *koinonia* when the community's faith, love, and hope shine through them. "What [the church] is, its mystery, its spiritual character, is not without manifestations and analogies in its generally visible form. But it is not unequivocally represented in any such generally visible manifestations and analogies" (*CD* IV/I, p. 657). Thus signs are both similar and dissimilar to *koinonia.* They reflect the inner reality of the church, though imperfectly and not without sin.

This brings us to a second distinction: how God and humans work together in the church. Formally speaking, the practices of the church are a *koinonia* of divine action and human action. In other words, God's work and human work are united in ecclesial practices. Like Jesus, who saw and heard and followed his Father, so the church is called to follow and join what Jesus is doing in its midst. Faithful and true actions of the church do not occur separate from Jesus' ongoing ministry of reconciliation unto *koinonia;* yet the church on its own strength and skill and stamina cannot follow Jesus. Even its best intentions are tainted by sin. And more often than not, it actively rebuffs its determination for *koinonia.*

Therefore, the mystery and miracle of the church lies in the fact that Jesus Christ actually encounters the church in its practices and enables it to join in God's communion-creating work of reconciliation. When Christ encounters the church (and its members), he affirms it, negates it, and reconstitutes it on a higher plane.[14] Christ affirms the members of his body as children of God. He confronts them when they contradict their true identity. He re-creates them as persons of faith, hope, and love. Consequently, they are freed to act in accordance with who they truly are, humans made for multidimensional *koinonia.* This freedom is not something that the church possesses as its own. The grace of God through which Jesus encounters and transforms the church is sheer gift. Even though the Holy Spirit empowers the church

---

14. The encounter between Christ and the church follows the Hegelian pattern of *Aufhebung:* affirmation, negation, and reconstitution on a higher plane. As George Hunsinger notes, Barth orders the relationship between nature and grace, and by extension between God and humanity, via a kind of *Aufhebung.* "In its distinction as a reality other than and over against grace, nature is affirmed. In its corruption as a reality that supposes itself to be autonomously grounded apart from grace, nature is negated. In its destiny as a reality to be drawn beyond itself into genuine fellowship with grace, the negation is negated, and nature is miraculously reconstituted on a higher plane" (Hunsinger, *How to Read Karl Barth,* p. 98).

to participate in the life of God, or to subjectively realize its ontological status, grace is not infused into human nature in such a way that *koinonia* becomes an inherent capacity for the church. The church lives in perpetual dependence on God's Spirit. *Koinonia* cannot be conjured up, created, or controlled by the church or its members. No ecclesial practices can instantiate *koinonia.* Therefore, the church prays and waits for Christ to encounter it again and again in the power of the Spirit. It trusts that Jesus Christ through the power of the Spirit will "make use" of its otherwise sinful action. For God's grace is so abundant that even the Bible "can speak and make itself heard in spite of all its maltreatment at the hands of the half-blind and arbitrary and officious" (*CD* IV/2, pp. 660, 674).

Though the possibility for participating in God's ongoing ministry lies outside itself, the church's action is always genuine and free. In the encounter with Christ, the Holy Spirit does not overpower, coerce, or humiliate the church. Its members are not "mere spectators, let alone puppets" (*CD* IV/3.2, p. 528). Their identity is not subsumed in Christ. Rather, the Holy Spirit places the church and its members in an I-thou relationality with its head. Christ becomes their "contemporary" and they his "companions." They correspond to him. Their lives are reoriented on Christ and on the world for which he died. The church does not act on its own or for its own sake. It does not seek even to propagate itself. Like the Holy Spirit, from whose work its actions spring, the church points away from itself toward Jesus Christ. When it finds itself participating in divine action, it responds with wonder, praise, and gratitude. As Barth says about the work of theology,

> The theologian does not have [the power of the Spirit] in his control. This power is by no means a further theological assumption that he, much like a magician, could employ or not employ according to need or desire. He should be happy if, while brooding over his work, he hears the hidden power rushing, and finds his statements determined, ruled, and controlled by it. But he does not know "whence it comes or whither it goes." He can wish only to follow its work, not to precede it. While he lets his thought and speech be controlled by it, he gladly renounces the temptation to exert control over it.[15]

15. Karl Barth, *Evangelical Theology: An Introduction* (Grand Rapids: Eerdmans, 1963), pp. 51-52.

A final distinct characteristic of the church is its relationship to time and space. The church *both* exists in time and space *and* transcends the normal bounds of time and space. Though it takes a particular communal form, it is located in Christ. It belongs in Christ, not in any building. It does not belong to any particular territory or social grouping. It does not belong to any nation or ethnic group. James Loder describes it eloquently:

> To be in Christ is to be in "the promised land," to be "at home" wherever you are. Furthermore, to be in Christ is to be in communion with the saints everywhere in the world and through all time. To be in Christ is to be participating already in the end of time. All space and time are relative to him; he radicalizes space and time, and should awaken us from our Newtonian slumber.[16]

As a human society, the church participates in the ebb and flow of chronological time. Yet its being is established in another time, the time of the *parousia,* the coming of Christ and attendant transformation of world history. *"Parousia,"* Barth writes, "means the immediate presence and action of the living Jesus Christ Himself" (*CD* IV/1, p. 725). The church's origin is Easter, the first form of the *parousia;* its *telos* is the consummation of all things, the final form of the *parousia,* when God will be all in all. It exists "in the time between the times," in the second form of the *parousia.* This is the time of Christ's coming to the world in the power of the Holy Spirit through the ministry of the church. The church "waits" for the final *parousia;* it "hastens" toward Jesus Christ; it prayerfully yearns for the full revelation of *koinonia* and the full reconciliation accomplished in Christ. As I have observed above, this means that the church's existence is provisional. It rushes toward its own end. It will cease to exist when God is all in all, when *koinonia* is fully manifest in all its beauty, creativity, love, and knowledge.

The church's relationship to time is both its strength and its weakness. The past fulfillment of its *telos* is the church's strength. It is impelled by a teleological orientation qualitatively different from other human organizations. "The Christian community has the advantage that in its beginning it already has behind it the end which it awaits. To that extent it proceeds from the fulfillment of its hope. Its hope is not

16. James E. Loder, *Educational Ministry in the Logic of the Spirit* (unpublished ms.), ch. 7, p. 24.

the expression of a longing and striving. It is the expression of the impetus by which it exists" (*CD* IV/1, p. 727). In the face of temptation and conflict, therefore, the church knows its predetermined, good, and joyful outcome. However, the christological time of the church also pricks its side like a thorn in its flesh. It requires the church to walk by faith, not by sight, to hear and see Christ not directly but through creaturely mediation, such as the proclamation of Scripture and celebration of the sacraments. As the apostle Paul puts it, this mediated sight occurs "through a glass darkly" (1 Cor. 13:12). Like the disciples adrift on the stormy sea, the church must trust that its captain is the Lord of creation rather than an apparition of its imagining. "The community moves from [the first *parousia*] to [the final *parousia*] like a ship sailing over an ocean a thousand fathoms deep" (*CD* IV/1, p. 728).

Koinonia and the Crisis of Community

Now that we have interpreted the essence of the church and distinguished it from other institutions and communities, we can consider how this theology of *koinonia* might help us interpret and guide the church's work in the midst of the crisis of community. What is the significance of the church's *koinonia* in the present context? How does *koinonia* compare to sociality in late modernity? To answer these questions, I will dialogue with the sociological framework set forth in chapter 1.

First, the extreme time-space distantiation of late modernity is analogous (both similar and dissimilar) to *koinonia*. Relationships today transcend time and place. People can communicate and carry out complex social and economic transactions even though they live at opposite ends of the earth. Similarly, the communion of saints is not bound to time and space. Believers are united to each other, belonging first to each other, not to the countries in which they live. But the communion of saints is not merely global in reach. *Koinonia* means that the church belongs to and participates in the life of believers from *all* places and times — past, present, and future. The church lives out its communion in the living presence of a "great cloud of witnesses" that has preceded it in life and death. Concretely, this communion occurs by means of the written Word of God and work of the Spirit. As we read, study, and hear the Word of God in Scripture, the Spirit grafts our life history into the life history of all God's people. Biblical narratives shape our identities.

In other words, the church's *koinonia* has an apostolic character. The church encounters the apostles who "are still before us in living speech and action" through the witness of Scripture (*CD* IV/1, p. 712). The church enters into a history with the apostles, and through their witness, with Jesus Christ. "Accepting the word of the apostles, it allows Him to speak. Being led by them, it is led by Him. His Holy Spirit acts and works in the concrete form of the power and truth of their word" (*CD* IV/1, p. 718). The church lives under the written and preached forms of the Word of God; it experiences the Bible's piercing gaze. It does so not in a slavish imitation of biblical forms of ministry but rather by following after the life history of the apostles. In this regard, it is important to note, then, that the *koinonia* with the communion of saints, particularly the apostles and prophets, is mediated by written and spoken speech. In contrast, relationships in late modernity increasingly are mediated digitally.

Second, relationships in late modernity become increasingly "faceless" as a result of time-space distantiation. People relate to one another without ever encountering one another face to face. This gets transposed to patterns of religious affiliation. People believe in God and seek intimacy with God outside of the context of local communities of faith. This pattern of believing without belonging contradicts *koinonia:* if we take *koinonia* seriously, we cannot separate ourselves from the church. In the here and now, *koinonia* exists in, under, and against the structure of the congregation. We can know *koinonia* only in a gathered and ordered life; therefore, Christians do not exist in isolation from one another. They are joined to Christ as they are joined to Christ's body. They cannot belong to Christ without simultaneously belonging to Christ's members. Just as infants cannot thrive without the support, nurture, and care of their mothers (or other primary caregivers), so Christians cannot thrive spiritually without the support, nurture, and care of local faith communities.

The late-modern pattern of believing without belonging is related to the end of tradition as well. The end of tradition refers to the fact that people today freely and actively choose their beliefs, customs, and practices. Tradition is not a given; nor is it infallible. In fact, beliefs and practices are challenged constantly by incoming information and diverse perspectives. How does this end of tradition compare to our theology of *koinonia?* On the one hand, this theology is a normative claim, an assertion about the church's identity as well as an assertion about what is good and right for the church and world. On the other hand, this theology openly acknowledges that the church's beliefs and practices change — indeed, they must change. There is a certain reflexivity to the church. The church is *semper reformanda ecclesia reformata:* once reformed and always *being* reformed by the Word and Spirit of God. While Jesus Christ remains the same yesterday, today, and forever, our knowledge of him regularly undergoes transformation. We cannot capture Jesus in a fixed image. He is multivalent, diverse, and richly surprising in his manifestations to us. Because Jesus coexists in and with the world, knowledge and practices arising outside the church may more faithfully reflect the reality of *koinonia* than the knowledge and practices within the church.[17] In these instances, our knowledge of God is affirmed, negated, and reconstituted again and again. All of this calls the church to a radical openness to critique from within and without.

Third, the church lives in the midst of late-modern risks, and it also experiences its own form of vulnerability and riskiness. Life today is risky. Try as we may to control our future, unexpected challenges emerge that confound us personally and communally. Global economics alter our life plans, illnesses become pandemic, the ozone layer erodes, and most of us can do little about it. The church experiences these risks and more, because its existence is precarious. It is threatened from within and without. As creature, it teeters on the brink of annihilation. In anxious awareness of its own limits and finitude, the church often attempts to usurp God by preserving itself. That is, the church sins. Its anxious response to its own riskiness often takes two forms — what Barth identifies as secularization and sacralization.[18]

---

17. In *Church Dogmatics* IV/3.1, Barth suggests that knowledge arising outside of the church may function as secular parables of the truth. Because all things coexist and coinhere with Christ, the world may — unknowingly — actually witness to the Word and work of God in Jesus Christ. The world may more faithfully practice what we have called *koinonia* than the church does. The church is admonished to recognize truth wherever it is found and to reform its own life in light of this truth. For an exposition of secular parables of the truth, see Hunsinger, *How to Read Karl Barth,* pp. 234-80.

18. In his 1948 Amsterdam lecture entitled "The Church: The Living Congregation of the Living Lord Jesus Christ," Barth vividly describes the church that has fallen prey to these temptations as "sleepy-eyed, squint-eyed, and blind." The "sleepy-eyed" church fails to connect the promises of God with the needs and tasks of the present world. The squint-eyed church fails to differentiate its own yearnings from the will of God. It has

The church succumbs to secularization when it follows the voice of a stranger rather than the voice of its Shepherd: that is, when it adopts a particular philosophy as a lens for interpreting the Word and work of God; when it aligns itself with a particular ideology, or with a political or economic force; and when its proclamation is determined solely by what seems to be the most pressing desires of its environment. Underneath secularization lurks a secret respect for the fashion of the world, a secret longing for the world's glory, or a secret fear that it cannot live solely by Jesus Christ. In sacralization, instead of serving the world, the church, "towers over" the world and promotes itself with self-righteous airs. It thereby "sets itself most terribly in the wrong" and "supremely jeopardises its true life and growth" (*CD* IV/2, pp. 663-69).

By virtue of its *koinonia* with the world, the church is at risk; however, by virtue of its *koinonia* with Christ, the church will not die. Herein lies its ontological security: "In him, all things hold together" (Col. 1:17). As Barth says, the *totus Christus* (the head and body of Christ) lives and cannot die. Providence prevails. Sin is no obstacle for God. The light of God dispels the very darkest of sin. Where sin abounds, grace abounds all the more. Jesus Christ, the Word of God, speaks through Scripture (again and again) in the power of the Holy Spirit, challenging and confronting the church. The Word of God will not remain silent even if it must admonish the church in the form of "an echo awakened in the outside world" (*CD* IV/2, p. 674).

The crisis of community is a wide-open door for the church's ministry in the world. It provides concrete entry points for connecting the gospel to people's harried and fragmented lives. It does so in a profoundly meaningful and healing manner. The crisis of community provides a way of pointing to our true identity and existence in *koinonia*. Time-space distantiation, the effects of which we feel daily, can signify the ontological reality of *koinonia*, our communion with the saints from all times and places. Perhaps in no other time in history could persons grasp the concept of the *communio sanctorum* in such a visceral way. *Koinonia* might be a plausible and compelling ontology in a world in which people near and far are linked by unseen digital connections.

"fallen in love" with itself or some particular form of its self-expression in the world. The blind church bends inward and defines itself anthropocentrically rather than Christologically ("The Church: The Living Congregation of the Living Lord Jesus Christ," in *Barth: God Here and Now* [London and New York: Routledge, 2003]).

Doesn't the "interconnection of all things through a living, luminous system of internal yet diverse relations" resonate with our lived experience and our deepest longings?[19] And what about our experience of ongoing, all-pervasive reflexivity? This can remind the church of its need for ongoing reform. The dynamism and multivalence of Jesus Christ, in whom we live and move and have our being, warns us against retreating from risk into fundamentalist thinking or rigid practices. It warns us against explaining unforeseen consequences as signs of God's displeasure or wrath. The church can accept risk and its inexplicability because it ultimately rests secure in *koinonia*. As I will unpack further in chapter 6, the ontological security of the church and the world is sure. In our present context, this security — this trust — may be the one thing that is needful in all our speech and action.

If the crisis of community creates an opportunity for seriously considering the plausibility of *koinonia*, then *koinonia* potentially transforms our understanding and experience of this crisis. An ecclesiology grounded in *koinonia* affirms, confronts, and transforms life in late modernity. Consider intimacy. *Koinonia* would affirm the democracy of intimacy in late modernity. This intimacy is marked by reciprocal self-disclosure, emotional resonance, parity, commitment, and freedom from coercion. The mutuality at the heart of this intimacy reflects, in part, the mutual freedom, openness, communication, and knowledge of the triune God. The *koinonia* among church members mirrors the *koinonia* of the Trinity. For theirs is a radically interdependent relationship of equals. At the same time, *koinonia* negates certain aspects of late-modern intimacy. Intimacy takes shape in the form of pure relationships. These relationships typically lack economic, communal, religious, and political supports. Moreover, they can be aborted with ease. If an intimate relationship no longer provides emotional support and meaning-making, we can leave it in search of another. In stark contrast, we cannot leave the *communio sanctorum*, neither objectively nor faithfully. That is, we belong to the communion of saints objectively (in Christ); ontologically, we cannot separate ourselves from Christ or one another. Subjectively, in our lived experience, we cannot faithfully depart from the church to pursue our own individual Christianity. If we do, we contradict our identity. While this does not mean that there is no justification for changing congregational affiliation, it does mean

19. Hunsinger, *Disruptive Grace*, p. 257.

that Christianity practiced outside of the community of faith (when there is one that gathers) is not true Christianity.[20] It also means that leaving a particular community of faith should be done only with the utmost seriousness, prayerful discernment, and penitent heart.

Koinonia transforms intimacy in late modernity so that it is no longer dyadic. Even friendship and marriage are not comprised merely of two persons. For Jesus Christ in the power of the Holy Spirit stands between them and unites them. "Where two or three are gathered in my name, I am there in the midst of them" (Matt. 18:20). "The living presence of God as a shared reality" transforms their intimacy so that they see each other through Christ's eyes, care for each other with Christ's compassion, and gladly assist each other with Christ's service.[21] They pray with Saint Patrick:

> The eye of God betwixt me and each eye,
> The purpose of God 'twixt me and each purpose,
> The hand of God betwixt me and each hand,
> The desire of God betwixt me and each desire.
>
> I sing as I arise today
> God be in every breath,
> As the mist scatters on the crest of the hill,
> May each ill haze clear from my soul today.
>
> The dearness of Christ 'twixt me and each dearness,
> The wish of Christ 'twixt me and each wish,
> The pain of Christ 'twixt me and each pain,
> The kindness of Christ 'twixt me and each kindness.
>
> I sing as I arise today
> God be in every breath.
> As I clothe my body with wool
> Cover my soul with thy love, O God.

20. With this comment I am leaving open the possibility of certain exigencies in which a Christian cannot gather with a group of fellow believers for physical, emotional, mental, or demographic reasons. While such situations may be tragic, it would be unfortunate to label them as unfaithful.

21. James E. Loder, *The Logic of the Spirit: Human Development in Theological Perspective* (San Francisco: Jossey-Bass, 1998), p. 197 (hereafter, page references to this work appear in parentheses in the text).

The eye of God 'twixt me and each eye,
The purpose of God 'twixt me and each purpose,
The hand of God 'twixt me and each hand,
The desire of God 'twixt me and each desire.[22]

Koinonia also transforms self-disclosure. In the context of *koinonia,* we can risk self-disclosure and authenticity in spite of the instability of the pure relationship. For our life history, our meaning, and our purpose is in *koinonia,* which has been, will be, and is real for us in Jesus Christ. We can know and be known not naively but trusting in our coming redemption. We can speak of our sin and suffering without fear, shame, or guilt. But we do so, as James Loder says in *The Logic of the Spirit,* not "simply disgorging one's dark side to another person." Instead we "reenvision our past through the eyes of faith . . . through a relationality of love whose present existence proleptically embodies the nullification of the dark side of one's past" (pp. 275, 264). "It is finished!" Our sin and suffering have been eradicated. We have been freed from guilt and healed of our wounds. Again, as we will explore further in chapter 6, in *koinonia* Jesus Christ "is able to establish genuine intimacy at the point where all other forms of intimacy have gone wrong . . . [because] the intimacy of the Spirit runs deeper than family violence and neglect and has immense restorative power" (p. 265).

Finally, *koinonia* enables authentic intimacy in the church by transforming role structures. According to Loder, life in *koinonia* calls for role reversibility. Roles are functional but not ontologically definitive. While a pastor may be ordained to a particular set of functions in the church — for example, preaching, teaching the Word, and administering the sacraments — she is always a member of the communion of saints, equivalent to and dependent on all the other members. She needs them and their gifts in order to fulfill her particular vocation. As Loder says, "The spiritual presence of Jesus Christ becomes the relationality among persons, so that their interaction is simultaneously profoundly intimate and thoroughly functional" (p. 194). This upends the clergy paradigm in favor of the priesthood of all believers. In fact, *koinonia* judges the clergy paradigm as a form of disordered divine and human action. When pastors act as if the well-being of the

---

22. Saint Patrick, "The Eye of God," quoted in Deborah van Deusen Hunsinger, *Pray Without Ceasing: Revitalizing Pastoral Care* (Grand Rapids: Eerdmans, 2006), pp. 10-12.

community of faith depends on their work, not to mention their over-work, they contradict the fact that Jesus Christ is the head of the church, the one who upholds his body, the one who initiates all minis-try in the world. *Koinonia* reminds pastors that while they are called to an office or role of shepherding, there is one true shepherd who keeps guard over his flock. To whatever degree their ministry corresponds to God's shepherding, it is a gift of grace. For they, too, are sheep.

In short, *koinonia* is the answer to the crisis of community. Fissures in our communal, interpersonal, and intrapersonal existence cry out for a life of the greatest possible intimacy and integrity. They may heighten awareness of our need for *koinonia*. We should not be sur-prised if the Spirit of God uses the difficulties of our context to awaken us to our determination for life in multidimensional *koinonia*. In our runaway world, *koinonia* can ground our identity in Christ and through Christ in our relationships with one another. In the face of the threat of personal meaninglessness, Christ calls us into purposeful mission in the world, a mission characterized by the practice of *koinonia*.

CHAPTER 5

Practicing Koinonia *in Small Groups*

> Let the same mind be in you that was in Christ Jesus, who though he was in the form of God, did not regard equality with God as something to be exploited, but emptied himself, taking the form of a servant, being born in human likeness. And being found in human form, he humbled himself and became obedient to the point of death — even death on a cross. Therefore God also highly exalted him and gave him the name that is above every name, so that at the name of Jesus every knee should bend, in heaven and on earth and under the earth, and every tongue should confess that Jesus Christ is Lord, to the glory of God the Father.
>
> Therefore, my beloved, . . . work out your own salvation with fear and trembling; for it is God who is at work in you, enabling you both to will and to work for his good pleasure.
>
> Philippians 2:5-13

This early hymn of the church encapsulates the vocation of the church in the present tense of reconciliation. While the church's *koinonia* with Christ, among its members, and with the world is an objective reality, it also must be lived out in the here and now. The church is called to correspond to Christ in his life, death, and resurrection, and in so doing become what it is. While practicing *koinonia* is not something that the church can carry out on its own, it nevertheless is called to act. Empowered by Jesus Christ in the presence of the Holy Spirit, the church is called to live in multidimensional *koinonia*.

In this chapter I will explore the church's practice of *koinonia* in three dynamic modes: gathering, upbuilding, and sending.[1] As framed by Karl Barth, the one church of Jesus Christ exists in three modes; that is, it has a Trinitarian shape. Building on Barth, I argue in this chapter that the members of the church realize their *koinonia* with Christ, with one another, and with the world in each of these modes. Though the church lives out all dimensions of its *koinonia* simultaneously, one of the *koinonia* relationships will be in the foreground of our thinking as we discuss each mode. In the mode of gathering, I will focus on the church's *koinonia* with Christ; in the mode of upbuilding, the *koinonia* among its members; and, in the mode of sending, its *koinonia* with the world.[2] To put it another way, as the church practices *koinonia* in each of these three modes, it serves Christ, itself, and the world. In its gathering, the church most strictly serves God; in its upbuilding, it serves God in its mutual service; and in its sending, it serves God and itself by serving the world. As it practices *koinonia* in its gathering, upbuilding, and sending and thus serves Christ, itself, and the world, the church

---

1. In using the word "mode," I am drawing on Barth's Trinitarian language and a limited number of quotations in reference to the church. Barth does not consistently use this word in speaking of the gathering, upbuilding, and sending of the church, but he does use it in a few instances such as the following: "The upbuilding of the Christian community is a particular aspect and mode of operation of the sanctification in which, whatever may have to be said about the human subject and his work, it is God Himself who is primarily at work" (Karl Barth, *CD* IV/2, p. 632). Further, it is important to note that for Barth each of these vantage points describes Christ's one saving work as a whole in and through the church as a whole.

2. Considered from another angle, we also can say that the church practices *koinonia* with Christ in one aspect of his threefold office in each of its three modes. In its gathering, the church practices *koinonia* with Christ our High Priest. In its upbuilding, it practices *koinonia* with Christ our King. In its sending, it lives *koinonia* with Christ our Prophet. See Phil Butin, "Two Early Reformed Catechisms, the Threefold Office, and the Shape of Karl Barth's Ecclesiology," *Scottish Journal of Theology* 44 (1991): 195-214. In that essay Butin demonstrates that each part of vol. IV of the *CD* develops the work of Christ under one aspect of the *munus triplex*. Part I, "Jesus Christ the Lord as Servant," pertains to the priestly office; Part II, "Jesus Christ the Servant as Lord," pertains to the royal office; Part III, "Jesus Christ the True Witness," pertains to the prophetic office. Each office, according to Butin, illuminates the following: a particular aspect of the objective reconciliation wrought in the life history of Jesus Christ, an application of this objective reconciliation, and a corresponding communal and individual enactment.

becomes a provisional representation of the justification, sanctification, and vocation of all humanity. It witnesses to the completed work of reconciliation in Christ.

By delineating the practice of *koinonia* in the gathering, upbuilding, and sending of the church, we will move toward more concrete normative guidelines for practicing *koinonia* in small groups. We will see how small groups can be shaped by the church's gathering, upbuilding, and sending. At the same time, we will explore how small groups might enhance these dimensions of the church's existence, helping the church to become a countercultural community of authenticity, intimacy, and compassion. We will bring the practice of *koinonia* into dialogue with our study of well-developed small groups, constructing guidelines for small-group ministries in light of the positive functions and limitations of well-developed groups. Because small groups are not a cure-all for all the church's challenges, we will not assume that that they can contribute equally to each of the three modes of the church's existence. In fact, this chapter will suggest that small groups are positioned uniquely to enhance *koinonia* among church members in the mode of upbuilding.

Gathering of the Church

The first mode of the church's existence is its gathering. Jesus Christ through the power of the Holy Spirit gathers persons into a concrete form of community, a fellowship of preaching, teaching, prayer, and partaking of the sacraments. In its gathering, the church thus becomes a visible historical reality. The church's practices, polity, leaders, art, and media are visible, while its *koinonia* is invisible. In the gathering of the church, people are awakened to faith in God and God's *koinonia*-creating work of reconciliation. They are awakened to the invisible and essential dimension of their existence as they assemble in a visible community. The church is gathered by the work of the Spirit and, in response, it attests its life in multidimensional *koinonia*.

The gathering of the church is a consequence of grace, the unmerited favor of God. Persons enter the church by means of grace. They join Christ and the church in baptism, in which they are incorporated into the death and resurrection of Christ in the here and now. Indwelling Christ, they indwell one another. Persons do not enter into *koinonia* with

Christ (and hence each other) through socialization patterns. As James Loder preaches, baptism is a judgment against socialization: "[Baptism] is a demonstration of the truth that we do not create this social unit, the church. We do not perpetuate it. Its inherent life has nothing to do with us." Likewise, the Eucharist is a judgment on kinship: "You are not finally a member of your family. You do not belong to them. You belong to Christ. Christ separates you from your family and so enables you to really love them."[3] In other words, in its gathering the church's identity is reordered. To whatever degree persons derive their identity from their families, educational backgrounds, socioeconomic status, gender, or race, these factors get decentered with respect to *koinonia* with Christ. Members of the church discover their identity first and foremost in Christ, in whom all the dividing walls of race, gender, nationality, and socioeconomic status are demolished.

By virtue of its *koinonia* with Christ, the church is "one, holy, catholic, and apostolic" body. These four marks shape the church's identity. The church is *one*. This is an objective reality. The church is united to Christ, who exists in the present tense of reconciliation as one body. The Holy Spirit grafts us into this body and thus into the communion of saints from all times and places. Division in the church is a contradiction of the church's identity: it is scandalous, perverse, and distressing, a tearing asunder of Christ's body. The church is *holy*. It is set apart from other communities and called to a particular task. Its holiness has to do with its vocation, its calling to serve God, the world, and thus itself. Its holiness never consists in sectarian posturing. "It is holy in its openness to the street and even the alley, in its turning to the profanity of all human life," says Barth, "when it rejoices with them that do rejoice and weeps with them that weep."[4] The church is *catholic*. The church's catholicity has to do with "an identity, a continuity, a universality, which is maintained in all the differences" (*CD* IV/1, p. 701). The church's essence, its *koinonia*, remains constant in its manifold expressions. It discerns whether or not its various activities reflect its invisible dimension. In this way it upholds its identity in Christ. It resists definition by, alignment with, and dependence on alien social, historical, or

3. James E. Loder, *Educational Ministry in the Logic of the Spirit* (unpublished ms), ch. 7, pp. 25-26.

4. Karl Barth, *Church Dogmatics*, ed. G. W. Bromiley and T. F. Torrance, trans. G. W. Bromiley (Edinburgh: T. & T. Clark, 1956), IV/1, p. 725 (hereafter, volume, part, and page references to the *CD* appear in parentheses in the text).

political categories. It does not conform to the order or objectives of other human societies. It accompanies them insofar as doing so contributes to multidimensional *koinonia*. The church is *apostolic*. As I suggested in the previous chapter, the church encounters Christ through the witness of the apostles and prophets. It enters into a history with Christ and with them. It does not live in *koinonia* with Christ separate from them.

Koinonia with Christ in the gathering of the one, holy, catholic, and apostolic church takes the form of faith. Through the work of the Spirit, the church recognizes and acknowledges its *koinonia* with Christ, each other, and all humanity. It turns to Scripture as a witness to Jesus and his work of reconciliation. At the same time, it recognizes the vastness of Jesus Christ. It opens itself to seeing Christ anew again and again. "For all His singularity and unity He is inexhaustibly rich, so that it is not merely legitimate but obligatory that believers should continually see and understand [its faith and its Lord] in new lights and aspects" (*CD* IV/1, p. 763). When the Spirit opens the church's blind eyes to see Christ's magnificence, the church breaks forth in praise. Having tasted and seen that the Lord is good, church members strive to be theologians, "having a true vision of the One in whom [they] believe, having true thoughts concerning Him, and finding the right words to express those thoughts" (*CD* IV/1, p. 765).

Faith also means that the church recognizes that Jesus Christ has carried away its guilt and shame. By virtue of our *koinonia* with Christ and through Christ with the triune God, we have been put to death and raised to new life. While we have participated in Jesus' death and resurrection, the effects are not yet fully manifest in our lives. We participate fully in Christ, though Christ is not yet fully formed in us. Faith trusts in the completed work of *koinonia* in the past, anticipates its future coming, and prays for its present in-breaking. As such, faith is a matter of the heart. It creates a particular disposition in the church: "a comforted and strong and joyful confidence"; a trust in the completed work of God for all; a cheerfulness, peacefulness, and thankfulness (*CD* IV/1, p. 774).

Faith includes public confession in the mode of gathering. As it is brought together by the Holy Spirit, the church confesses its complete reorientation on Christ. Church members acknowledge that they belong to Christ, and when they contradict their *koinonia* with Christ, they groan and exult with the apostle Paul:

I delight in the law of God in my inmost self, but I see in my members another law at war with the law of my mind, making me captive to the law of sin that dwells in my members. Wretched man that I am! Who will rescue me from this body of death? Thanks be to God through Jesus Christ our Lord! . . . For the law of the Spirit of life in Christ Jesus has set me free from the law of sin and death. (Rom. 7:22-24; 8:2)

In this way the church practices *koinonia* with Christ in his death and resurrection. It acknowledges its cruciform identity as a reflection of the crucified Lord. By trusting in God's forgiveness and the reconciliation wrought in him, the church witnesses to the universal reach of God's love.

In summary, the church's *koinonia* with Christ expresses itself in and through faith in the mode of gathering. The church practices its *koinonia* with Christ as it accepts the verdict pronounced in the incarnation — that the world has been reconciled to God in Jesus Christ — and as it accepts its consequent new being, its daily dying and rising with Christ. The church lives out its *koinonia* with Jesus Christ in its joyful confidence in Christ's finished work. The church lives out its *koinonia* with Christ as it confesses this new reality in its corporate gathering. The church also lives out its *koinonia* with Christ when it confesses its objective status as one, holy, catholic, and apostolic church, and when based on this objective reality, it prays for its fulfillment, submits itself to examination by the Word and work of God, and listens and reaches out to other congregations from whom it is disconnected. Finally, the church lives out its *koinonia* with Christ and the *communio sanctorum* in the mode of gathering when it submits itself to the testimony of the apostles and prophets recorded in Scripture.

We now consider the place of small-group ministry vis-à-vis the church's *koinonia* with Christ in the mode of gathering. What normative guidelines for small-group practice emerge from this definition of the gathering of the church? Can small groups contribute to the gathering of the one, holy, catholic, and apostolic church? How might small groups nurture the kind of faith that reflects the church's *koinonia* with Christ?

To begin with, we already know from a sociological perspective that small groups are not the answer to all the challenges faced by the church in our present context. We now add to that a theological argument. First, small groups are not synonymous with the gathering of the church. Nor can they replace it. They lack constitutive ecclesial practices, such as baptism, the Lord's Supper, and preaching. They may be communities of faith, and they may contribute to the church's ministry; but they are not equivalent to the church.

Second, participants in small groups often describe their groups as "family" or "closer than family." From a sociological perspective, identifying one's family outside biological bonds is a unique characteristic of late modernity. We choose our family as part of creating and re-creating our own life narratives. We may disassociate with biological relatives as part of rewriting our own history and creating the future that we desire. From a theological perspective, such statements by small-group members are quite accurate. As Jesus himself said, "Here are my mother and brothers! Whoever does the will of God is my brother and sister and mother" (Mark 3:34-35). *Koinonia* is more definitive than biology; *koinonia* is the locale in which we belong. It comprises the people to whom we are bound ontologically.

If baptism is the normative means of entry into *koinonia* with Christ and with the communion of saints on the subjective level, then we do not choose to whom we belong. We are chosen, called, and set apart by God and God's people. This radically challenges the late-modern tendency to choose family as a means of personal fulfillment. Moreover, it undoes the late-modern religious tendency to believe without belonging or before belonging. From a baptismal perspective, we belong before we believe. God's love claims us before we respond in faith. When we are baptized into Christ's death and resurrection, we are placed in God's family so that we can learn to practice *koinonia*, so that we can respond with faith to God's gracious initiative in claiming us as God's own.

Small-group ministry should reflect the grace by which people enter *koinonia* in the present tense of reconciliation. Too often small groups become self-selecting affinity groups, comprised of people of the same gender, race, socioeconomic status, political affiliation, and educational background. When all the participants in a congregation's small-group ministry are segregated into like-minded groups, then the ministry contradicts the baptismal quality of *koinonia*. As Loder reminds us, "*Koinonia* is not your core group of friends. . . . *Koinonia* is constituted by the Holy Spirit and includes the enemy and the stranger as well as the like-minded and the compliant."[5] Thus small groups should be outwardly open to persons of varying socioeconomic status, race, gender, ethnicity, and kin. While there may be instances in which affinity groups contribute to *koinonia,* such groups should not become the standard for an entire small-group ministry. For instance, some groups might consist of the same gender, but together all the groups in any congregation would not be characterized by a complete lack of diversity. Perpetual homogeneity would be interpreted and confessed openly as a symptom of the church's contradiction of its oneness in Christ. Along the same lines, groups would not devolve into cliques. Mutual belonging would involve openness and hospitality to others outside the group. While this does not mean that small groups must allow any interested person to join their group, in principle, they would be open to newcomers. They would be willing to risk their established bonds and to trust that, even if the group reorganizes, bonds remain among all who participate in the *communio sanctorum.*

This leads to a third normative guideline for small-group ministry. Church leaders should explore, strengthen, and act on the ecumenical longings of members of well-developed small groups. In this way groups would contribute to the church's capacity to live out its unity and catholicity. Small groups could be organized across congregational and denominational lines. In small groups, those from differing theological traditions could seek to hear God's voice together — in and through each other. They could acknowledge and mourn any ongoing dissension between their respective strands of Christianity as a contradiction of their *koinonia* with Christ. By the work of the Spirit in their midst, mutual recrimination and lingering judgments toward one another might melt away. Openness to seeing Christ anew in and through one another would be understood as integral to their discipleship. Christ is not captive to any particular theological tradition, scriptural interpretation, or culture. Rather, Christ is ever new, just as he is always the same. He wakens us out of our slumber, frees us from our ecclesial ruts, even and perhaps especially those ruts we fail to see. Ecumenical small groups could provide space for the Spirit to work in this way.

5. Loder, *Educational Ministry,* chap. 7, p. 18.

Upbuilding of the Church

In this mode of the church's existence, Jesus Christ in the power of the Holy Spirit causes the church to grow, integrates its members into one body, and forms its practices according to its inner life of *koinonia*. The church participates in its own upbuilding as its members live in mutual dependence and support, engage in common worship and prayer, and remain open to the ongoing reformation of all their practices. In these ways, the church lives in mutual self-giving love, a love that mirrors Christ's love as well as the love that is the Trinity.

The Nature of Church Growth

The church grows by virtue of its *koinonia* with Christ. Jesus Christ, through the Holy Spirit, is the indwelling power of the church's growth. According to Barth, there are two kinds of church growth: extensive (outward) and intensive (inward and upward). The church extends itself into the world and thereby acquires more members so that it can fulfill its vocation. However, extensive growth in and of itself is not true growth. It must be accompanied by intensive growth, growth in relationship to Christ and in the relationships among church members. Furthermore, numerical growth is not equivalent to spiritual growth, in which members of the church together receive and exercise their spiritual gifts and reflect the self-giving love of Christ.

Spiritual growth is a mystery. It cannot be controlled by the church or guaranteed by any of its practices. There is no instructional curriculum, ministerial program, or set of practices that can be transposed from one context to another in guarantee of growth. In fact, the church's extensive and intensive growth is limited. "[It] is not ordained to give a perfect but only a provisional and therefore imperfect representation of the new humanity, God having reserved the definitive and perfect representation for His kingdom which comes in the final manifestation" (*CD* IV/2, p. 649). The church's spiritual growth may even "have the appearance of its opposite" (*CD* IV/2, p. 601). For the Christian life is one of death and resurrection, a dying and rising in and with Christ. That is, the cross is at the heart of the Christian life. *Koinonia* with Christ means *koinonia* in Christ's cross. By the power of the Spirit, we have been united to Jesus in his death and resurrection (i.e., in the past). By the power of the Spirit, we live in correspondence to his death and resurrection (i.e., in the present). In so doing, we practice *koinonia* with Christ. As Barth writes, the cross of the Christian "is the most concrete form of the fellowship between Christ and the Christian" (*CD* IV/2, p. 599). We take up our cross in whatever form it may come: grief and loss; temptation; rejection from the world or, more likely, from fellow church members; and persecution. All these forms of the cross may serve as a kind of pruning for future growth.[6] Death and loss may precede significant flourishing. As Jesus said, "Unless a grain of wheat falls into the earth and dies, it remains just a single grain; but if it dies, it bears much fruit" (John 12:24).

Given this, let us consider the role of small groups in church growth. In what sense might small groups contribute to church growth? How might this theological understanding of church growth shape small-group practice?

First of all, inward growth rather than numerical growth should be the priority. Small groups should first contribute to the church's growth in conformity to Christ's likeness. This is the essence of growth; this is spiritual growth. Orienting small-group ministries to the inward or spiritual growth of a congregation should not be difficult either. For, as our research suggests, small groups do not by and large help the church to grow numerically (in spite of claims to the contrary by some small-group resources).

Second, church leaders should not expect small-group ministry or any particular model of small groups to guarantee growth. Many small-group models have been marketed widely on the basis of their success in a particular congregation. It often is assumed that, with a few minor tweaks, these programs will yield similar results in other contexts. This assumption fails to recognize the priority of God's action in bringing about church growth. It may encourage church leaders to bypass the process of prayerfully discerning how best to join God's ministry in their community of faith. The mystery and grace of church growth actually encourages ministers to slow down, to learn about the

---

6. This is not to suggest that suffering in and of itself is good. Nor is it to suggest that the way of the cross is synonymous with passive acceptance of injustice. Suffering, in fact, is a negation of God's good intent for creation. But none of us can escape it. Thus we can steward our suffering as participation in the cross of Christ. See Theresa F. Latini, "Grief-Work in Light of the Cross: Illustrating Transformational Interdisciplinarity," *Journal of Psychology and Theology* 36, no. 2 (Summer 2009): 87-95.

gifts given to their members, and to hear the passions of church members as part of deciding how God is moving in their midst. Perhaps small groups are not the most appropriate practice for them right now. Perhaps some small-group models would be fitting and others not. In any case, small groups should be implemented with a healthy dose of humility when it comes to expectations for church growth. As one pastor who established well-developed small groups in his congregation says, "We tried multiple small-group models out there. We followed them to a 'T,' but group leaders and members got frustrated. After about five years of that, we learned to let go of our expectations and trust the groups to unfold and grow in an organic way."

Third, small groups could contribute to the kind of church growth that appears in the guise of its opposite. They could become a primary site for learning to live the way of the cross. Small groups excel at caring for church members in the midst of grief, loss, and personal crises. They actively and holistically support those who are suffering. They contribute to the emotional, social, physical, and spiritual needs of their members. What if small-group leaders and members learned to interpret this compassionate service as *koinonia* with Christ and each other in the form of the cross? Pastors and Christian educators could develop training materials that help small-group leaders understand Christian life and particularly small groups as a venue for living the way of the cross. Preaching and teaching on the cross could support small-group participants in having a theological framework for their own lives. In this way, small groups might contribute to authentic spiritual growth and simultaneously counter the trend of separation from the richness of their theological tradition.

Mutual Integration

The church practices *koinonia* as its members are "brought together, constituted, established and maintained as a common being — one people capable of unanimous action" (*CD* IV/2, p. 635). In the upbuilding of the church, Christ fits the members of his body together in mutual dependence and support. They respond by submitting to one another in self-giving love. The unity that emerges from this mutual submission does not swallow up their diversity. Rather, their diversity and concomitant mutual adaptation are essential to the fulfillment of their vocation. "Without this integration and mutual adaptation, there can be no reciprocal dependence and support. And without this the community will inevitably fall apart and collapse" (*CD* IV/2, p. 636).

Church members are united in worship; in worship their life together takes shape. Thus the upbuilding of the church flows from its common worship. The church's integration and edification in worship determines its entire life-act, all its relationships and practices. From its center in worship, the church's life of *koinonia* "spreads to the wider circle of the daily life of Christians and their individual relationships" (*CD* IV/2, p. 639). If edified in worship, it edifies itself elsewhere. Church members will be knit together in a series of I-Thou encounters of love marked by the following attitudes and actions: they live in peace with each other; they admonish one another; they forgive one another; they subject themselves to one another; they practice hospitality toward one another; and they bear each other's burdens. As the church "adopts these attitudes and actions," says Barth, it is built up. Such integration is a normative guideline for all ecclesial practices. "Everything that Christians do is to be judged by the standard whether it serves this integration" (*CD* IV/2, pp. 636-37).

Just as the upbuilding of the church happens in worship, it also happens in special practices of *koinonia*. *Koinonia* is the origin, *telos,* and content of the church's life-act. All its work is fundamentally a *koinonia* of divine and human action. At the same time, certain communal activities may be considered "special practices" of *koinonia* among church members. In these activities, members of the church embody their *koinonia* with one another. These activities include — but are not limited to — confession and forgiveness of sin, bearing one another's burdens (or mutual forbearance), praise, prayers of thanksgiving, petition, and intercession, service, and theological dialogue. In other words, the practice of *koinonia* entails communal activities that are centered in Jesus Christ. Potlucks, book clubs, and social gatherings do not, in themselves, reflect our union and communion with Christ; nor do they necessarily have anything to do with union and communion with each other in Christ.

Given that, let's consider the role of small groups in the integration of church members. How can small groups weave together the lives of Christians into one tapestry of *koinonia*? How might this vision of integration challenge small-group ministry?

First, small-group ministry should on the whole reflect the unity and diversity characteristic of *koinonia*. As I have suggested above, small groups should be outwardly open to diversity in membership. They should also be inwardly open to the variety of talents, personalities, and perspectives of their members. Small groups should not deny or suppress difference, disagreement, or conflict; rather, they should celebrate difference as an expression of the diversity inherent in the body of Christ. Small groups could practice *koinonia* by acknowledging and appreciating the radical particularity of each group member. Each person would be accepted in all of her complexity as an essential part of the body of Christ. Accepting the uniqueness of each member should lead small groups to accept conflict as a potential catapult into new life. Conflict would not be squelched for the sake of superficial peace, which really is no peace at all. Tension between groups or individuals would be embraced as an opportunity for new vision to emerge. Group members could pray that their conflicts become a means through which Christ transforms their self-understanding so that they live more authentically in *koinonia*. Rather than suppressing discussion of "tough topics," such as politics, small groups should enter into more authentic dialogue. In this, they would know that their unity is not synonymous with uniformity. They would rest secure in their union and communion with each other in Christ — even when they struggle to understand and love one another. They would interpret disagreement as a sign of the finitude of human understanding. Members would acknowledge their faltering insight and knowledge, and they would avoid simplistic answers to life struggles. They would take a generous posture toward those with whom they disagree. In response to their differences of opinion, belief, and action, they would practice mutual forbearance as an aspect of their *koinonia* with each other. As the Presbyterian Church (USA) Book of Order declares, "[T]here are truths and forms with respect to which persons of good character and principles may differ. And in all these we think it is the duty both of private Christians and societies to exercise mutual forbearance toward each other."[7]

This leads to the special practices of *koinonia* for which small groups are uniquely positioned. Given the depth of sharing that occurs

---

7. *Book of Order: Constitution of the Presbyterian Church (USA), Part II* (Louisville: Presbyterian Church USA, 2007), G-1.0305.

in small groups and their members' desire for mutual accountability, groups should become places where confession and forgiveness are practiced along with mutual forbearance. As revealed in our study of well-developed groups, leaders and members shy away from the confession of sin. Therefore, it is incumbent on ministers and church educators to teach and preach about sin in ways that enable congregants (1) to understand sin in the context of grace and thus (2) to experience conviction as liberating. To confess our sin means to acknowledge honestly the ways in which we fall short of God's good intention for our lives. It is to admit openly those things that we deeply regret having said or done (or not said or done). To confess means to bare our souls to God and to one another. To confess means to tell our inner truth. Saint Augustine provides a clear example of this kind of confessing. In his memoirs Augustine shares the story of his doubts about the Christian faith, his troubled relationship with his mother, his son born out of wedlock, the mistress he never married, and what today we might call his sexual addiction.[8] When we dare to be as honest as Augustine, then and only then will we experience true communion with one another, because then we will know and be known in ways that really matter. As Dietrich Bonhoeffer says in *Life Together,* we often do not experience authentic fellowship in the church because we do not break through to authentic confession in the presence of one another.[9]

To put it another way, confession is inextricably linked to *koinonia.* When we pour out our hearts to one another, we are united in love in the present mode of reconciliation. Failure to be real, to be fully human, to acknowledge our sin to one another limits not only our fellowship with each other but also our fellowship with God. For we experience the presence of Jesus in each other. As I have observed above, Jesus Christ lives in the present in a body. He lives in the here and now, in you and me. Jesus comes to us through each other. There is no way of knowing the love of Jesus in isolation from each other, and thus confessing leads to communion with God and each other.

Confession of sin in small groups might bring healing to church members as well. When we lock up our distress and disappointment in some secret compartment of our hearts and minds, then our separation

---

8. Saint Augustine of Hippo, *Confessions,* trans. R. S. Pine-Coffin (New York: Penguin Books, 1961).

9. Dietrich Bonhoeffer, *Life Together* (New York: Harper and Row, 1954), pp. 110-13.

from God and each other only increases. But when we take the risk to speak about what is the source of our shame, whether it is something we have done or something that has been done to us, we move out of isolation and loneliness and into connection. When we are accepted fully by someone who sees us in the depths of our being, then we experience grace; and in the presence of grace our self-judgments melt away: "Perfect love casts out fear" (1 John 4:18). As small-group members confess their guilt and their grief to one another, they do so grounded in christological time. That is, they understand their sin and suffering in light of the kingdom of God, which has already come and which will come in its fullness. Small groups can risk self-disclosure when they trust in Christ's past, present, and future coming. If they see and hear each other fully, they will participate in Jesus' ministry of forgiveness and healing in the here and now. They will become who they are: Christ's ambassadors of reconciliation living in multidimensional *koinonia*.

Finally, small groups should add forgiveness to these practices of mutual forbearance and confession of sin. Again, groups are situated to live out this particular dimension of *koinonia* among church members. Consider the fictitious yet recognizable small-group member who continually subverts discussion. He may dismiss others' opinions, resort to ad hominem attacks, demand the group's attention, or storm out of meetings. Instead of labeling him as "disruptive, inappropriate, narcissistic," small groups might (1) recognize the needs behind his behavior; (2) challenge the behavior by clearly stating its effects on the group; (3) provide space for all involved to share their feelings; (4) express mutual forgiveness; (5) pray for each other; and (6) commit to holding group members accountable to this kind of process whenever conflict arises.

Formation of Ecclesial Practices

A crucial dimension of the church's upbuilding is the ongoing and intentional ordering or formation of its ministry.[10] The church is re-

10. In paragraph 67.4, "The Ordering of the Community," Barth writes: "The upbuilding of the community, the event of the communion of saints, is accomplished in definite relationships and connexions, and to that extent in order. Let us again put it in another way. In the upbuilding of the community we have to do with that which is law-

formed and always being reformed, and this formation follows three normative guidelines: *diakonia, liturgia,* and dynamic excellence, or as Barth puts it, living and exemplary law. As the church actively forms and reforms its practices according to these norms, it reflects its inner life of *koinonia* by the grace of God.

Diakonia. In all of its activities, the church serves Christ, the world, and its members. This service is total, determining "its being in all its functions."

> Nothing that is done or takes place can escape the question whether and how far within it the community serves its Lord and His work in the world, and its members serve one another by mutual liberation for participation in the service of the whole. That which does not stand the test of this question but is done merely because, even though it does not serve, it has always been done or is regarded as a possible line of action, is quite unlawful, and it must either be jettisoned as inessential and harmful ballast or made to serve (which is often easier said than done). (*CD* IV/2, p. 692)

This service is universal and differentiated. Each person, with his or her unique mix of gifts, is indispensable to the whole; she/he cannot delegate nor denigrate her/his responsibilities, for no one kind of service is more important than another. Just as each person is indispensable to the whole body of Christ, so also is each ministry indispensable to the whole. Each form of ministry must be integrated with all the others. Each form serves the others even as it serves God and the world. In other words, the various ministries of a congregation must consider and be concerned for their common vocation.

Leitourgia. As discussed above, all ecclesial practices are bound to and flow from the church's life of worship. In keeping with Barth, we might say that ecclesial practices should support or recapitulate "four concrete elements" of worship in which Jesus Christ is really present: confession, baptism, the Lord's Supper, and prayer (*CD* IV/2, p. 710).

---

ful and right" (*CD* IV/2, p. 677). Throughout this section, the words "order" and "law" — and less frequently "form" — describe the church's proper relationship to Christ, itself, and the world. Barth implicitly admonishes the church to order itself according to its basic and derivative laws. His concern for the proper ordering of the church's action, i.e., its living according to its basic and derivative laws, may be described as the "formation" of the church.

In worship the church hears the Word of God and responds with public confession. In this way it simultaneously expresses gratitude to God and builds itself up. This confession happens in multiple liturgical acts: recitation of the creed, singing, reading of Scripture, preaching, and teaching. Ecclesial practices grounded in worship support public confession and response to the Word of God in other contexts. Liturgical forms of confession provide a general shape for confession in other ecclesial practices.

In worship the sacraments of baptism and the Lord's Supper confirm members' twofold belonging to Christ and to one another. The sacraments establish their relationships in trust: though they are cognizant of each other's sins and shortcomings, members accept one another as sisters and brothers in Christ. The sacraments place them on equal footing beneath the judgment and liberation of the Word of the cross. The real presence of Christ sustains them in the promises of eternal life. Their Lord nourishes and strengthens their faith as they gather in the bosom of the church. Ecclesial practices grounded in worship build on the trust engendered by mutual participation in the sacraments.

In the common prayer during worship, church members are constituted as the body of Christ. They are "taken up" into the prayer of Jesus Christ, and through him they commune with God. In prayer they participate in the work of the triune God, specifically the in-breaking of the kingdom. From its grounding in its common prayer in worship, the church can pray without ceasing and in accord with God's will. "The prayer of individuals and groups can be true and serious calling upon God only as it derives from the prayer of the assembled community" (*CD* IV/2, p. 705). Ecclesial practices should emerge from and be deepened by common prayer.

Dynamic excellence is the third guideline for the formation of ecclesial practice: church practices that faithfully reflect *koinonia* are dynamic. They are reformed and always being reformed according to the Word of God and the work of the Spirit. The body listens continually to its head in an attitude of openness. The church never presumes that today's practices, which the community chooses in obedience to its Lord, "[are] therefore universally valid for the Christian community at all times and in all places" (*CD* IV/2, p. 717). The church recognizes the exigencies of context and reshapes its practices according to the work of the living Christ in its particular time and space. The church also remembers and admits its own fallibility. Its obedience is "never unadulterated," and thus it "must always be improved and reformed" (*CD* IV/2, p. 715). In an attitude of free humility, the church lives in the transition between its past and future practices. It holds its practices lightly, in a readiness to receive from its Lord a new command. At the same time, the church "honours its past" (*CD* IV/2, p. 716). It neither hastily nor flippantly discards old practices; nor does it idolize them.

Not only is the church living and dynamic, but it is also exemplary in all its practices. It should be "a pattern for the formation and administration of human law generally and therefore of the law of other political, economic, cultural and other human societies" (*CD* IV/2, p. 719). The church knows its responsibility to the world: it converses with the world without imposing its lifestyle on the world. By living out (forming its practices according to) its inner life, the church presents a concrete, though imperfect and provisional, witness to life in multidimensional *koinonia*. According to Barth, the church models *koinonia* to other communities in its mutual service, trust, and commitment; in its differentiated unity; and in its fluidity and openness to change. These actions of communal love signify *koinonia* (*CD* IV/2, pp. 719-26). They attest the reconciliation of the world to God in Christ and joyfully invite others to join the dance in which they become who they truly are.

How might small-group ministries be formed according to these three guidelines? How might service, worship, and dynamic excellence shape small groups? First, small groups should be marked by mutual service. Each small-group member should care for the other according to the gifts they have been given by God. One member may give financially; another may listen with empathy; another may share the comfort of an open home and laughter; and all will intercede for one another. Our research suggests that this is in fact what well-developed small groups do. They serve each other in multiple ways, and in doing so they practice *koinonia* with each other and with Christ.

Second, small groups should be connected integrally to the worshiping life of the community of faith. Small groups isolated from the congregation's worship need to be reintegrated into the congregation. Leaders and members of such groups can be encouraged to join in worship as central to their Christian discipleship. Even those groups embedded in the larger congregational-ministry design could more intentionally connect group life with worship. Congregational care practiced in small groups could be grounded in members' common partaking of the Lord's Supper. Eating from the one loaf and drinking from the one cup symbolizes and enacts their mutual belonging and calls them to share all that they have with one another. Similarly, small groups could acknowledge their ministry of care as emerging from and reinforcing the giving of alms in worship services.

Small groups could grow in their capacity to confess the faith by studying their practice of confession in worship. What if they contemplated the meaning of the creed or their favorite hymns? In this way they could transform mindless repetition into meaningful declarations of Christian identity and purpose. Likewise, prayer in small groups should flow from the multiple forms of prayer expressed in worship, for example, invocation, thanksgiving, petition, intercession, and lament. Research on well-developed small groups suggests that one of their primary functions is providing space for church members to learn to pray. Small-group leaders could build on this inherent capacity of groups by practicing a wider variety of prayer in small groups. Pastors and church educators could provide leadership training on various kinds of prayer, as well as recommend multiple resources for group prayer.

Third, small groups should be dynamic and exemplary in practicing *koinonia* with one another. The stagnation of so many groups contradicts the church's call to ongoing formation and reformation, and church leaders must take this stagnation seriously. By saying this, I am not suggesting that pastors and Christian educators condemn or judge such groups. Rather, I am suggesting that they have dialogues with such groups (1) to understand the causes of stagnation and the needs and passions of group members, and (2) to express honestly their concerns about the group's spiritual growth. A number of well-developed small-group ministries encourage groups to assess their growth on a yearly basis. Self-assessment tools can be adapted for a variety of small groups, thereby enabling group members to discern the ways in which they are and are not practicing multidimensional *koinonia*.

In summary, the church practices *koinonia* among its members in the mode of upbuilding. It becomes the provisional representation of the sanctification of all humanity in Christ as its members (a) are integrated and integrate themselves into one organism; (b) participate together in Christ-centered activities; (c) are formed by God and responsively form their common activities according to the "law" of *koinonia;*

(d) pursue faithfulness and thus intensive growth instead of "success"; and (e) submit themselves to Word and Spirit (and never one without the other). In all this the church works out its unity, holiness, catholicity, and apostolicity. Well-developed small-group ministries are suited to foster each of these dimensions of *koinonia* among church members and thus contribute to the church's capacity to reflect the self-giving love of God in Jesus Christ.

Sending of the Church

In its mode of gathering, the church provisionally represents the *justification* of all humanity; in its mode of upbuilding, it provisionally represents the *sanctification* of all humanity. Now, in its mode of sending, the church provisionally represents the *vocation* of all humanity. Jesus Christ in the power of the Holy Spirit sends the church into the world to witness to humanity's reconciliation to God and its determination for multidimensional *koinonia*. It participates in the prophetic work of Christ by living out its solidarity with the world and thereby becoming the *communio vocatorum*. Its work in the world flows from hope in God's promises.

For Barth, the mode of sending constitutes the church's life-act. The church is fundamentally missional. As such, it follows in the footsteps of John the Baptist, the witness to the Light and Life of all humanity. So important is witness that Barth ascribes to it the status of a "true *nota ecclesiae* . . . an external sign by which the true community of Jesus Christ may be infallibly known" (*CD* IV/3.2, p. 772). As it is sent, the church experiences its fullest temporal fellowship with Christ (that is, other than its fellowship in his cross).[11] As it lives in solidarity with the world, practicing *koinonia* with the world, the church also practices *koinonia* with Christ. For the church is incarnational. It corresponds to Jesus as the "Man for others." It "resembles" and "imitates" and "cooperates" with Christ (*CD* IV/3.2, p. 777).

---

11. George Hunsinger writes: "The special vocation of the Christian is to share in the living self-witness of the Crucified. This sharing results in a fellowship of action and a fellowship of suffering. The act of witness will lead to suffering, and the suffering will function as an act of witness to the cross (*CD* IV/3, pp. 598, 608, 637-42)." Hunsinger, *How to Read Karl Barth: The Shape of His Theology* (New York: Oxford University Press, 1991), p. 183.

Living in Solidarity with the World

The church lives out its *koinonia* with the world as it exists for the world. As Barth puts it, the church is the community for the world. As such, the church knows the world, practices solidarity with the world, and is responsible for the world.

The church knows the world as it truly is. It knows that the origin and *telos* of the world is multidimensional *koinonia*. It knows that the world, like itself, spurns its determination for *koinonia*, thereby sinning against God and itself. It knows supremely that the world has been reconciled to God in Jesus Christ. Therefore, the church takes a generous posture toward the world, for it belongs to the world: like the world, it is creaturely. In other words, generosity is the church's normative disposition toward the world and central to its own life-act. The church takes a hospitable and merciful posture toward nonbelievers. It eschews any and all self-righteousness. It does not denigrate the world; in fact, it may acknowledge that practices outside its walls more faithfully reflect the gospel than its own activity. It may recognize the truth of God in the world and thus be called back to its right form and identity. In such loving openness, the church practices *koinonia* with the world. It also practices *koinonia* with Christ. In contrast, a lack of generosity toward the world may be "an alarming sign that something is decisively wrong in the inward relationship of the community to its own basis of existence" (*CD* IV/3.2, p. 772).

The church lives in *koinonia* as it practices solidarity with the world. It exists "only in the most genuine attachment" to the world (*CD* IV/3.2, p. 776). Church members enter into I-Thou relationships with members of the world, encountering them as joint heirs with Jesus Christ. "[T]hose who are genuinely righteous are not ashamed to sit down with the unrighteous as friends . . . those who are genuinely holy are not too good or irreproachable to go down 'into hell' in a very secular fashion" (*CD* IV/3.2, p. 774). Thus the church cannot avoid any dark corner in the world. A compassion parallel to that of its shepherd, which results from the power of the Holy Spirit in its midst, impels the church to act. It cannot close its eyes to suffering or its ears to cries for liberation. If it fails to live in this kind of solidarity, the church denies its *koinonia* with the incarnate one. "It manifests a remarkable conformity to the world if concern for its purity and reputation forbid it to compromise itself with it" (*CD* IV/3.2, p. 778).

In other words, the church is "under obligation to the world" (*CD* IV/3.2, p. 776). It is responsible, in a certain sense, for the future of the world, "for what becomes of it" (*CD* IV/3.2, p. 776). The church cannot be "neutral or passive" toward the world (*CD* IV/3.2, p. 777). Even though the church acknowledges the limited possibility of its own growth and of the world's transformation, nonetheless it acts in hope. The church grasps the outstretched hand of its neighbor wherever he may exist and whatever his condition may be. "It cannot leave [the world] in the lurch, nor to its own devices" (*CD* IV/3.2, p. 779). Moreover, as the church dies to itself by seeking not its own preservation but rather the humanization of the world, it is preserved. It lives. As Barth writes, "What it has to do in the world saves it from being lost in the world even though it is worldly" (*CD* IV/3.2, p. 776).

Confessing and Witnessing in the World

The church practices *koinonia,* not only in its solidarity with the world, but also in its work of confession and witness in the world. The church's confession takes two forms: authentic acknowledgment of its sin and suffering (as discussed above); and, public declaration of its beliefs and how it intends to act in light of its beliefs. In this second form of confession, the church communicates its understanding of God, itself, and all humanity on the basis of Jesus Christ — true God and true human. Jesus Christ is both the revelation of God and the revelation of humanity. Thus the content of the church's confession, as Barth elaborates, is twofold: God and humanity, that is, God and humanity in light of Jesus Christ.

Specifically, the church confesses God in Jesus Christ as "Friend, Helper, Savior, and Guarantor" of all (*CD* IV/3.2, p. 798). It confesses Christ not against humankind but with and for humankind. It joyfully proclaims the "yes" of God. The church confesses God's affirmation of humanity in the incarnation, God's negation of human sin in the cross, and God's re-creation of humanity in the resurrection. Thus the church sees and affirms humanity in its determination for *koinonia.* The church does not "take seriously" the "heathenism" of unbelievers, "refusing to consider [them] in this capacity" (*CD* IV/3.2, p. 805). Instead, it approaches others as *christianus designates,* those waiting (whether they know it or not) to be awakened, quickened, and enlightened by the power of the Holy Spirit.

The church's confession is contextual. It addresses the world and its members in a particular time and space. For Jesus Christ "penetrates each specific historical situation with a specific intention to be specifically received and attested by the community" (*CD* IV/3.2, p. 813). Jesus lives and works in the here and now. Therefore, "the Gospel on its lips cannot be perverted into an impartation of general, timeless and irrelevant Christian truth" (*CD* IV/3.2, p. 817). It cannot be "devoid of practical significance" (*CD* IV/3.2, p. 821). Conversely the Christian message cannot be "translated into the language and concepts and philosophy and notions of this age" (*CD* IV/3.2, p. 818). The gospel remains catholic — universal in its essence — as it is applied to particular contexts. The gospel is not an object mastered by the church; rather, it is a subject mastering the church and the world. Therefore, church practices are fueled by faithfulness to the gospel, not by concern for results or success as defined by the world (*CD* IV/3.2, p. 829).

In the mode of sending, the church's confession of God and humanity takes the form of witness. Witness is the sum of Christian ministry for Barth. Witness proclaims, explains, and applies the good news of the gospel in word and deed. First, witness includes proclamation of the gospel. In its act of witness the church confesses the reality of *koinonia*. It acquaints the world with its true identity in Christ. Second, witness includes explication: the church articulates its message intelligibly (with its own inner coherence) and contextually, that is, "in the constantly changing forms of human consideration, thought and expression" (*CD* IV/3.2, p. 849). Third, the church's proclamation and explication take the form of application. The church carries the world in its heart, bearing the world's burdens in prayer, and speaking to the world's suffering, sin, and perplexity. It comforts the world, on the one hand, and challenges it, on the other. In this way, the church "represent[s] a calm center of lodging and reflection in contrast to the world's activity and idleness, and . . . the source of prophetic unrest, admonition, and instigation, without which this transitory world could not endure."[12] Moreover, the church's witness — its proclamation, ex-

---

12. Karl Barth, "The Church: The Living Congregation of the Living Lord Jesus Christ," in *Barth: God Here and Now*, trans. Paul M. van Buren (New York: Routledge, 2003), p. 66.

plication, and application of the gospel — must take the form of both speech and action. The church witnesses to multidimensional *koinonia* in both word and deed and never one without the other.[13]

The church lives in hope as it practices *koinonia* with the world. Hope determines the church's knowledge of, solidarity with, responsibility for, and witness to the world. Hope means that the church expectantly awaits the final coming of Christ, when multidimensional *koinonia* will be completely manifest. Hope also means that the church yearns for the in-breaking of the kingdom in the present. Hope neither seeks refuge in the eternal nor overestimates transformation in the temporal. When fashioned by this hope, the church's sending signifies its *koinonia* with the world, its *koinonia* with the incarnate Christ, and the *koinonia* of its members in their common vocation.

To summarize, the church's *koinonia* with the world occurs most decisively in its mode of sending. It lives out its *koinonia* with the world as it takes a generous posture toward the world, emphasizing the "yes" of God and the world's ontological coexistence with Christ. It lives out its *koinonia* with the world as it practices solidarity with the world, when it knows the struggles, questions, pain, and sin of its context. It lives out its *koinonia* with the world in full witness, which includes the proclamation, explication, and application of the gospel. That witness is authentic when it combines speech and action. Finally, the church lives out multidimensional *koinonia* when hope undergirds and shapes all the above.

We now turn to the question of small groups in relationship to the church's *koinonia* with the world in the mode of sending. How do small groups contribute to the ministry of the church in the mode of sending? In what sense should they contribute to the church's *koinonia* with the world?

Research on well-developed small groups indicates that they help members witness in word and deed outside of the church. As members' lives are woven into the Christian narrative through small-group shar-

13. While acknowledging the multiplicity and changing forms of ecclesial practice, Barth outlines six ministries of speech (i.e., action by word) and six ministries of action (i.e., speech in deed) that have persisted throughout church history. The ministries of speech include: praise, preaching, teaching, evangelism, mission, and theology; the ministries of action include: prayer, the cure of souls, development of exemplary lives, solidarity with the helpless, prophetic action, and the establishment of fellowship (see *CD* IV/3.2, pp. 865-901).

ing, they acquire confidence and courage to convey their faith to friends, family members, and coworkers. Some of them become oriented toward — or ecstatically centered on — the world for which Christ died. Many well-developed groups adopt mission projects, covenanting together to care for those outside the walls of the church. This participation in the church's sending should become regularly practiced and integrated into the identity of small groups. In this sense, then, small groups would contribute to the church's capacity to confess its faith in speech and action.

Small groups could contribute indirectly to the church's witness in the world in at least two other ways. First, groups could nurture generosity, openness, and compassion among their members, emphasizing God's "yes" as central to the confession of Christian faith. Second, they could build on their strength in applying Scripture to their own lives. If small-group members appropriated Scripture in conversation with the preaching and teaching in the gathering of the church, then group members would grow in their capacities to interpret their own lives theologically. By understanding the implications of multidimensional *koinonia* for their own lives, they might be empowered to witness to *koinonia* more fully in communicating their faith to those outside the church.

Small-group ministry also could contribute indirectly to the church's capacity to live in solidarity with the world. In community with one another, small-group members discover the values of mutuality and interdependence. They learn to listen compassionately rather than judgmentally to others. Their enhanced relational skills overflow to persons outside their small groups. Pastors and Christian educators should interpret this aspect of the small group as a rudimentary sign of the image of God. The basic form of humanity, according to Barth, is "being-in-encounter." The image of God within us is this relationality. Though our capacity to be in perfect communion with God, each other, and the rest of creation has been marred by sin, the image of God in humanity has not been completely eradicated. We continue to exist in encounter with each other. This encounter consists of mutual seeing, hearing, speaking, and assisting one another with gladness (*CD* III/2, pp. 222-85). To put it another way, truly human and humanizing encounters that correspond to Jesus Christ, the true human, are characterized by mutual seeing, hearing, speaking, and assisting. In encounter we see and are seen, so that suspicions and prejudices melt away; we persist in speaking and listening in order to increase mutual understanding; we give and receive support and care in myriad ways. Small groups could become laboratories for practicing these four dimensions of "being-in-encounter," which we might call *koinonia* at the interpersonal level. Small-group members might, in this way and by the grace of God, reflect the *imago dei* and live in correspondence to Jesus, the true human. They might live in solidarity with our late-modern world by encountering the "others" in their full humanity, with all the dignity and respect that is due a child of God.

Conclusion

By now we have traveled far into the normative leg of our practical theological journey. I have defined the church as multidimensional *koinonia,* contrasted it to other communities and organizations, and argued that *koinonia* is the answer to the crisis of community. I have explored the Trinitarian shape of the church's life-act, its gathering, upbuilding, and sending in the present mode of reconciliation. We have seen how the church practices *koinonia* with Christ, among its members, and with the world in all three of these modes. In short, we have excavated Karl Barth's ecclesiology, have creatively reinterpreted it in light of *koinonia,* and have brought it into dialogue with both Anthony Giddens' interpretation of life in late modernity and with social-scientific research of small-group ministries. Consequently, we have constructed normative guidelines for practicing multidimensional *koinonia* in small groups. We have seen how small groups should be shaped by and enhance the church's practice of *koinonia* in each of these three modes. Small groups most clearly contribute to the upbuilding of the church. They should be developed further in light of this vision for living in *koinonia* within the church. By the grace of God, then, church-based small-group ministries might become one practice through which Jesus Christ transforms our broken and shallow forms of community into life-giving and life-sustaining communion.

CHAPTER 6

Healing in Small-Group Koinonia

In our small group, we have shared some very, very painful situations in the past. And the beauty of those situations hasn't been how terrible they were, even though they were. The beauty was seeing Jesus come into those situations and bring healing. And it's been a distinct honor and privilege for all of us to be a part of that.

Small-group leader

There would be no point in Christ's rescue work on the Cross if He had not retained on earth a fellowship, His Body, with its limbs, or members, to offer a new dynamic cycle of relationships to those whose natural cycle had broken down, and who, in any case, needed His divinity to replace their mortality.

Frank Lake, *Clinical Theology*

Well-developed small groups provide a context for personal healing and transformation, as is reflected in some of the narratives I presented in chapter 3. In one small group, Karen encountered the living Christ, whose overwhelming grace and love healed her shame, relieved her guilt, and propelled her into ministry to other wounded souls. As Emma's small group surrounded her with prayer, she experienced liberation from traumatic childhood memories that threatened to undo her. Other small-group members and leaders share similar stories. God's presence in fellow group members relieves their anxiety and weaves together the disparate threads of their lives to create a meaningful identity. From a psychosocial perspective, small-group community bolsters participants' ontological security — their sense of well-being and their experience of trust in themselves and others. But how are we to understand this aspect of small groups in light of our ecclesiology? What exactly is "ontological security"? Is this term compatible with our theology of *koinonia?* Does practicing *koinonia* in small groups enhance ontological security or heal ontological insecurity? Answering these questions will be the final aspect of the normative task of practical theology that I undertake in this book.

Defining "Ontological Security"

Scottish psychologist R. D. Laing coined the term "ontological security" in the mid-twentieth century. Influenced by object-relations theory and existential philosophy, Laing argued that ontological security has to do with a sense of being real, alive, vital, and creative, whereas ontological insecurity is a condition in which "the individual in the ordinary circumstances of living may feel more unreal than real; in a literal sense, more dead than alive, precariously differentiated from the rest of the world so that his identity and autonomy are always in question."[1] Similarly, British clinical theologian Frank Lake used the term "ontological anxiety" to describe the dilemma of those who suffer from "inner emptiness, inferiority, meaninglessness, and exhaustion."[2] More recently, Anthony Giddens has defined ontological security as "the confidence that most human beings have in the continuity of their self-identity and in the constancy of the surrounding social and material environments of action."[3] It is a primal sense of security and trust in the reliability of the world, which keeps us from being overwhelmed to the point of nonfunctioning.

The definitions of ontological security and insecurity presented by

1. R. D. Laing, *The Divided Self: An Existential Study in Sanity and Madness* (Baltimore: Penguin, 1965), p. 42.

2. Frank Lake, *Clinical Theology* (London: Darton, Longman, and Todd, 1966), p. 1058.

3. Anthony Giddens, *Consequences of Modernity* (Stanford: Stanford University Press, 1992), p. 92.

Laing, Lake, and Giddens emerge in part from their engagement with object-relations theory, particularly the work of D. W. Winnicott. Following their lead, I will define the psychological roots of ontological security on the basis of my own close reading of Winnicott. Then I will build on Giddens to describe the unique impact of late modernity on ontological security. Finally, I will bring this psychosocial definition of ontological security into dialogue with a theological definition of ontological security. My theology of *koinonia* will provide the larger context in which to understand the source of — and threats to — ontological security.

Psychological Roots of Ontological Security

For Winnicott, relationships are the source of human flourishing and the most significant motivating factor in human existence. While this may sound obvious to contemporary ears, his claim was groundbreaking in the early twentieth century. He dissented from the Freudian premise that persons are driven primarily by instinctual drives for food and sex. He declared that relationships are more fundamental to human being and doing than the powerful libidinal and food drives. Mere gratification of basic physical needs is not enough for human satisfaction, because people cannot be truly fed without love, affection, and connection. Winnicott also departed from Freud by focusing not on "curing symptoms" but on "whole living and loving persons." He explored the roots of dynamic, spontaneous, joyful aliveness. He sought to answer the questions "What is the goal of living?" and "What enables us to live creatively, passionately and productively?"

One of Winnicott's students, Harry Guntrip, summarizes his mentor's answer: "In the end . . . the solution [to living well] is not in the realm of medicine as professionally understood. It is in the realm of personal relationships, of the growth of personal reality within oneself, of life having a worthwhile meaning (because it can and does become significant only when, and in so far as, genuine personal relationships can be made)."[4] Such vital connection to oneself and others depends on ontological security. While ontological security is not a

---

4. Harry Guntrip, *Psychoanalytic Theory, Therapy and the Self* (New York: Basic Books, 1971), p. 123.

term that Winnicott himself used, his depiction of early childhood de-velopment can be read as a blueprint for it. The relationship between mother and child — or, as we might put it today, between primary caregiver and child — lays the foundation for either ontological secu-rity or ontological insecurity.[5]

Human beings begin life in an unintegrated state, merged with their mother. In the first months after birth, mother and child have a symbiotic relationship. Mothers identify with their infants, and infants reciprocally depend on their mothers as their source of being. After giv-ing birth, mothers enter a state of heightened physiological sensitivity to their infants. This "primary maternal preoccupation" is character-ized by near complete adaptation to the child's needs.[6] A mother keenly intuits and responds to her baby's need to eat or be changed at any hour of the day or night. By attending to her baby's bodily needs, par-ticularly the need for food, a mother creates the illusion that she is un-der the infant's control. For the infant, this translates into personal power and trust in the world.[7] Such routine care and attention to an in-fant's most basic needs lays the foundation for a sense of being and continuity of being or what we would call "ontological security."

Touch and mirroring also contribute to the development of onto-logical security in the earliest months of life. As an infant is held and handled by her mother, she experiences herself as alive. She delights in her mother's physicality as well as her own. She also gains a sense of self from the affectionate gaze of her mother. Her mother's counte-nance is her mirror, so that when she looks into her mother's eyes, she sees herself. Her most rudimentary sense of self emerges from face-to-face interaction with her primary caregiver. When truly seen and en-joyed — that is, delighted in — an infant senses that she is real, pleasur-able, and good.

Eventually, mothers recover from primary maternal preoccupa-

5. Throughout this section I have chosen to adopt Winnicott's language of the mother-child relationship with the knowledge that other caregivers may provide an en-vironment in which the child may thrive if the biological mother is unavoidably absent.

6. D. W. Winnicott, "Primary Maternal Preoccupation," in *Collected Papers: Through Paediatrics to Psycho-Analysis* (New York: Basic Books, 1958), p. 302.

7. Winnicott writes: "By her high degree of adaptation at the beginning, the mother enables the baby to experience omnipotence, to actually find what he creates, to create and link this up with what is actual" ("Living Creatively," in *Home Is Where We Start From* [New York: W. W. Norton, 1986], p. 49).

tion, and they falter in adapting to their infants' needs. Paradoxically, such faltering is actually adaptive. It facilitates the infant's movement out of a merged identity toward "the establishment of a personal identity."[8] Now the infant distinguishes the "me" from the "not-me"; and this capacity to distinguish develops gradually and is experienced when subject and object become differentiated. For this reason, healthy parenting is not synonymous with the permanent subordination of the mother's needs or loss of her own identity. In other words, to be a good mother does not mean mothers should subjugate their needs entirely, for at this stage "an infant does not thrive on perfect adaptation to need."[9]

Imperfect adaptation is critical for infants to develop not only a sense of self but also the "capacity for concern."[10] An infant will act aggressively toward her mother when the latter does not meet her needs immediately or flawlessly. This aggression is the flipside of love, and it signals that the child has come to depend on her mother. In more technical language, it signals the achievement of object permanence and trust in her mother. Winnicott says: "Adaptation failures have value *in so far as the infant can hate the object,* that is to say, can retain the idea of the object as potentially satisfying while recognizing its failure to behave satisfactorily."[11] This hatred is possible only on the basis of prior trust and love. And for this very reason it leads to guilt and reparation. Here it is important to note that aggression, or hate, is not opposed to love as much as it is integral to it. As a mother permits the infant to lovingly attack her body, time, and psychic energy in the first few months of life, she creates space for the experience and expression of both aggression and love. The development of this "simultaneous love-hate relationship" leads ultimately to the development of concern for the mother. For in later months, the infant recognizes that her mother is a human being distinct from herself. Her desire to possess the mother's time, energy, and body now may yield anxiety and a primitive

---

8. Winnicott, "Morals and Education," in *Maturational Processes and the Facilitating Environment: Studies in the Theory of Emotional Development* (London: Hogarth Press, 1965), pp. 96-97.

9. Winnicott, "Aggression in Relation to Emotional Development," in *Collected Papers,* p. 215.

10. Winnicott, "The Development of the Capacity for Concern," in *Maturational Processes,* p. 73.

11. Winnicott, "On Communication," in *Maturational Processes,* p. 181.

sense of guilt. If so, she will seek to make amends for her supposedly destructive impulses. In other words, the infant learns "to take responsibility for [her] own instinctual impulses" by repairing the relationship with her mother.[12] This capacity for concern, which includes the capacity to make amends, is essential for her future relationships and indeed the entire social fabric.

An infant's earliest self-differentiation emerges from imperfect adaptation to her needs, the freedom to respond aggressively, and then the opportunity to make amends. Mothers further support this differentiation by balancing freedom and support as their infants adjust to increasing amounts of physical separation from them. This balance enables infants to develop, first, the capacity to be alone in the presence of their mother and, second, the capacity to be separated from their mother. Infants creatively construct a "transitional object" (T.O.) — often a beloved blanket, stuffed animal, or pacifier — to accompany them on their journey from symbiosis to differentiation. With the T.O.'s comforting assistance, children make the transition from feeling secure when being physically held by their mother to feeling secure in her absence. They learn to tolerate separation without a disintegration in their sense of self. In Giddens's terminology, they learn to manage time-space distantiation. In so doing, they become ontologically secure.

In short, the experiences of holding and mirroring, being fed and changed in a routine and timely manner, expressing aggression and making amends, and learning to tolerate the mother's absence establish ontological security. These early developmental processes contribute to the fledgling human's trust in self and others; they enable the transition from a merged identity to a differentiated identity, thus laying the foundation for developing a coherent, flexible identity throughout life. Yet the development of a creative, vital self is a precarious process that can be undermined during these early years as well. Winnicott writes:

> All the processes of a live infant constitute a *going-on-being*, a kind of blueprint for existentialism. . . . Any impingement, or failure of adaptation, causes a reaction in the infant, and the reaction breaks up the going-on-being. If reacting to impingements is the pattern of an infant's life, then there is serious interference . . . in the infant [becom-

12. Winnicott, "Capacity for Concern," p. 75.

ing] an integrated unit, able to continue to have a self with a past, present, and future.[13]

In such instances, ontological *insecurity* prevails. For example, if his mother is absent for too long, a child may feel traumatized, or in Winnicott's words, "annihilated." In defensive response to repeated traumatic separation, he may build a false self, which will be characterized by an organized and rigid defense against dependency. If maintained throughout life, this false self typically results in isolation and meaninglessness. Or the infant may adopt a false self if a mother repeatedly fails to identify and respond to her child's needs during the first few months of life. If a mother repeatedly projects her own needs onto her child, the child will experience this as environmental impingement, a shocking rupture in his sense of peace and security. Adaptation then becomes inverted, so that the infant now responds to the mother's needs. Over time, the child learns to suppress his own needs and aggressive impulses, the source of his true self. He may cut off his anger and hence his love: as discussed above, anger and love are inextricable. He may disown his need for touch, holding, or intimacy so that authentic relationships become nearly impossible.

Throughout life, the false self may take the form of what I would call a caretaker, bully, or chameleon. The caretaker self appropriates the nurturing role that the environment failed to provide. The bully self creates a persecuting environment as a means of feeling alive. Since the child's internal impulses have been muted, he experiences aggression — and hence love — solely with respect to environmental impingement. Therefore, the bully self creates chaos and opposition in her relationships in order to secure some sense of continuity of being. By contrast, the chameleon is an extreme people-pleaser. "Through this [chameleon-like] False Self the infant builds up a false set of relationships, and by means of introjections even attains a show of being real, so that the child may grow to be just like mother, nurse, aunt, brother, or whoever at the time dominates the scene."[14]

In summary, object-relations theory suggests that we develop ontological security in the first two years of life in relationship with our

13. Winnicott, "From Dependence to Independence in the Development of the Individual," in *Maturational Processes,* p. 86.

14. Winnicott, "True and False Self," in *Maturational Processes,* p. 146.

mother or primary caregiver. We experience trust when our mother establishes for us a regular routine of eating, sleeping, and playing, and when she balances both time with us and time away from us. As infants, we transition from feeling secure when physically held by our mother to feeling secure in her absence. We learn to tolerate separation without a disintegration of our sense of self. We gain a sense of "being and going on being."[15] We become ontologically secure. We trust that the world is reliable, which enables us to participate in broader circles of community throughout life. Trusting the world and ourselves, we learn to balance autonomy and belonging, so that we can exist in a differentiated unity with others who are increasingly "other."

Ontological Security/Insecurity in Late Modernity

Life in late modernity is analogous to riding a juggernaut careening into an unforeseen future: unexpected questions and crises confront every level of our social existence. Former relational structures now function as mere shell institutions. With one hand, the pure relationship form gives us choice, and with the other hand, it takes away stability. We have lost trust in religious authorities (and just about every other authority, for that matter). We attempt to create our own life plan in a context of many threats — from personal meaninglessness to massive destruction and death on the global level. We face annihilation in our world — and in our very persons. In other words, the dynamics of late modernity threaten our primal sense of being and well-being. Our ontological security is assailed, thus simultaneously making it all the more critical for our flourishing.

As I have described above, we become ontologically secure as we learn to manage time-space distantiation, that is, separation from our mother, our source of being early in life. Ontological security depends on the ability to stay connected with others when separated from them. Late modernity requires persons to maintain a sense of connectedness across vast tracts of time and space. Persons must maintain continuity of being when living apart from family, friends, community, and coworkers. Ontological security must be strong enough for us to endure prolonged separation from the people, routines, and structures

---

15. Winnicott, "Primary Maternal Preoccupation," in *Collected Papers,* p. 303.

that once provided trust, security, and stability in the world. It must withstand impingement from multiple sources: (1) from global others, people whom we will never see from cultures we barely understand; (2) from experts (doctors, lawyers, economists, real estate and insurance agents) with conflicting advice; and (3) from media sources that bombard us with incoming information. Without sufficient ontological security, all these dissenting opinions about lifestyle choices will lead to pervasive doubt, mistrust, and helplessness.

New relational forms in late modernity also erode ontological security. While ontological security depends on mirroring from our primary caregivers, face-to-face interaction remains a persistent psychosocial need throughout life. Mirroring from the larger family system, friends, and community sustains our sense of security and well-being as we venture out into larger social circles.[16] In late modernity these larger social circles often consist of faceless relationships, which tend to deplete ontological security. Faceless relationships are not reliable sources of mirroring, for they force us to trust persons whom we do not know and systems that we do not understand. The pure relationship is an attempt to compensate for this loss of adequate mirroring. The pure relationship is the most common face-to-face encounter in late modernity. Friendship, marriage, and parenting supply emotional intimacy, face-to-face communication, and affirmation of our life narratives. Though Giddens does not say it, the pure relationship may represent not only a substitution for the loss of communal ties but also an attempt to retrieve the security once found in the mother-child dyad. It may be an unconscious return to a primal experience of connection. But this return is precarious, for the pure relationship is fragile: it can be terminated at will. In this sense, the pure relationship is a double-edged sword, threatening ontological security in its very attempt to reinforce it.

Similar to the predictability and dependability of our mother's response to our needs, continuity of routine throughout life helps maintain ontological security. In late modernity, mediated experience, the loss of tradition, and thoroughgoing reflexivity have the effect of

16. Winnicott says: "When a family is intact . . . each child derives benefit from being able to see himself or herself in the attitude of the individual members or in the attitudes of the family as a whole" ("Mirror Role of Mother and Family in Child Development," in *Playing and Reality* [London: Tavistock/Routledge, 1971], p. 118).

constantly undoing routine. Social practices and the knowledge on which they are built are inherently unstable. Today's truths may be altered or even nullified by tomorrow's discoveries. Experts inundate us with competing opinions regarding the most basic needs, such as physical health, challenging us to change our most basic practices. In practice, marriage and family function like shell institutions, contributing to high divorce rates and fiery public discourse. With all the freedoms of modernity comes the anxiety-producing obligation to create a meaningful and consistent personal narrative in the context of perpetual change, leading to a sense that one's very personhood is rickety.

Finally, ontological security depends on the continued ability to bracket out "unthinkable anxieties," as Winnicott puts it.[17] It functions as an "emotional inoculation" against anxieties that arise throughout life. It provides a "protective cocoon" that safeguards us against crises that would intrude.[18] In late modernity, this ability becomes all the more important, on the one hand, and all the more difficult to achieve, on the other. Late modernity instantiates risk and crisis. Due to bureaucratization, the institutionalization of war, and globalization, modern people become — or at least perceive themselves to be — powerless in the face of high-consequence risks. "No amount of bracketing out is likely altogether to overcome the background anxieties produced by a world which could literally destroy itself."[19] Further, abstract systems such as the stock market and insurance companies institutionalize risk, thereby weaving it into the fabric of daily life. One's future security is entrusted to experts, who effectively are strangers. Risk and doubt are inescapable. If one's basic ontological trust is fragile, contemplating a small risk, especially with regard to a cherished aim, may be psychologically unbearable.[20]

In summary, Giddens's interpretation of the effects of late modernity on the self suggests that the psychological development of ontological security determines one's ability to survive and thrive in an era of uncertainty and crisis. The uncertainties of modernity potentially jeopardize *both* the establishment of ontological security in early child-

17. Winnicott, *Maturational Processes,* p. 60.
18. Anthony Giddens, *Modernity and Self-Identity: Self and Society in the Late Modern Age* (Stanford: Stanford University Press, 1991), pp. 39, 40.
19. Giddens, *Modernity and Self-Identity,* p. 183.
20. Giddens, *Modernity and Self-Identity,* pp. 181-82.

hood, as gender roles, marriage, and parenting become "shell institutions," *and* the maintenance of ontological security throughout life, as people face impingement, unstable sources of mirroring, and uncontrollable risk.

Ontological Security in Theological Perspective

If ontological security is a psychological reality for Winnicott and a sociological reality for Giddens, then it would be a theological reality for Barth. While "ontological security" is neither a term Barth used or an issue that concerned him directly, he does give us a theology from which we can extrapolate a theological definition of ontological security.

Embedded within Barth's thought is the ontological reality of *koinonia*. Recall George Hunsinger's explanation:

> *Koinonia* in Barth's sense, as in the New Testament, means that we are not related to God or to one another like ball bearings in a bucket, through a system of external relations. We are, rather, something like relational fields that interpenetrate, form, and participate in each other in countless real though often elusive ways. *Koinonia*, both as a term and as a reality, is remarkable for its range and flexibility and inexhaustible depth. In Barth's theology I think it may fairly be said that *koinonia* is the ground of all being. *Koinonia* stands for the final reconciliation and interconnection of all things through a living, luminous system of internal yet diverse relations.[21]

Koinonia means that the entire cosmos somehow coexists with and coinheres in Jesus Christ. All creation indwells Christ. We exist in the greatest possible intimacy with Christ, and through Christ with God and each other. We exist in a series of *koinonia* relationships, all of which are inseparable from one another — with Christ, with God, with the church, with the world (including all creation).

On the one hand, multidimensional *koinonia* is an actual (objective) reality: "In Christ all things hold together" (Col. 1:17). Jesus Christ bridges all the divides between God and humanity and within human-

---

21. George Hunsinger, *Disruptive Grace: Studies in the Theology of Karl Barth* (Grand Rapids: Eerdmans, 2000), p. 257.

ity. If sin alienates humanity from God, Jesus reconciles them. He stands on the ontological divide between divinity and humanity, and he brings them together in his own person. In the incarnation, God and humanity come face to face, and they are reconciled. Jesus Christ is the self-revealing face of God to humankind and the fully responsive (i.e., trusting and obedient) face of humankind to God. Consequently, the ontological divide is overcome, and our ontological security is established for eternity. We are secure in *koinonia* with Christ, and through Christ we are secure in *koinonia* with God and each other.

On the other hand, multidimensional *koinonia* is not yet fully manifest existentially (subjectively) in creation. Sin and suffering persist. Sin has no ultimate being, no real eternal existence; nonetheless, it continues to isolate humans from God and each other in their lived experience. Suffering haunts us, leaving us to lament, "Where is God?" On account of the continued presence of sin and suffering, we may experience ontological insecurity. Only in the future, in the *eschaton,* will our security in *koinonia* be realized fully. In the here and now, the church has been awakened to the reality of *koinonia*. Jesus Christ, the Word of God, reveals to us through the power of the Holy Spirit that all creation is secure in him. In Word and sacrament primarily, and other church practices secondarily, we glimpse *koinonia*. We experience the real presence of Jesus Christ in our midst, united to us and uniting us to God and to each other. We practice this *koinonia* and thus witness to it in the world when we live in solidarity with others who are suffering and when we interpret our own suffering as a fellowship with Christ in his cross. Though the church loses sight of *koinonia* — for its faith is weak and its sight is frequently dim — the knowledge of God's communion-creating work is nevertheless trustworthy. As the apostle Paul wrote, "For now we see in a mirror, dimly, but then we will see face to face. Now I know only in part; then I will know fully, even as I have been fully known" (1 Cor. 13:12).

From a theological perspective, then, ontological security, like *koinonia* itself, must be differentiated in view of the three tenses of reconciliation and the absurdity of sin, so that we may speak of two dimensions of ontological security: actual (objective) ontological security and existential (subjective) ontological security. In contrast, our psychosocial definition of ontological security only addresses the existential dimension of ontological security. Neither Winnicott nor Giddens considers the question about ultimate security in the cosmos, and rightly so, for doing so would transgress the boundaries of their own disciplines.[22]

To claim ontological security on the basis of the church's interpretation of the self-revelation of God in Jesus Christ is the work of theology alone. With that said, we can make the following theological assertions about ontological security: (1) Humanity has no ontological security outside of Christ. We have come from the dust of the earth (or more accurately, the cosmos), and we shall all return to it. Death is the end of our story, our annihilation, if God does not preserve us. We are contingent beings who have no being in and of ourselves, that is, apart from God. (2) Because God has chosen to exist with us and not without us, humanity is ontologically secure (as is the cosmos). Objectively speaking, our being and continuity of being are secure because we are upheld on all sides by the love of God. (3) There is nothing that human beings can do to alter their objective ontological status. We are ontologically secure whether we know it or not, whether we feel it or not, whether we experience it or not. (4) We know that we are ontologically secure because God has revealed it to us in Jesus Christ and awakened us to this reality by the power of the Holy Spirit. Though faith is an awakening to this status, it is not a condition for it. (5) Our actual ontological security is the ground and *telos* of the experience of ontological security in the here and now. If we experience ourselves as ontologically secure in the face of violence and crises, then it is because we actually are ontologically secure whether we know it or not. (6) We may suffer from ontological insecurity on an existential level, for the reality of *koinonia* and its effects are not fully manifest in our lives. Yet any experience of ontological insecurity does not nullify our objective ontological security. (7) Jesus Christ — in, through, and in spite of the church — can strengthen ontological security and heal ontological insecurity at the level of our lived experience. This occurs primarily — but not exclusively — through Word and sacrament. (8) In the future, when God is all in all, our actual ontological security will be realized in all its fullness and beauty.

22. For a further discussion of the interdisciplinary method implicit in this statement, see the Epilogue of this book.

Healing Ontological Insecurity in the Context of *Koinonia*

Objectively speaking, ontological security is a reality, but subjectively speaking, ontological insecurity persists in human life. In fact, the propensity for ontological insecurity increases in late modernity. Giddens and Winnicott propose means of healing ontological insecurity through the creation of new social practices (Giddens) and therapy (Winnicott). Social practices, such as small groups, consist of trust relationships and routine activity, both of which contribute to personal and societal stability. Therapy enables persons to regress to early stages of development in the context of acceptance; counseling sessions become holding environments in which persons move from dependence to interdependence. The therapist becomes a mirror for his clients as he affirms their value and inherent goodness. As clients construct a meaningful life narrative, their ontological anxiety diminishes, and their ontological security congeals.

The church is a social institution and thus it can provide some — though not all — of the components of healing ontological insecurity. At the same time, it is more than a social institution. It is the communion of saints. It exists because of *koinonia*. It has an inner life that is connected to and mirrors the inner life of God. For this reason, then, healing ontological insecurity in the context of *koinonia* reconfigures healing ontological insecurity understood only from a psychosocial perspective. At the same time, our psychosocial understanding of ontological insecurity reconfigures our understanding of the church's ministry of healing in late modernity. In this way, our psychosocial and theological definitions of ontological security and approaches to the healing of ontological insecurity become mutually illuminating. Most relevant to our concerns here, our psychosocial definition of ontological security illuminates how multidimensional *koinonia* strengthens ontological security and heals ontological insecurity.

Theologically speaking, the healing of ontological insecurity depends on God's action through Jesus Christ by the power of the Holy Spirit. In his cross and resurrection, Jesus has saved us from sin and healed our suffering. By virtue of our union with Christ, we have been made ontologically secure, yet this is not yet fully manifest in human existence. We may experience ourselves as fragile, on the verge of annihilation, or overwhelmed by dread and despair. Jesus Christ breaks into our midst, in the here and now, by the power of the Holy Spirit to heal us of this ontological insecurity. The church joins Christ in this ministry of healing. The church is caught up in this healing by virtue of its union and communion with the triune God. As the church lives out its communion with God, among its own members, and with the world, it becomes "a new dynamic cycle of loving relatedness,"[23] through which persons are delivered from annihilation and restored to life. Practicing *koinonia* in baptism, the Lord's Supper, preaching, and other expressions of fellowship frees us to become who we are: persons secure in and created for eternal intimacy with God and each other. As Frank Lake writes, "[I]n fellowship with God, through Christ and His Church, there are available personal resources which transform relationships and personality. We claim that there is, here, an inflow of being and well-being" (p. 15).

The church participates in the healing of ontological insecurity when it points persons to Jesus Christ, the face of God that never goes away. Our mother's face goes away, leaving us with a yearning for the continual presence of love. As James Loder explains, there is consequently in human nature "a cosmic loneliness that longs for a Face that will do all that the mother's face did for the child, but now a Face that will transfigure human existence, inspire worship, and not go away, even in and through the ultimate separation of death."[24] Jesus has become this face for all humanity. He is present with us at all times, in all places. As the psalmist declares, "Even if I make my bed in Sheol, you, God, are there with me" (Ps. 139:8). Through the power and presence of the Holy Spirit, Jesus is our constant companion, our contemporary. Every time the church pronounces the Aaronic blessing, it encourages us to open ourselves to the face of God, the loving presence of God in our midst: "The Lord bless you and keep you; the Lord make his face to shine upon you, and be gracious to you; the Lord lift up his countenance upon you, and give you peace" (Num. 6:24-26).

The face of God in Jesus Christ is an enduring, eternal, and ultimately reliable source of mirroring. Of course, we do not actually see Jesus' face as his disciples did. Our seeing Christ in the church, that is, in the present tense of reconciliation, is mediated by Word and sacra-

---

23. Lake, *Clinical Theology,* p. 206 (hereafter, page references to this work appear in parentheses in the text).

24. James E. Loder, *Logic of the Spirit: Human Development in Theological Perspective* (San Francisco: Jossey-Bass, 1998), p. 119.

ment through the power of the Holy Spirit. In its preaching, the church points all persons to the face of God in Jesus Christ, through whom we behold God's delight, joy, and pleasure. Jesus becomes our mirror through the preached Word, and we discover our true identity as children of God. We internalize the reality that, as part of God's good creation and as those reconciled to God and one another, we are indeed accepted and called to both a common and particular vocation. Our lives become reoriented to Christ and the world for which Christ died. For the creative power of the preached Word creates truth in our inward parts. It bestows on us purpose and a secure identity that withstands the vicissitudes of late modernity. This mirroring and consequent bestowal of an identity and vocation contributes to the healing of ontological insecurity. Lake writes: "When a neurotic sufferer realizes that under God he has become a significant channel of help to someone else, and continues both to receive and to give on deeply interpersonal levels, he is well on the way to recovery" (p. 39).

Encountering the face of God in Jesus Christ potentially rescues late-modern people from despair and intrapersonal disintegration. The word of the cross, the affirmation that Christ has put death to death and given us well-being in the place of nonbeing, can heal ontological insecurity. Knowledge of Christ's ontological identification with human suffering on the cross may topple every distorted notion of God's omnipotence and wrath; it may inspire trust, the essence of ontological security. For some sufferers, "nothing less than the deliberate identification of the Son of God with them, entering into every form of mental pain by which personal being is slowly annihilated and every aspect of well-being squeezed out cruelly to the last drop, can convince them of the creative justice of the love of God" (pp. 1116-17). Outside of the knowledge of God's passion in Jesus Christ, some individuals may never confront the source of their ontological insecurity. Jesus' descent into hell, his utter passivity in the presence of sheer terror and nonbeing, and his triumph over death and destruction may be the only reality that enables some individuals to trust that God's love is deeper and wider than the abyss of their own anxiety and dread.

Even the presence of a sympathetic therapist may be inadequate to support the patient sufficiently for his mind and central being to permit the return of so much pain to his consciousness. In our experience it has not been possible, though we have often genuinely attempted this, to enable patients in the deeper reaches of mental pain to permit the emergence of this experience without specific appeal to the saving companionship of Christ. (p. 1138)

The church's sacramental ministry also is a means by which God heals ontological insecurity. In baptism, God grants us a new, durable, and flexible identity. We are joined publicly to Christ and thus to Christ's body in baptism. This union transforms our identity. We no longer belong primarily to ourselves, to our biological families, to our nation, to our careers, academic guilds, or any other social category. We belong to Christ. We exist "in Christ." We find our true identity in Christ's death and resurrection. Consequently, our identity becomes cruciform, that is, baptismal. We daily die to our sin and are raised to new life in Christ. We "strip off the old self" and "clothe ourselves with the new self . . . according to the image of [our] creator" (Col. 3:9-10). In so doing, we may be liberated from the false selves we have constructed earlier in life. The persecuted and persecuting self may be freed to live out the words of the apostle Paul: "But thanks be to God through Jesus Christ our Lord, who has set us free from the law of sin and death" (1 Cor. 15:57; Rom. 8:2). The caregiver may be delivered of her incessant need to ensure the well-being of others, instead prayerfully entrusting them to the one and only Messiah. The people-pleaser may discover that he is the apple of God's eye and accepted as beloved. The bully may trade in his sword for a ploughshare as he practices confession and penitence in the context of acceptance and love.

We reaffirm and celebrate in the Lord's Supper this transformation of our identity in baptism. Here we are nurtured by the real presence of Christ. As the infant receives physical and psychological sustenance in the combination of mirroring and nursing, so — on another level — the church receives ontological sustenance in eating the bread and drinking the wine. We see Christ and feed on Christ. Christ's broken body and shed blood, of which we partake, establishes Christian identity as communal, not individual. It establishes the church as Christ's broken body, the communion of sinners and saints called to fellowship with Christ in his suffering and to live in solidarity with others in their suffering.

In the Lord's Supper anxious souls are folded into a relational field of loving-kindness and mutual care. This is good news for those suffering from ontological insecurity, those who, as Lake says, "need, as the decisive therapeutic and ontogenic factor, to experience satisfying dependence on a personal Other, in the context of a positively caring, family-like community" (p. 1031). The church is just such a community of spiritual siblings born of the same womb. Every time church members partake of the Lord's Supper they remember their *koinonia* with Christ, and they feed from the same spiritual bosom. They are empowered to be with one another in the midst of grief and unbearable psychological pain. The abiding presence of the communion of saints may encourage persons to plunge into the abyss of their ontological insecurity and thereby find themselves upheld by the love of God in Jesus Christ.

> [W]hen the parishioner's dynamic strength of spirit is enhanced, as a result of the being and well-being which flow into him through the life and fellowship of the Christian community, the patient will himself recognize that the power of being is now such that this deep threat of non-being can be entered, and indeed must be entered, in such a way as to vanquish it. (p. 432)

The church contributes to the healing of ontological insecurity by facing dread and despair rather than retreating from it, on the one hand, or being consumed by it, on the other. To put it another way, the healing of ontological insecurity in the context of *koinonia* is related to the church's perspective on death and nonbeing. From a psychological perspective, ontological insecurity has to do with the fear of nonbeing, the sense that one's very existence is fragile. From a sociological perspective, ontological security is threatened in late modernity partly because death is sequestered from our experience. Hospitals, not communities, deal with the sick and dying. Yet death cannot be avoided forever. When finally facing death, late-modern people may be overwhelmed to the point of nonfunctioning. They may lack the community support and frameworks of meaning that enable them to cope with death without being thrown into despair. In contrast to this avoidance, death is at the center of Christian faith and life. The second person of the Trinity endures a tortured death. God suffers. While the cross puts death to death, its marks endure for all eternity. "The wounds of Christ are his identity. They tell us who he is. He did not lose them. They went down into the grave with him — visible, tangible, palpable. Rising did not remove them. He who broke the bonds of death kept his wounds."[25]

It is this very capacity of the church to acknowledge the suffering of God and the suffering of the world that brings healing. Through its practice of *koinonia* in Word and sacrament, the church creates space for the ontologically insecure to encounter the crucified God. Miraculously, their anxieties diminish so that they are freed to live connected to God, themselves, and others, even in the high-risk culture of late modernity. The one whose world has been reframed or reconstructed according to the promises of God may experience continuity of being in the presence of multiple sources of anxiety. This is not to be confused with the spiritualized form of denial of people who are psychologically dissociated from their real anxieties in pseudofaith. Faith is not denial; instead, faith is an unshakable trust in both the goodness of God and God's preservation of all creation. It is an anchor in stormy times, in the midst of the unknown. Trust enables us to live in the present moment. We are not overwhelmed with anxiety about the future; nor do we despair about our past actions. Trust instills the virtue of serenity, and from trust flows this acclamation: "All is well; all manner of things are well; all manner of things shall be well."[26]

In summary, multidimensional *koinonia* establishes the being and well-being of all persons. *Koinonia* with Christ is the source of healing ontological insecurity; the *koinonia* of the church — that is, among church members — is the context in which this healing occurs. In its *koinonia* with the world, the church witnesses to and participates in Christ's ministry of healing, including the healing of ontological insecurity. In the midst of the upheavals of late modernity, the *koinonia* among church members is a new dynamic cycle of loving relatedness that corresponds to the love of God in Jesus Christ. The church embodies this love as it practices multidimensional *koinonia* in Word and sacrament and mutual integration of its members. In a runaway world, the church grounds our identity in Christ and through Christ in relationship with one another, and through Christ it calls us into purpose-

25. Nicholas Wolterstorff, *Lament for a Son* (Grand Rapids: Eerdmans, 1987), p. 92.

26. Edmund Colledge, James Walsh, and Jean Leclerq, *Julian of Norwich: Showings* (Mahwah, NJ: Paulist Press, 1978), p. 225.

ful mission in the world. In the context of being uprooted and displaced, the church knows the secret of humanity — that we are united ontologically to Christ and one another. In the midst of faceless relationships, the church points us to the face of God in Jesus Christ, a face that never goes away. In a world that sequesters suffering and death from daily experience and attempts to control the trajectory of life, the church accepts loss as participation in the cross of Jesus Christ. To have *koinonia* with Christ means that we partake in Christ's death and resurrection. In the context of high anxiety, identity crises, and pervasive self-reflexivity, the preaching of the Word, administration of the sacraments, and practices of service and fellowship foster healing and restoration and peace. Consequently, ontological security as an existential reality is not dependent solely on early childhood experiences. Jesus Christ, through the power of the Holy Spirit, who is bound to neither time nor space, may reestablish ontological security in the context of *koinonia*. As Frank Lake demonstrates in one of his most poignant cases, even those whose ontological insecurity manifests itself as a personality disorder may be healed. Referring to a client afflicted with obsessive-compulsive disorder, he says:

> The radical change occurred when he was invited by the Hospital Chaplain, an Anglican of the High variety, . . . to attend and partake in the Sacrament of Holy Communion with other patients and staff. All his life he had attempted to cleanse himself from without. He had attempted to curtail his evil; to separate it off from the little good he contained. The truth suddenly poured in upon him that there never could be cleansing that way. It could only come by drinking in the life of a loving person to the full. As he ate and drank the symbols of Christ's self-giving, he gained a new identity and a new source of personal sustenance. He knew himself to be accepted both by God and by the congregation, in such a way that the whole of his past "badness" became progressively irrelevant to him. Not that he has been entirely free of anxiety. Some roots of it undoubtedly remain, though for the last ten years he has lived a full and active life without recourse either to medicines or physicians. In spite of what seemed to him insurmountable obstacles, he married a girl who shared his Christian faith and they have a happy family. The Holy Communion has remained for him a central experience of his life. (p. 45)

Guidelines for Healing in Small Groups

The preceding chapter suggested that all ecclesiastical practices are bound to and flow from the church's life of worship. Small-group ministries should be connected intrinsically to the worshiping life of congregations. Building on this, we can now claim that the healing of ontological insecurity by means of Word and sacrament can flow into, inform, and be expanded in small groups.

To begin with, small groups could point persons to the face of God in Jesus Christ. By doing so, they would build on an inherent strength and simultaneously counter one of the theological weaknesses in how groups frame connection to God. Our research indicates that well-developed small groups already practice communion with a personal God in prayer and the reading and study of Scripture. Scripture could be read out loud, pondered, discussed, or meditated on via such ancient practices as *lectio divina* in small groups. The gospel narratives would be the controlling interpretive center of this engagement with Scripture, pointing group members again and again to the face of God in Jesus Christ. Small-group members should pray for one another, petitioning Christ to break through their self-protective defenses that keep God's love at a distance. They should bring before God and each other their insecurities, shame, and guilt. They could learn not to rush in to fix one another. Instead, they could grow in their capacity to trust that healing would come simply by creating space for the expression of their deepest yearnings in the context of *koinonia*. At the same time, pastoral staff should trust that the Spirit speaks through the written Word of God, often despite and against errors in human interpretation. The Bible will make itself heard in spite of all its maltreatment.

This focus on the face of God in Jesus Christ could counter the tendency of groups to transpose the pure relationship onto God. As a result of this transposition, group members' existential connection to God depends on their internal sense of emotional intimacy with God. Not only does this make one's perceived connection to God vulnerable to the inherent frailties of the pure relationship and the vagaries of human emotion, but it also reduces God to the interpersonal level. In response, groups should distinguish the pure relationship from the face of God in Jesus Christ. Small groups have a unique opportunity to point out the futility of seeking ontological security primarily or solely from any human relationship. Group members are well aware of the shortcomings and disappointments associated with their relationships with spouses, children, parents, and sometimes friends. Mutual confession of sin against one's loved ones should become a regular part of small-group practice, especially for couples' groups. Instead of trying to fix marital problems, small groups could acknowledge our common need for a face that never goes away — the face of God in Jesus Christ. Or small groups should highlight the analogy between broken marital relationships and the breach in relationship with God because of human sin. They could allow the loss and breakdown in relationship to point to our qualitatively distinct and greater disconnection from and antipathy toward God. Small groups could acknowledge the brokenness inherent in temporal relationships, pray for the kingdom of God to come in these relationships, and hope for the future when *koinonia* becomes a fully manifest reality. Thus might ontological security be strengthened as group members accept the shortcomings of the pure relationship form and simultaneously buttress their trust in God.

Second, small-group members could function as mirrors for one another. Seeing the face of God in Jesus Christ in Scripture and prayer does not ultimately occur in isolation. It occurs in the context of Christ's body. Jesus does not exist as a disembodied or abstract spirit, but as a diverse community of love. Seeing delight, acceptance, and tender care in the face of fellow small-group members might point ontologically insecure persons to the face of God in Jesus Christ. For the former mirrors the latter. We all, with unveiled faces, reflect the glory of God to one another (2 Cor. 3:18). "Unveiled faces" means, at the very least, that group participants should express themselves honestly and openly. Mirroring will be hindered if group members hide from one another in fear, guilt, and shame. For this reason, it will be important for group leaders to receive education and support in facilitating authentic dialogue in their groups.[27] "Reflect" means that this mirroring among small group members should be understood as imperfect but nevertheless trustworthy. As such, it should convey unconditional acceptance of the very being of others. But it should not be reduced to affirmation of every action. Small-group members can acknowledge openly that some choices contradict our life in *koinonia*. Such acknowledgment should eschew judgment or condemnation. No choice — no

27. I address this subject in more detail in chapter 7.

sin — should be seen as placing one outside the bounds of God's love. Naming what contradicts *koinonia* would flow from knowledge of our created goodness and our reconciliation to God and each other, which is complete and cannot be eradicated. It needs to come from a longing for each group member to become who he or she is. In this way, confessing our faults to one another in small groups would be an expression of mirroring. Accountability to life in *koinonia* would be liberating and joyful rather than onerous and fearful.

Third, small-group members could contribute to the healing of ontological insecurity by functioning analogously to mothers who receive their infants' attacks and then provide opportunity for making amends. The small-group practices of confession, forgiveness, and mutual forbearance (as I outlined in the preceding chapter) would contribute to the healing of ontological insecurity. Group members know that they, like their mothers, will falter in providing mirroring. They know that they are capable of saying and doing things that stimulate pain, disappointment, and frustration in one another. Accepting themselves and each other, they can welcome the expression of these feelings in the service of reconciliation. All the while they can rest assured they will experience *koinonia* fully in the future. If a member of the group repeatedly communicates in a harsh or aggressive manner, the group may compassionately interpret this as a subconscious attempt to create an opportunity for reparation with his unavailable mother. Truculence is a reparable drive emerging from unfulfilled needs for the kind of relationships that can withstand hurt and disappointment. By responding to aggression by way of creating space for forgiveness and reconciliation, small groups potentially would participate in Christ's ministry of healing ontological insecurity.

Fourth, small groups could further deepen and expand on what they do best: being present with each other in the midst of loss. Groups provide myriad forms of support for those who are sick, dying, or grieving, yet they do not necessarily connect this aspect of their life together with Christ's suffering. If the church's overall ministry design teaches group members to interpret suffering as participation in the death and resurrection of Christ, then small-group members could plunge into their common and particular sorrows with greater fullness. Not only do groups provide meals and visitation; they also create space for the full expression of lament, doubt, and fear. If the Son of God bewailed God's absence on the cross, then certainly small-group members can do the same. In the presence of one another, they can drain the bitterness of their suffering to its dregs. They can learn to lament in prayer following the psalms. And group leaders should be prepared to make referrals to specialists, such as counselors or therapy groups, if those experiencing loss became depressed or showed signs of mental instability.

Fifth, small groups might strengthen ontological security simply by providing continuity of routine. By covenanting together to meet over a set period of time (e.g., twelve weeks, six months, one year, and so on), they might contribute to a felt sense of security and stability in a runaway world. Routine and commitment build trust among group members. At the group's inception, they can explore how regular attendance meets their common needs for dependability, reliability, and stability. Group leaders can encourage members to avoid the twin traps of disconnecting from the group when other demands arise or of participating in the group out of guilt, which often breeds resentment. In other words, group members should be encouraged to make choices on the basis of the meaning that their participation holds for them and for the group. Similarly, the group should establish a flexible pattern to govern their time together, for example, prayer, study, dialogue, meditation, and eating. This pattern would provide continuity over time and thus potentially strengthen ontological security.

Finally, small groups can connect their regular practice of eating with the sacrament of communion. They can explore how their meals together are about more than physical sustenance (though they are that, of course). Their table fellowship can be approached as mutual feeding analogous to Christ's feeding of us in the Eucharist. Accordingly, their meals would take on the flavor of spiritual as well as physical nourishment. Nourished in the bosom of the body of Christ, bound to each other through the waters of baptism, beholding the face of God in each other — they might become ontologically secure. Such security would not be threatened by wars and rumors of wars, by the worst environmental hazards, or by the heinous crimes of any national government. Rather, ontologically secure small-group members would express faith that we are held at all points and at all times in the arms of the one who upholds the universe, who has risen from the dead, and who continues to feed us with his own being.

Then, perhaps, this feeding would expand beyond the borders of their group. Some groups might volunteer to feed others at homeless shelters or together donate money to charities that fight hunger and poverty. They could do this with the knowledge that they are participating in Christ's feeding of the whole world. They could prayerfully anticipate the messianic banquet when all humanity sits down to feast together in the fullness of *koinonia*. As small groups care for those who are deprived of the most basic sustenance, they would become beacons of hope in God's *koinonia*-creating reconciliation, a reconciliation that in its ultimate eschatological form will include physical, emotional, and — most profoundly — ontological healing.

CHAPTER 7

Strategies for Implementing Small Groups

How can small groups concretely practice multidimensional *koinonia* and thereby contribute to the healing of fractured communities, families, and persons in late modernity? How can churches support and develop small groups as communities of *koinonia?* With these practical questions, we commence the final leg of our practical-theology journey. I will seek to make the normative guidelines for practicing *koinonia* that I have set forth in the preceding two chapters operational. To do so, I will return to the research of well-developed small-group ministries, drawing on their use of mission statements, small-group leaders' training, congregational-ministry design, and assessment tools. From this I will present strategies for (1) constructing small-group mission statements that encourage *koinonia;* (2) training small-group leaders to practice *koinonia;* (3) practicing *koinonia* in the congregation by creatively linking small groups to other congregational ministries; and (4) assessing the growth of small groups in practicing *koinonia.*

Before constructing these strategies, however, I believe it is important to clarify the posture with which we develop and implement them. Otherwise, we run the risk of trying to implement small-group *koinonia* in a way that contradicts the spirit and nature of *koinonia.* The ends do not justify the means. So what must we consider about the nature of *koinonia* action? First, *koinonia* is a flow of life: it is dynamic and on the move. Static rules or rigid regulations are antithetical to *koinonia.* So is the assumption that all strategies can be applied equally to all contexts. To put it another way, God does not meet hu-

149

manity through external demands. Instead, God meets us in the incarnation, through the most intimate union of divinity and humanity possible, and incorporates us into the humanity of Jesus Christ. The Spirit of God awakens us to the reality that we are related internally to God, each other, and the whole cosmos. In the context of intimacy, acceptance, mutual communication, and knowing, God calls us to become who we are. This calling does not come in the form of law but rather grace. Thus it would be contrary to *koinonia* to take the strategies suggested in this chapter and force them onto a small-group ministry. They should not function as a demand, as proof of the "rightness" of the group, or as a way to guarantee spiritual growth (if that were possible). For instance, mission statements for small groups should emerge organically from the shared life of the group; they should not be imposed by the pastoral staff or simply grafted on from another source (including this book).

Second, faithful and true ecclesial action is a mutual indwelling of divine action and human action. Its very nature is *koinonia;* for *koinonia* is an event, a communion of divine action and human action that happens again and again. There is a particular order to this communion of action: God initiates, humans respond. Human action is dependent and contingent on God's prior action, an action that creates space within which humans can participate. Thus there is no guarantee that any particular human action (or practice) is a participation in divine action. *Koinonia* cannot be conjured up, created, or controlled by the church or its members; no ecclesial practices can instantiate or guarantee *koinonia.* Therefore, small groups should not assume that their actions are *koinonia* actions. Leaders cannot assume that strategies that once seemed to foster *koinonia* will always do so. Small groups must enter into prayerful reflection about their actions, asking whether or not their life together *today* shows signs of *koinonia.* Similarly, congregations should precede implementation of small groups with prayer, meditation, and communal discernment of some kind. In this kind of discernment each person would hold his or her agendas for the small-group ministry lightly. Each would petition the Spirit of God to affirm the decision and actions that contribute to *koinonia,* negate those that contradict *koinonia,* and reconstitute the group's mission and structure so as to support *koinonia* in fuller ways.

Third, faithful and true ecclesial action lives at the intersection of divine action and societal action. The church exists for the sake of the world, not merely for its own internal edification. And it exists for the world in a particular time and place. Congregations are situated in particular locales so that the gospel can be lived out in a way that connects to the deepest longings, confusion, and sorrows of the community outside the church. This means that context shapes ecclesial action profoundly. Therefore, strategies for implementing small groups should consider the larger setting in which small groups operate. Topics of study and group activities should be shaped by the members' deep engagement with family, friends, neighbors, and coworkers, as well as with political, economic, and larger social structures. For this to happen, group members and leaders will need space to name and explore their questions and concerns with respect to the world outside the church, which, of course, is not merely outside but also inside the church by virtue of the fact that church members are simultaneously members of other communities. With these caveats, we now turn to strategies for implementing well-developed small groups.

Congregational-Ministry Design

Congregational-ministry design, at the most basic level, is the intentional planning and organization of a congregation's activities in light of its particular mission and vision. Some congregations have highly structured ministry designs that could be presented in a flow chart of sorts; others have more free-flowing, emergent designs. Church activities are chosen and implemented with intentionality, but with less explicit ordering. Still others carry out congregational activities without any intentional formation in light of a particular vision of ministry. These congregations do what they have always done without creative, proactive responsiveness to their current situation.

All of the well-developed small-group ministries I studied for this project were part of a larger congregational-ministry design. Some designs were tightly ordered; others were loosely ordered. None included all of the same elements, but all included some of the same elements. In other words, these congregations demonstrate both continuity and distinction in their ministry designs. Small groups had an explicit place in the overall ministry design of these congregations. They were linked to the mission and organization of the congregation, and they were embedded within it. The small-group ministry was not the sole carrier of the church's mission, but it was a core practice that enhanced members' connection to and participation in the congregation.

Our normative ecclesiology suggests that congregational-ministry designs should reflect and nurture all dimensions of the church's *koinonia: koinonia* through Christ with the triune God; *koinonia* among church members; and *koinonia* in, with, and for the world. The three modes of the church's existence — gathering, upbuilding, and sending — should be evident in the ministry design. Small-group ministry should be connected to one or more of these modes and the corresponding *koinonia* relationship with the understanding that the *koinonia* relationships are not actually separable from each other. For instance, practicing *koinonia* among church members is simultaneously a practice of *koinonia* with Christ: it is simply that the former is the focus, in the foreground of our intention, while the latter is in the background even as it provides the foundation and possibility for the former.

Some of the specific normative guidelines for practicing *koinonia* in small groups can be implemented by embedding small groups in the overall congregational-ministry design. Congregational-ministry design can connect small groups to the worship life of the congregation. Congregational-ministry design can help small groups contribute indirectly, if not directly, to the church's solidarity with the world. Congregational-ministry design can reflect the church's ecumenical nature, and it can provide avenues for small groups to contribute to the oneness of the larger body of Christ. And congregational-ministry design can ensure teaching about *koinonia*, which supports the practice of *koinonia* in the small groups.

I will now summarize the ministry designs from three congregations that I studied for this book, and I will note if and how these congregational-ministry designs potentially foster the practice of *koinonia*. Do they nurture all dimensions of *koinonia* or only some? How fully and theologically do they understand life in multidimensional *koinonia*? This kind of analysis will demonstrate that using the word *koinonia* in one's ministry design is not essential, yet the depth, complexity, and beauty of *koinonia* can be used as a theological framework to guide the development of a congregational-ministry design. I will also note how the congregational-ministry designs could be developed further in order to implement the normative guidelines for small groups listed above.

First Presbyterian Church

First Presbyterian Church is a congregation of 800 members situated in a midsize Northeastern city.[1] It has a four-part congregational-ministry design: defining vision; defining practices; large-group/small-group balance; and ministry-team leadership. The congregation's leadership training material says this: "Vision is seeing what God wants to do through *you*. Vision is seeing what God wants to do through *us*." Simply put, the vision of this church is "to glorify God by making disciples and meeting human need." Discipleship is defined in terms of three key practices: *reaching* those uninvolved in the congregation or not committed to Christ; *growing* with one another through prayer, the study of Scripture, and mutual care; and *sending* each other to serve the church and the world. These defining practices (reach, grow, send) are emphasized in large groups (fifteen or more persons) and small groups (fourteen or fewer persons). Large-group settings excel at inspirational and celebratory events; they allow some anonymity and the development of acquaintances or friendly relationships. Small groups excel in providing support, intimacy, and quality relationships with a few persons.[2] Ministry teams, the fourth component of this congregational-ministry design, combine the fellowship and discipleship typical of most small groups with the task-orientation of committees. They empower congregation members to carry out the ministry of the church while simultaneously ministering to one another.[3]

This congregational-ministry design is quite similar conceptually and linguistically to the three modes of the church's existence that I presented in our normative ecclesiology. Two of the core practices, growing and sending, are nearly synonymous with the modes of upbuilding and sending. Like the three modes of the church's existence, reach-grow-send are not three separate activities. Rather, they permeate — and stem from — all that the congregation does. Thus small groups reach, grow, and send, even though they focus on growing disciples. Ministry teams reach, grow, and send even as they focus on sending disciples. Reaching, as described in the ministry design, would

1. Throughout this chapter I have used substitute church names to protect their anonymity.

2. E. Stanley Ott, *The Vibrant Church* (Ventura, CA: Regal, 1989), p. 166.

3. See E. Stanley Ott, *Transform Your Church with Ministry Teams* (Grand Rapids: Eerdmans, 2004).

be considered part of sending in the ecclesiology developed in this book. One of the weaknesses of using the language of "reaching" rather than "gathering" is that the former does not emphasize the corporate and public worship of the congregation, even though worship is actually a central part of the ministry of First Presbyterian Church.

Ministry-team leadership also is consistent with *koinonia.* "The power of ministry teams rests in their success in mobilizing ordinary people for ministry. The vast majority of church members haven't come to terms with their call to ministry, their gifts for ministry, or their opportunities for ministry."[4] As I discussed in chapter 4, Christ empowers members of his body to become the *communio vocatorum,* the communion of persons called to participate in Christ's ministry in the world. In multidimensional *koinonia,* the priesthood of all believers overturns the "clericalizing" of ministry. Ministry teams are a specific strategy for living out this reality. Furthermore, ministry teams hold together *koinonia* with Christ, *koinonia* among Christ's members, and solidarity with the world. Unlike many committees, which function as though these *koinonia* relationships can be severed from one another, ministry teams (1) provide mutual care and support, (2) encourage meditation on Scripture and prayer, and (3) engage in mutual service to the church and world. In other words, they are holistic and reflective of the unity of all the *koinonia* relationships.

Small groups are mentioned explicitly in the congregational-ministry design of First Presbyterian Church. To what extent is this design consistent with the normative guidelines for small-group ministry? First, small groups are paired with large-group worship and teaching in light of the fact that small groups cannot fulfill all of the educational needs of a congregation. In this regard, the ministry design provides opportunity for extensive teaching about life in multidimensional *koinonia.* Aspects of this teaching could be practiced in small groups. Second, the connection between small groups and corporate worship could be strengthened if the ministry design itself somehow emphasized worship. As I have mentioned above, the core practices could be altered slightly to "gather, grow, and send." Gathering could be defined as the large-group (or corporate) joining together for worship, prayer, and teaching. Gathering in small groups could be seen as derivative of and dependent on large-group gathering. Third, the

4. Ott, *Transform Your Church,* p. 14.

congregational-ministry design does not explicitly highlight the ecumenical nature of the church. However, growing and sending could be explained and practiced in such a way as to promote connections with other congregations. That is, *koinonia* with church members transcends the time-space boundaries of any one congregation. Similarly, solidarity with the world is a common vocation of all Christians. On the basis of this, small groups or ministry teams could be encouraged to partner with members of other congregations, including those of other Christian traditions. Fourth, ministry teams, as a specialized type of small group, contribute to the church's solidarity with the world. Though not mentioned in the ministry design, the covenant statements of other small groups at First Presbyterian Church also include commitment to a group-service project, which is a form of witness.

Fourth Reformed Church

Fourth Reformed Church is a congregation of one thousand members with multiple campuses in a small Midwestern city. It does not use the language of "ministry design," but it clearly has one. Its congregational-ministry design consists of core values, a mission statement, core practices, a vision statement, and a vision path. Fourth Reformed defines values as "the foundation on which our ministry is built, the glue that holds our ministry together, [and] the nonnegotiable characteristics which define who we are, who we want to be, or the kind of character we wish to possess." These values guide their decision-making, including the development and assessment of all their activities. Small-group ministry is one of their ten core values. Fourth Reformed Church's mission is: "To Know Christ and to make Him Known." The central practices for carrying out this mission include prayer, worship, education, mutual encouragement, support and service, and witness. The vision statement is more specific than the mission statement. It has been revised in response to the changing demographics of the congregation and the community in which it is embedded. At the time of my research, the congregation's vision was the following:

> We, the members of [Fourth] Reformed Church, motivated by the love of God and empowered by the Holy Spirit, have been uniquely endowed and called by God to be a large, regional church in the

_____ area, committed to evangelizing and discipling an ever-increasing percentage of the population who have yet to experience the transforming power of Jesus Christ. We accept the responsibility of prayerfully, patiently, and lovingly nurturing those who come to faith in Christ and call [Fourth] Reformed Church their home.

The current vision statement is a shorter, simplified version: "The body of Christ [at Fourth Reformed Church] will love people where they are, using all means to introduce pre-Christians to God's transforming love. Together, we will intentionally and patiently guide one another as we continue in the process of becoming Faithful Followers of Jesus Christ." The vision path (or strategic actions) for fulfilling this vision include multi-site and creative worship, community partnerships, equipping congregants to share their faith, encouraging all members to participate in an in-house ministry and an outside mission, and spiritual formation. Fourth Reformed encapsulates all the above in a "big dream," that is, to be "the most successful church in the country at inspiring, equipping, and deploying faithful followers of Jesus Christ to passionately share the Good News of Jesus Christ with pre-Christians."

The congregational-ministry design of Fourth Reformed Church is seemingly less similar to our normative ecclesiology than that of First Presbyterian Church. Nevertheless, the basic meanings of gathering, upbuilding, and sending are evident in it. The central practices resonate with these three moments of the church's life in *koinonia*. Their mission statement, vision statement, and vision path prioritize the moment of sending — and thus the church's *koinonia* in the world. This is consistent with the thought of Karl Barth, who claims that in all of its activities the church must have its gaze directed outward toward the world. The church exists as it witnesses to the reconciliation of God with the world. The mission statement links *koinonia* with the world to *koinonia* with Christ. In fact, *koinonia* with Christ is central to both the mission and the vision statements. Similarly, the previous vision statement was explicitly Trinitarian, consistent with our claim that the origin and *telos* of the church is the *koinonia* of the Trinity. The current vision statement has lost this explicit Trinitarian character.

Fourth Reformed Church's "big dream" statement is problematic from the perspective of *koinonia*. It reflects an uncritical use of advice from a leadership-theory book.[5] In this regard, Fourth Reformed seems to fall prey to what Barth would call one of the primary threats to the church, that is, *secularization*, or a secret longing for the glory and success of the world.[6] As I have suggested in chapter 4, the church, by virtue of its *koinonia*, is both like and unlike other social organizations. Even if the church adopts practices developed in the business world, for instance, it must do so in a way that those practices are transformed by the church's inner life. The *koinonia*-creating work of Christ, by the power of the Holy Spirit, seeks expression in and — if necessary — against ecclesial practices. Ecclesial practices shaped by *koinonia* are not self-aggrandizing. Churches practicing *koinonia* do not compete with other churches; rather, they join those churches as essential partners in fulfilling their common vocation in the world. Their *koinonia* with Christ is expressed in the posture of John the Baptist, who decreased so that Christ could increase. In all that the church does, it is called to point persons to Christ, not to itself. And it humbly acknowledges that its life is discovered precisely in its dying. It knows that its growth may have the appearance of its opposite. For spiritual growth is not synonymous with numerical or programmatic growth.

Small groups are listed underneath two parts of the congregational-ministry design at Fourth Reformed Church. As I have observed above, small-group ministry is one of the congregation's ten core values: "We value small group ministry because we believe that in the large church small groups are the best places for people to feel a part of the body of Christ, to be cared for, and to experience the life-changing power of Jesus Christ." As a core value, small groups are a nonnegotiable practice of this congregation. Small groups also are highlighted as a primary means for practicing mutual encouragement, support, and service. "Through discipling relationships, large group gatherings, and especially small groups, the Holy Spirit will move through His people to impart encouragement, healing, and wholeness. Authentic Christ-centered friendships will develop that will draw others to Him." Both of these references suggest that small groups contribute to the upbuilding of the church. The second statement suggests that small groups potentially contribute to

5. Jim Collins, *Good to Great: Why Some Companies Make the Leap . . . and Others Don't* (San Francisco: Harper Business, 2001).

6. See the section in chapter 4 above entitled "*Koinonia* and the Crisis of Community" for a fuller explication of secularization as one of the threats to the church's existence.

the healing of ontological insecurity. It potentially encourages small-group members to be present to one another in sorrow and suffering. Moreover, this statement explicitly links the upbuilding and the sending of the church, the *koinonia* among church members and *koinonia* with the world in the form of witness.

Fourth Reformed Church's congregational-ministry design implicitly connects small groups and worship as well. Worship is one of the six core practices of the church: the vision path indicates that creative, culturally relevant worship is a priority for this church. It also relates worship to witness, connecting the mode of gathering (though it is not explicitly named as such) with the mode of sending. It also links small groups to the teaching ministry of the church. Like the congregational-ministry design of First Presbyterian Church, this suggests that small groups cannot fulfill all of the educational needs of a congregation. In this sense, the ministry design provides opportunity for extensive teaching about (1) life in multidimensional *koinonia* and (2) the influence of Word and sacrament on other ecclesial practices, such as small groups.

Second Presbyterian Church

Second Presbyterian Church is a midsize congregation (250 or more people attending worship regularly) that is located in an urban setting in the Northeast. Unlike First Presbyterian and Fourth Reformed, its congregational-ministry design is implicit more than explicit. Its mission influences all that it does, but with less structure. Based on my observations, the ministry design of Second Presbyterian Church consists of a mission statement, core values, and three areas of ministry focus. Its mission is threefold: "To glorify and enjoy God forever; to preach Christ-crucified, dead and buried to pay the price for our sins, risen from the dead so that we might live with Him forever, and coming again in judgment; and to provide a Christ-centered home and family for all of God's children." The exposition of the third part of its mission says: "We are committed to making this church a safe haven for all of God's wounded, frightened, and stressed-out children." This part of the mission statement functions as a deep metaphor for all the practices of the congregation.

Second Presbyterian supports personal transformation so that the people of God may be healed in heart and formed for service. This may be the congregation's core value. Other values of Second Presbyterian Church include a biblical and Reformed understanding of God, the church, and the world, and ministry to those who are most vulnerable in church and society, such as children and the elderly. Its three areas of ministry focus are worship (Sunday morning and Sunday evening in differing formats), children and youth (daycare, midweek program, and youth-group program), and pastoral and congregational care (including brief counseling, education geared toward transformation, small groups, and a prayer-and-visitation ministry team).

Overall, Second Presbyterian's congregational-ministry design supports the gathering and upbuilding of the church. Corporate worship is central to its identity. It is the primary means for practicing *koinonia* with God through Christ, as revealed in the church's mission statement and key areas of ministry. The mission statement also emphasizes *koinonia* with Christ. In contrast to First Presbyterian Church and Fourth Reformed, Second Presbyterian refers to the crucified Christ. The cross is at the heart of their understanding of the church's relationship with God. This ministry design thus provides a foundation for delineating the implications of practicing *koinonia* with Christ on the cross for congregational life in general and small groups in particular.

The mode of sending is latent within this congregational-ministry design. Reference to the church as a "safe haven for all of God's wounded, frightened, and stressed-out children" sounds like solidarity with and compassionate service to persons living in a runaway world, that is, late modernity. If this were more explicitly connected to the church's witness in the world, then the ministry design would be more complete in terms of our normative ecclesiology. It would include all three modes of the church's existence and thus all three *koinonia* relationships: with Christ and through Christ with God; with each other; and for the world.

Small groups fall within the pastoral and congregational-care ministries at Second Presbyterian Church. Pastoral and congregational care flows from the third aspect of the congregation's mission statement above. Small groups provide a spiritual home, a familylike atmosphere of healing, comfort, and rest for congregation members. A reworking of the mission statement and/or explicit delineation of focused areas of ministry could promote intentional links among worship, education, ministry teams, and other small groups. This would prevent potential fragmentation or siloing of ministry areas. Second, as I have suggested for First Presbyterian Church and Fourth Reformed Church, the ministry design at Second Presbyterian Church could incorporate a fuller theology of the body of Christ, one that emphasizes the unity of the communion of saints that transcends the bounds of any single congregation. This would be in keeping with the men's ministry team, which collaborates with another local (non-Presbyterian) congregation. It also would encourage other ecumenical partnerships.

In summary, congregational-ministry designs package a variety of elements — core values, mission and/or vision statements, core practices and strategies — along a continuum from highly structured to loosely structured. Small-group ministries may be considered a core value, a core practice, or even part of the mission statement. They might be embedded underneath a broader set of practices, such as mutual care and encouragement among church members. However they are structured into an overall ministry design, small groups should flow from the gathering of the church and contribute directly to the upbuilding of the church and indirectly to the sending of the church. In this way, small groups can become part of the congregation's overall life of multidimensional *koinonia*.

Mission and Covenant Statements

Well-developed small groups maintain a sense of purpose and contribution to the larger congregation, partly by means of mission statements or covenant statements. Though closely related, mission statements and covenant statements differ in emphasis. Mission statements tend to set forth the vision and objectives for a group or community, whereas covenant statements emphasize the responsibilities and commitments of each group member to the whole. In the best of circumstances, each small group in a congregation would have a group covenant that is linked to the overall mission statement for the entire small-group ministry. Small-group members and leaders can be cognizant of their connection to other groups, as well as to the congregation at large. Not all circumstances will be amenable to this integration of mission statements and group covenants. In such cases, individual groups are encouraged to construct a group covenant that incorporates an overall vision for their life together.

Mission statements and covenant statements for individual small groups and entire small-group ministries should emerge organically from the shared life of the group or the larger congregation. Church leaders can listen to the yearnings of the congregation, the ideas bubbling up in formal and informal settings, and the passions expressed by members as they live out their faith in their daily lives. At Second Presbyterian Church, pastors and lay leaders progressively moved toward the development of a prayer-and-visitation ministry team as they listened to themselves and their context. One year they sponsored a prayer vigil for members who were sick or had been marginalized from the church's life in some way. The next year they built on that, adding phone calls and letters to these members; the following year they developed a prayer-and-visitation ministry team. As a ministry team, it was a task-oriented small group that attended very carefully to its own communal life. It had a core group of people whose vision had been shaped through working together over a period of three years. For this reason, its purpose statement came together quite seamlessly: "The Prayer and Visitation Ministry Team empowers lay leaders to provide basic listening, prayer support, and care to their fellow congregation members."

Besides listening to the passions of congregation members, small-group leaders and members can facilitate the development of covenant statements at the group's inception. To jump-start the writing of a group covenant, one might ask group members to reflect on and/or write answers to the following questions:

- Think of the group you most want to be associated with. What do you want from the group? What are you prepared to give to it? What does the group want from you? What does it give to you?
- Think of a group you recently left or are considering leaving. What did you want from this group? What were you prepared to give to it? What did the group want from you? What did it give to you?
- How do these different situations influence your commitment to and participation in these groups?[7]

Answers to these questions can be harvested for shared values, commitments, and ideas for group activities to be drafted into a group covenant.

7. Adapted from Rodney W. Napier and Matty K. Gershenfeld, *Groups: Theory and Experience*, 4th ed. (Boston: Houghton Mifflin, 1992), pp. 186-87.

The content of covenant statements will vary from group to group, depending on their particularities. However, most group covenants will be effective in guiding the group if they contain the following elements:

- Concise statement of the group's purpose
- Activities or tasks that the group will undertake in fulfillment of that purpose (Bible study, prayer, meditation, sharing meals, outreach, etc.)
- Membership criteria
- Responsibilities of group members
- Responsibilities of the group's leader(s) or facilitator(s)
- Meeting logistics (where, when, how frequently, and for how long the group will gather)
- Qualities of the group's internal dialogue (confidentiality, openness, honesty, etc.)

Each of these components of the covenant statement can be constructed in light of our normative guidelines for living in multidimensional *koinonia*. These covenant statements might explicitly refer to practicing *koinonia* as the purpose of the group(s). Or they might express in more colloquial language the essence of practicing *koinonia*. The rest of this section considers how each element of a group covenant could be crafted to support *koinonia* — either explicitly or implicitly (colloquially).

Concise statement of the group's purpose. This part of the covenant statement should clarify which dimension of *koinonia* will be the focus of the group; that is, *koinonia* with God through Christ; *koinonia* among church members through Christ; or *koinonia* with the world through Christ. While these *koinonia* relationships cannot be severed from one another, one or more can be in the foreground of a group's purpose. A spiritual-direction group might emphasize members' *koinonia* with Christ, though of course they would experience *koinonia* with each other as well. A support group might emphasize *koinonia* among group members, though of course their entrance into one another's sorrows would be one of the most concrete forms of *koinonia* with Christ in this life. A couples' group open to the larger community might be a form of *koinonia* with the world even as it fosters *koinonia* among life partners in the congregation.

Activities or tasks undertaken in order to fulfill the group's purpose. In crafting this part of a covenant statement, groups should be encouraged to consider both the activities that they imagine are typical for small groups (e.g., Bible study, discussion, intercessory prayer) and other kinds of activities that give them life and simultaneously contribute to the practice of *koinonia*. Perhaps a couples group wishes to practice *koinonia* with the world, specifically solidarity with other couples struggling to form authentic, intimate relationships outside of the church. If so, their group might sponsor an educational event, workshop, or retreat on marriage for the larger community. Similarly, they might advertise their group to people outside the congregation.

Membership criteria. One of the normative guidelines for small groups is that they reflect the grace through which we enter *koinonia*. Small-group ministries that practice *koinonia* are not established on the basis of social status or any particular demographic factor, such as age, race, gender, educational background, or economic status. Instead, people are welcomed into small groups because God's arms are stretched open wide to them — and indeed to all. While some groups may seek to serve particular social groups — women, youth, married couples, those who are grieving, and so forth — their covenant statements can express openness to considering as members those who do not fit these categories. The covenant statement of a small group may state that, though the group is intended for married couples seeking to grow in their relationship to God and to one another, the group will consider members who are not married but nevertheless want to grow in their capacity to live as faithful disciples in intimate relationships. Thus someone who is engaged, widowed, or single and interested in establishing a lifelong partnership could participate in the group and enrich it through her unique life experience.

At the same time, it is important to consider the optimal size of a small group. Julie Gorman writes: "Size is best determined by the objective of the group. Those desiring to stimulate individual thinking and questioning require a small group, while objectives that incorporate broad exposure with many points of view will be best achieved in a larger group."[8] In general, groups of five to seven people allow for sig-

8. Julie Gorman, *Community That Is Christian: A Handbook on Small Groups,* 2nd ed. (Grand Rapids: Baker, 2002), p. 117.

nificant intimate conversation, while those of fifteen to twenty people inhibit intimate conversation.[9]

Responsibilities of group members. These might include the following commitments: to participate regularly in group meetings; to assist with facilitation of group discussion on some sort of rotating basis; to bring snacks or prepare meals; to participate in a group mission project (such as volunteering at a local homeless shelter); to contribute financially in order to provide childcare during the group meeting times, and so on. All of these responsibilities could be couched in the theological language of mutual service, which is characteristic of *koinonia.* They could also be connected explicitly to the establishment of trust in the group. The covenant could state that group members seek to build trust with one another by keeping these commitments to each other. In this way, the group covenant implicitly would contribute to the strengthening of ontological security, which is dependent on continuity of routine.

Responsibilities of the group leader/facilitator. Potential small-group leaders often fear that they are not equipped to lead. They may assume that leaders need to be biblical scholars or erudite communicators, whereas in reality they need to listen, facilitate discussion, plan group meetings, and maintain communication between the small-group and pastoral staff. They may delegate certain group activities to other group members, from the preparation of food and drinks to leading a Bible study. Depending on the nature of the group, the leader may have more extensive responsibilities based on his or her training. A spiritual-direction group leader most likely will plan, facilitate, and guide group meetings in light of her training in spiritual formation. In any case, this part of the covenant statement should reflect the reversibility of roles in *koinonia.* Role reversibility refers to the capacity of leaders — whether they are small-group leaders or pastors — to recognize that their leadership role is not definitive for their identity.[10] They can move in and out of functioning as a leader. Their sense of self-worth does not depend on any position of leadership. This is because their primary identity is as members of the body of Christ, persons whose existence is determined through and through by the communion-creating love of

9. Gorman, *Community That Is Christian,* p. 117.

10. For an extended discussion of role reversibility, see James E. Loder, *Logic of the Spirit: Human Development in Theological Perspective* (San Francisco: Jossey-Bass, 1998).

God. To put it another way, their role as leaders is a functional not an ontological distinction.

Meeting logistics. Organizational structure and logistics are not synonymous with *koinonia,* but the *koinonia* of the group cannot exist in the temporal realm without them. The organization of the small group, in the best of circumstances, supports the practice of *koinonia.* This part of a group covenant would include items such as start date and end date of the group; days, times, and frequency of group meetings; and location of the meetings.

Quality of the group's communication. Establishing trust in small groups depends on confidentiality and authentic dialogue. Confidentiality is grounded in respect for the autonomy and integrity of others; it is intended to support and honor honest self-disclosure for the sake of compassionate care. Ordained clergy and other congregational staff members are expected to keep confidences in the course of pastoral care. The Evangelical Lutheran Church in America bylaws state it this way: "No ordained minister of this church shall divulge any confidential disclosure received in the course of the care of souls or otherwise in a professional capacity . . . except with the express permission of the person who has given confidential information to the ordained minister or who was observed by the ordained minister, or if the person intends great harm to self or others."[11] In cases where persons intend to harm themselves or others, or they reveal that someone else is being harmed (sexually, physically, or emotionally), clergy function, under the law, as mandated reporters. They are mandated to notify proper authorities of abuse and neglect.[12]

Confidentiality in small groups should follow the same basic principles as do confidentialities in pastoral care and counseling settings. What is said in the group stays in the group, unless a person's well-being is at grave risk or permission has been given otherwise. Small groups should discuss this commitment in order to prevent unintentional sharing of information outside the group or, conversely, in order to prevent sharing outside information inside the group. Consider the following example. Justine and Meg are close friends. Their kids go to

11. *Constitutions, Bylaws and Continuing Resolutions of the Evangelical Lutheran Church in America* (Minneapolis: Augsburg Fortress, 2008), 7.45.

12. For information on mandating reporting, see Marie Fortune, "Confidentiality and Mandatory Reporting: A Clergy Dilemma?": www.faithtrustinstitute.org/downloads/confidentiality_and_mandatory_reporting.pdf (accessed Aug. 3, 2005).

the same school, and they participate in a small group at their church together. Meg shares with Justine that she and her husband are quarreling constantly and that one of their children is performing poorly in school. Justine feels distraught by this information, and she is eager to support Meg. At their next small-group meeting, which Meg is unable to attend, Justine asks the group — without first asking Meg's permission — to pray for Meg's home life. What Meg has shared in confidence has now sparked curiosity and concern within the small group. Justine could have kept confidentiality by simply asking the group to pray for a struggling family whom she knows. Or she could have asked Meg's permission to share this information inside the group.

Confidentiality and attentive listening in small groups create an atmosphere conducive to honest expression. Attentive listening and honest expression are means of living in truly humanizing encounter with others. As I observed in chapter 5, the image of God is "being-in-encounter." We live as those made in God's image when our relationships with others are characterized by mutual seeing, hearing, speaking, and assisting one another with gladness.[13] When small-group members set aside their biases and judgments of one another, and when they throw off their own masks and facades, they enter into mutual seeing. When small-group members persist in understanding each other's point of view, especially in the midst of disagreement and difference, they enter into mutual hearing and speaking. When they gratefully make and receive requests of each other, they enter into mutual assistance.[14] When their communication is characterized by these four traits, they reflect God to one another, that is, they image God, who in Jesus Christ has entered into the most intimate relationship possible with us.

Training Leaders

Training for small-group leaders can take a variety of forms, depending on the particularities of both the congregation and the small-group

13. Karl Barth, *Church Dogmatics,* ed. G. W. Bromiley and T. F. Torrance, trans. G. W. Bromiley (Edinburgh: T. & T. Clark, 1960), III/2, pp. 222-85 (hereafter, volume, part, and page references to the *CD* appear in parentheses in the text).

14. See below for a description of specific communication skills related to these four aspects of humanizing encounter.

ministry. In general, the small-group ministries studied for this book combined numerous venues for equipping and empowering small-group leaders, for example, annual weekend retreats, monthly meetings, intensive six-week training sessions, off-site specialized training, and short articles sent via email.

The types of leadership roles will also vary according to the size of the congregation and its small-group ministry. One congregation with a thousand members participating in small groups had a full-time staff member designated as the small-group coordinator, as well as individual small-group leaders. Another congregation had over five hundred members in small groups and had a nested leadership structure: small-group apprentices working closely with small-group leaders as part of their training to become leaders; small-group leaders facilitating group meetings; small-group coaches supporting small-group leaders in their choice of study materials and in response to any challenging interpersonal situations arising in the group; and a member of the pastoral team empowering small-group coaches and working with them to plan yearly training events for all small-group leaders and apprentices. Julie Gorman suggests a similar typology of small-group leaders: group facilitators, group coordinators or coaches, and group strategists/equippers. Small-group facilitators plan group meetings, lead discussions, and coordinate outside events for the group. Gorman notes that there are two kinds of group facilitators: (1) those who prepare content for group meetings, facilitate the various activities of each group (i.e., discussion, prayer, study), and guide the group process (i.e., dialogue); (2) those who host the meetings, arrange the space, organize the food, and plan outside events. Group coaches/coordinators oversee more than one group, though they typically participate in a small group or serve as a group facilitator as well. Group coaches set goals for the overall group ministry, encourage assessment of small groups, help recruit new group facilitators, provide support and counsel for group facilitators as needed. Strategists/equippers may be a member of the pastoral staff. These leaders help connect the small-group ministry to the larger congregational-ministry design. They offer or organize training activities for group coaches and group facilitators. They create assessment tools for the small-group ministry.[15]

15. Gorman, *Community That Is Christian*, pp. 214-16.

The types of leadership needed also may depend on the specialized nature of some groups. Leadership of the prayer-and-visitation ministry team mentioned above consists of the following people and roles: coordinator of visitation, who links team members with congregation members in consultation with the pastor and chair of the board of deacons; prayer-and-visitation ministry team trainer, who leads monthly meetings of the caregivers, focusing on listening skills and community-building; and a pastoral supervisor, who receives and reviews written records of all visitations. Recovery groups and spiritual-direction groups similarly require specialized leadership training.

In order to support the practice of multidimensional *koinonia* in small groups, most leaders will need training in both the content and process of small-group dynamics. They also may need support in leading spiritual practices, such as Bible study and various forms of prayer. Much (not all) of the content of the small-group leaders' training can be gleaned from the previous chapters in this book and adapted in light of the language used to describe *koinonia* within the congregation. I have listed specific topics for the content of training with appropriate references to previous sections of this book, as well as references to supporting Scripture passages. However, I have not thoroughly addressed the group-process skills in this book. I list them below, provide a short overview, and refer to other resources that will be helpful in training small-group leaders.

Basic Level of Content: Small Groups and the Identity of the Church

- The church as a spiritual community whose inner life is *koinonia* (John 17). Here I recommend a basic definition of *koinonia* as intimacy, integrity, mutual indwelling, and coexistence, along with a brief overview of the multiple *koinonia* relationships: with God through Christ; with one another through Christ; with the world through Christ (chap. 4 above).
- Three modes of the church's existence: gathering (Acts 2:44-47), upbuilding (Eph. 4:1-16), and sending (Matt. 28:18-20)
- What small groups do well and not so well (chap. 3 above)
- Small groups as contributing predominantly to the upbuilding of the church (chap. 5 above, "The Upbuilding of the Church")
- Church growth and small-group growth as intensive growth (John 12:20-26; 15:1-17) (chap. 5 above, "The Nature of Church Growth")

More Specific Content:
The Mission of Small Groups in Today's World

- Brief overview of the crisis of community (chap. 1 above)
- The church in contrast to other communities (Col. 1:1-20) (chap. 4 above)
- Small groups as communities that participate in the church's ministry of care and healing (chap. 2 above, "Enhancing Congregational Care" (and chap. 6 above)
- Suffering as participation in the cross of Christ; entering into one another's grief and suffering as a way of practicing *koinonia* with Christ and *koinonia* with each other (Mark 8:34-47; Gal. 6:1-2; Heb. 12) (chap. 6 above).
- How to engage in confession, forgiveness, and mutual forbearance in small groups (I John 1:1–2:14) (chap. 5 above, "Mutual Integration"; chap. 6 above, "Guidelines for Healing in Small Groups")
- Building trust and healing guilt, shame, and trauma in small groups (Mark 5) (chap. 6 above)

Spiritual Practices for Small Groups:

- *Reading and studying the Bible* (chap. 4 above, "*Koinonia* and the Crisis of Community"; chap. 5 above, "Gathering of the Church"; chap. 6 above, "Guidelines for Healing in Small Groups").
- *Meditating on the Bible. Lectio divina* (meaning divine — or spiritual — reading) is an ancient practice of meditation on Scripture that can be carried out in small groups. It consists of four movements: *lectio, meditatio, oratio, contemplatio.* In the first movement *(lectio),* the group leader (or member) reads a short passage of Scripture slowly and carefully, encouraging group members to note any words, phrases, or images that grab their attention. The group leader then asks members simply to speak the word, phrase, or image. In the second movement *(meditatio),* the group leader reads the passage a second time; group members then ponder the words, phrases, or images silently and then share them with each other again. In the third movement *(oratio),* group members petition God to meet their needs on the basis of the Scripture meditation. They may even pray for each other's needs in light of their group sharing. In the fourth movement *(contemplatio),* the group leader encourages

members to use the words, phrases, or images as a lens for discerning God's action in their midst throughout the coming days and weeks. Or the leader encourages members to rest silently in the knowledge that God knows all their needs.[16]

- *Variety of prayer forms:* confession (honest acknowledgment of our sin and suffering before God, accompanied by requests for forgiveness and healing); thanksgiving (expressions of gratitude to God); petition (requests for God to meet our basic needs, the Lord's Prayer being a prime example); intercession (praying on behalf of others whether in their presence or absence); lament (pouring out our sorrow, despair, rage to God with full honesty).[17]

Process Skills for Small Groups:

- *Modeling and encouraging honest expression.* Honest expression is contingent on our ability to make observations, name our feelings, identify our needs, and make requests on the basis of those needs. These four steps are the basic skills in compassionate communication, and they correspond to the four aspects of humanizing encounters, that is, mutual seeing, hearing, speaking, and assisting.[18] Briefly, observations are devoid of judgment: they are statements of what we have seen, heard, said, remembered, and so on. Feelings are distinct from thoughts. Often we use the word "feel" to express an opinion ("I feel like you are ignoring me") rather than to express our inner reality ("I feel frustrated because I just answered that question and I didn't hear any response from you"). Needs are basic qualities that contribute to the flourishing of human life. Needs include such things as community, peace, health, autonomy, and so forth. Needs are the underlying reason for our feelings. We tend to have so-called "negative" feelings when our needs are not being met and "positive" feelings when they are being met. If we have identified our needs, we can make requests to God, others, or ourselves to meet them.[19]

16. Deborah van Deusen Hunsinger, *Pray Without Ceasing: Revitalizing Pastoral Care* (Grand Rapids: Eerdmans, 2006), pp. 201-3.

17. For a full explication of each of these types of prayer, as well as instructions for leading groups to pray in these ways, see van Deusen Hunsinger, *Pray Without Ceasing.*

18. Marshall Rosenberg, *Nonviolent Communication: A Language of Life* (Encinitas, CA: Puddle Dancer Press, 2003).

19. See Theresa F. Latini, "Nonviolent Communication and the Image of God," *Per-*

- *Modeling and encouraging empathy.* Contrary to popular opinion, empathy is not the capacity to "get inside another person's skin" or "put on another person's shoes." Empathy is not about feeling our way inside another person. Rather, empathy is a listening skill that enables us to be fully present to other people, hearing and reflecting back to them their feelings and needs. Often it is called "mirroring." In mirroring we reflect back to a person what we have heard him say. We may reflect back the basic content of what we have heard, the meaning of what we have heard, or the feelings and needs embedded in what we have heard. When we empathize in these ways, we convey full acceptance, understanding, and compassion to others, and we foster an atmosphere conducive to trust, and thus to healing and transformation.

- *Responding to conflict without anxiety.* Training in this process skill should begin with an overview of the potentially positive outcomes of conflict, for example, new learning, greater faithfulness to the group's mission, increased commitment to the group, and the deepening of authenticity. It would build on the skills of honest expression and empathic listening. If two or more group members are stuck in conflict with each other, the group leader could facilitate a discussion between them within the group setting. Of course, the capacity to enter such a process would depend on the prior establishment of trust in the group. This discussion should involve the following: (1) vulnerability: asking each person to share his or her observations, feelings, and needs; (2) empathy: asking each person to mirror back what she or he heard the other person say; (3) acknowledging the value of both sets of needs; (4) empathy from the group: asking other group members to share what they heard each person saying; (5) vulnerability from the group: asking the group to identify how they feel about the tension and conflict in the group and what they are needing in response to it; and (6) prayer for God to bring understanding, healing, and reconciliation.[20]

---

spectives (May 2007): 10-17; Theresa F. Latini, "Nonviolent Communication: A Humanizing Educational and Ecclesial Practice," *Journal of Education and Christian Belief* 13, no. 1 (2009): 19-31. See also Deborah van Deusen Hunsinger, "Practicing *Koinonia*," *Theology Today* 66, no. 3 (October 2009): 346-67.

20. See David Augsburger, *Caring Enough to Confront,* 3rd ed. (Ventura, CA: Regal, 2009).

• *Making referrals.* Sometimes group members will need the support of trained professionals, for example, therapists, spiritual directors, social workers, and so forth. The church should have a referral network that includes marriage-and-family therapists; counselors who work with children and youth; counselors who specialize in certain areas, such as abuse, drug and alcohol addiction, or depression; psychiatrists; support groups; and twelve-step groups. Group leaders could refer small-group members, as needed, to the pastor, who then would make a referral to another specialist, or group leaders could be trained to make referrals using the church's referral network.

Assessment

The six well-developed small-group ministries I investigated for this book all engage in some form of self-assessment. Four of these congregations have created specific self-assessment tools for their small groups. Three of these assessment tools are linked to the congregation's overall mission and ministry design. We will examine one of these assessment tools in detail. Then we will consider assessment in light of our normative ecclesiology of *koinonia*.

Assessing Discipleship

Community Presbyterian Church has a highly structured and integrated mission, ministry design, and assessment plan. Its mission statement reads: "We are called together by God to make disciples and to release them for service in our broken world." The strategy for fulfilling this mission is "to connect people together in large group, small group, and one-on-one relationships so that an ever growing number of men, women, youth and children experience the grace of Christ, grow in the Six Marks of a Disciple, receive discipleship training, and choose to become disciple-makers themselves." In other words, Community's ministry design combines large-group, small-group, and personal activities that aim at growth in discipleship for congregants of all ages. They intentionally "[d]esign *large group* teaching so that participants become empowered toward realizing [CPC] goals and outcomes

[and] reinforce teaching through coordinated efforts in *small group* and *one-on-one relationships*" (emphasis in original).

At Community Presbyterian Church, worship, Christian education, small groups, and individual pastoral care flow from and are assessed in light of a robust definition of discipleship. Disciples are those who have the following six traits:

- *A heart for Christ alone.* Jesus, as the one-and-only Son of God, becomes the priority in all of life: we worship him with all our heart, soul, mind, and strength.
- *A mind transformed by the Word.* We progressively come to view the world as God views it, setting aside the world's values as our minds are continually renewed by God's Word.
- *Arms of love.* As the hands and feet of Jesus in the world, we come alongside others in need, extend compassion, welcome the stranger, and live in a community of mutual care with other disciples.
- *Knees for prayer.* Our posture before God is one of continual dependence, trusting deeply that God is in charge of everything, conversing always about what he and we are accomplishing together.
- *A voice to speak the Good News.* We embrace the call to share Jesus with those who do not know him, leading them to faith and answering questions and providing hope and encouragement for those who already know the truth.
- *A spirit of servanthood and stewardship.* We live as servants of God and each other, doing good through the gifts the Spirit has given us, living generously and simply, seeking to bring about the fullest expression of God's rule in our culture.[21]

All newly formed small groups study these traits of discipleship. They receive a "Small Group Starter Kit," which contains a six-week detailed study of each of these marks. Each week includes a definition of the mark, Scripture texts that illuminate the mark, practical ways to grow in the mark, and the personal and relational effects of practicing the mark. The church session (i.e., board of elders) sets yearly objectives based on one of the marks. Preaching, teaching, and small groups fo-

---

21. Glenn McDonald, *The Disciple-Making Church: From Dry Bones to Spiritual Vitality* (Grand Haven, MI: Faith Walk Publishers, 2004).

cus on a particular mark in a given year. To support small groups in their study of this mark, the pastors write and distribute weekly group-discussion guides based on the sermon and corresponding biblical texts. The small groups are not required to use these discussion guides, but over 50 percent of them do.

Small groups at Community Presbyterian Church are encouraged to evaluate themselves formally in light of these six marks of discipleship and subsequently to focus their studies and activities on growth in weak areas. The pastoral staff has developed an assessment tool that is called "Six Marks of a Disciple Gap Analysis."[22] The assessment consists of a matrix defining each of the six marks along a continuum of discipleship, from seeker to beginner to intermediate to mature disciple. Small-group members are encouraged to identify themselves along this continuum in reference to each mark. They also answer questions such as, "Which mark(s) do you feel are your strongest? What are some of the ways that God has moved in your life to bring this/these mark(s) to a point of strength? Which mark(s) is/are the most challenging for you? What are some things you could do to grow in this/these mark(s)? In which mark(s) do you sense God's Spirit is desiring to work in your life right now?" Small-group leaders collect the assessments and tally the group's strengths and opportunities for growth. Small-group leaders also answer questions such as, "What activities related to these strengths does your group tend to do well? What activities could your group do . . . in order to grow in this/these mark(s) in service to Christ?" All of the information gleaned from answers to these questions then guides the group's discernment regarding future topics to study and activities to undertake.

Overall, the greatest strength of this assessment tool may be its thorough integration into the congregation's mission and ministry design. Not only small groups but also the session and various ministry teams at Community Presbyterian Church use the same matrix to guide their own growth in discipleship. A second strength of this as-

---

22. Gap analysis is a common form of assessment in business. It is a "technique for determining the steps to be taken in moving from a current state to a desired future-state. It begins with (1) listing of characteristic factors (such as attributes, competencies, performance levels) of the present situation ('what is'); (2) cross-lists factors required to achieve future objectives ('what should be'); and then (3) highlights the 'gaps' that exist and need to be 'filled'" ("Gap Analysis," *Business Dictionary:* http://www.businessdictionary.com/definition/gap-analysis.html [accessed Nov. 27, 2009]).

sessment is its robust biblical definition of discipleship. Discipleship is holistic: it entails the formation of one's head, heart, and hands according to the likeness of Jesus Christ.

The assessment tool could be strengthened theologically in three ways. First, it could prioritize discernment of Trinitarian practice. As it is written, small-group leaders and members are asked to consider what God is doing in their midst. But this is only one among many questions. It is not the central question. The practical theology of *koinonia* set forth in this book suggests that discernment of God's action in our midst is the primary and guiding question for shaping all ecclesial practice. Furthermore, God's practice is Trinitarian as well as christological. The definition of discipleship and the assessment tool lack even colloquial Trinitarian language. Second, the assessment needs a fuller understanding of mission. The fifth mark reduces the church's witness to evangelism. While public confession of one's faith is central to the mission of the church, it does not encompass the fullness of the church's vocation in the world. As I have argued throughout this book, the church is called into solidarity with the world. This intimate connection with the world is missing in the definition and assessment of discipleship at Community Presbyterian Church. Third, the assessment tends toward an individualistic understanding of Christian faith and discipleship. Whereas the definition of discipleship uses the pronoun "we," the assessment tool refers over and over to "me," "my," and "I." It focuses on the individual disciple and marginalizes the assessment of the *community* of disciples. It asks questions about what the group does well, but it does not assess the quality of communal life itself. This could be remedied, at least in part, if the assessment tool asked questions about small-group life as defined by the six marks.

Assessing Koinonia

Our ecclesiology grounded in *koinonia* calls for regular ongoing assessment of church practices. The church is called to discern whether or not its practices reflect its invisible dimension, that is, its *koinonia*. It kneels in supplication for its own peace, purity, and unity. Recognizing its contingency, fallibility, and potential self-deception, it humbly submits to the Refiner's fire whether ignited from above or from outside. "The Church stands in the fire of the criticism of its Lord. It is also ex-

posed to the criticism of the world, and this criticism has never been altogether false and unjust. It has always needed, and it always will need,
self-examination and self-correction. It cannot exist except as *ecclesia
semper reformanda*" (*CD* IV/1, p. 690).

As I observed in the section on the upbuilding of the church (chapter 5), assessment flows from the normative guideline of dynamic excellence. Church practices are called to be dynamic — once reformed and
always being reformed by the Word and work of God, Jesus Christ.
Church practices are called to excellence, meaning that they demonstrate the reality of *koinonia* to the world. It is not that ecclesial practices do so perfectly or without sin; rather, they do so adequately, in
such a way that the self-giving love, mutual forbearance, and service
characteristic of *koinonia* shine through them. Multidimensional
koinonia cannot be grasped in fullness in this life, because it is seen primarily by faith not sight. As Barth writes, it "takes place only as we can
see and read the dark letters of an electric sign as the current is passed
through it" (*CD* IV/2, p. 619).

How might a congregation discern signs of *koinonia* in its midst?
How might small groups assess their practice of multidimensional
koinonia? They can do so on the basis of the normative guidelines for
small groups constructed throughout this book: in other words, the
guidelines for small-group practice can be translated into self-
assessment questions. The chart below lists the small-group guidelines that emerged from my delineation of the three moments of the
church's existence: the gathering, upbuilding, and sending of the
church by the Holy Spirit. Those guidelines related to healing and
transformation in small groups have been included as part of the
church's upbuilding. The chart includes assessment questions related
to each of these normative guidelines. The chart is by no means ex-
haustive, but it provides enough sample questions with which a small
group can embark on a process of mutual discernment and self-
reflection. In other words, small-group members and leaders could
discuss these questions together on a regular (e.g., yearly) basis. Like
Community Presbyterian Church, they could ask God to illuminate
the strengths, weaknesses, opportunities for growth, and threats to
their life together in light of their discussion.[23] They could make deci-

---

23. Here I am implicitly referring to SWOT analysis, i.e., "Situation analysis in
which internal strengths and weaknesses of an organization, and external opportunities

sions for future study and activities on the basis of their longing to grow in practicing some dimension of *koinonia*.[24] Above all, this assessment would be clothed in humility, an acknowledgment of the fallibility of all human discernment, and prayerful recognition that growth in practicing *koinonia* ultimately depends on the grace of God. Groups would remember that spiritual growth is both a mystery and a gift. Their assessment would be in service of working out their salvation with fear and trembling, trusting that God is at work in their midst (Phil. 2:13).

	Normative Guidelines for Small Groups	**Related Assessment Questions**
Gathering of the Church	Small groups are not a substitute for the church's overall ministry.	In what sense does your small group remain connected to the larger congregation? Do group members participate regularly in corporate worship? How does your group support the overall ministry of the church?
	Small-group membership should reflect the grace through which we enter *koinonia*.	What kind of diversity exists in your small group? How does your small group remain open to new members, especially those who may appear different from you?

---

and threats faced by it are closely examined to chart a strategy" ("SWOT Analysis," *Business Dictionary:* http://www.businessdictionary.com/definition/SWOT-analysis.html [accessed Nov. 27, 2009]).

24. Churches might also adopt appreciative inquiry as a process for assessing small groups and other practices. Appreciative inquiry focuses on the strengths and values of an organization or team. "Appreciative Inquiry is about the co-evolutionary search for the best in people, their organizations, and the relevant world around them. In its broadest focus, it involves systematic discovery of what gives 'life' to a living system when it is most alive, most effective, and most constructively capable in economic, ecological, and human terms. AI involves, in a central way, the art and practice of asking questions that strengthen a system's capacity to apprehend, anticipate, and heighten positive potential" ("What is Appreciative Inquiry?" *Appreciative Inquiry Commons:* http://appreciativeinquiry.case.edu/intro/whatisai.cfm [accessed Nov. 27, 2009]). For information about using appreciative inquiry in congregations, see Mark Lau Branson, *Memories, Hopes, Conversations: Appreciative Inquiry and Congregational Change* (Herndon, VA: Alban Institute, 2004).

Normative Guidelines for Small Groups	Related Assessment Questions
Small-group ministries (as a whole) should encourage ecumenical relationships.	Do any groups in your church include members from other congregations or church traditions? Do any of your groups engage in interfaith dialogue or mission projects? Are any of your small groups intentionally ecumenical?

Upbuilding of the Church

Small groups should live the way of the cross in mutual care.	How do small-group members care for each other? What kind of theological language do they use to interpret their ministry of care? What are the limits of their mutual caregiving?
Small-group life should reflect the unity and diversity of *koinonia*.	What differences exist among group members (age, race, gender, socioeconomic status, etc.)? How does your small group deal with difference and disagreement?
Small groups should practice confession, forgiveness, and mutual forbearance.	How and when does your small group talk about sin? How does your small group engage in mutual confession of sin? Tell a story about a time when your small group practiced forgiveness. How does your small group deal with hurt feelings and anger among members? Tell a story about how group members have learned to love each other after having offended one another.
Small groups should be connected integrally to the worship life of the congregation.	How often does your small group eat meals together? Where is God in the midst of your table fellowship? How, if at all, do you understand the relationship between your small group fellowship and receiving the Lord's Supper in church? Does your small group ever discuss subjects related to sermons or other aspects of worship? If so, what subjects? What kinds of prayer does your group engage in?

Normative Guidelines for Small Groups	*Related Assessment Questions*
Small groups should point their members to the face of God in Jesus Christ.	What aspects of Jesus' life does your group discuss? What would you say is the image of Jesus held by members of your group? If your group is the body of Jesus, then how does Jesus live in your group?
Small-group members should accept one another unconditionally.	What, if anything, would you not feel safe enough to talk about with your small group? What kinds of pain, secrets, struggles, and sin have members of your group been willing to share with one another? How would your group be different if members knew and accepted each other fully?

Sending of the Church

Small groups should nurture generosity, openness, and compassion among their members.	Share a story that demonstrates generosity in your group. Share a story that demonstrates openness in your group. Share a story that demonstrates compassion in your group.
Small groups should encourage humanizing encounters that would become the basis for living in solidarity with the world.	Tell a story about a time when members of your group truly saw, listened to, and heard each other fully. How has your participation in this small group changed the way you relate to people outside the church?

Conclusion

The church of Jesus Christ, by virtue of its multidimensional *koinonia,* is a countercultural, humanizing, missional community. It is a communion of saints and sinners called to the deepest possible intimacy, authenticity, solidarity, and radical equality. It is a communion of love, a love that corresponds to God's love in Jesus Christ, a long-suffering love that knows no bounds. This love is lived out in the ministry of well-developed small groups, through which the church is built up and empowered for witness in and solidarity with the world. Congregational-ministry designs, mission and covenant statements, leadership training, and regular assessment help small groups contribute to the upbuilding and sending of the church. When small groups live the way of the cross in mutual care, practice confession and mutual forbearance, and reflect the unity and diversity of *koinonia,* they help the church grow in mutual integration and edification. When small groups nurture generosity, compassion, and openness to the world and find creative ways to witness to God's love in both word and deed, they help the church fulfill its vocation of participating in Christ's ongoing ministry of reconciliation unto *koinonia.* Furthermore, when small groups practice multidimensional *koinonia,* they participate in God's transformation of the crisis of community in late modernity. In the midst of faceless relationships, small groups can point us to the one face that never goes away, the face of God in Jesus Christ. In the context of being uprooted and displaced, small groups become a spiritual family characterized by the unity and diversity of *koinonia.* Where anxiety runs high and crises confront us at every level of our common existence, small groups provide a venue through which God grounds us in Christ and heals our ontological insecurity.

These conclusions about small-group ministry, the church, and life in late modernity have emerged from carrying out four tasks of practical theology: descriptive-empirical, interpretive, normative, and pragmatic. We began our practical theological journey with this question: How can small groups (ecclesial practice) faithfully participate in the practice of God (Trinitarian practice) for the sake of the world (societal practice)? This question sets in motion all four movements (or tasks) in our journey. This journey not only has developed a practical theology of small-group ministry but also has demonstrated *how to do* practical theology. Each of these four tasks can be carried out whenever a crisis or persistent question arises in ministry. Pastors, Christian educators, lay leaders, and practical theologians can step back and ask four questions whenever they encounter a ministerial challenge: What is happening? Why is it happening? What should be happening? How can we put this into action? That said, it is important to note that our theological precommitments, as well as our social location, will shape how we answer each one of these questions. Therefore, it is time to make explicit what has been implicit throughout this book, that is, my own neo-Barthian approach to practical theology. I will define what I mean by "neo-Barthian practical theology," and then I will summarize how I have constructed guidelines for small-group ministry in light of this precommitment.

Basic Definition of Neo-Barthian Practical Theology

Karl Barth is widely considered to be one of the most significant theologians of the twentieth century. He spent his early years teaching in Germany and then later in Switzerland. He is known for his defiance of Hitler, his writing of the Barmen Declaration, his thirteen-volume *Church Dogmatics,* and a multitude of other books, essays, and articles. It would not be an overstatement to say that every serious Protestant systematic theologian today must grapple with Barth's work, for he innovatively reworked Reformation theology in light of modern hermeneutics, the liberal methodology of his theological forebears, and the orthodoxy of the early church councils.

Though Barth was not a practical theologian, he is an invaluable dialogue partner for practical theologians for numerous reasons: (1) the clarity, creativity, and expansiveness of his thought; (2) his affinity with the currently prevailing postmodern epistemology;[1] (3) the largely untapped potential, especially within Barth's later theology, for interdisciplinary and ecumenical dialogue;[2] and (4) the implicit connections between the core of Barth's ecclesiology — the *koinonia* relationship — and both Eastern Orthodox and Roman Catholic ecclesiologies.[3] Because Barth was not a practical theologian, and because he lived and wrote prior to the late-modern resurgence of practical theology as a field of study, he does not ask the same questions that practical theologians ask today. He does not develop an interdisciplinary method, nor does he explicitly reflect on the epistemic significance of practices. This has led me to construct a "neo-Barthian practical theology," defining practical theology differently from but in continuity with Barth's theology. (See the Epilogue for a full explication of neo-Barthian practical theology.)

At the most basic level, by "neo-Barthian practical theology" I mean critical reflection on and interpretation of three forms of action or practice — ecclesial, Trinitarian, and societal — with the goal of reforming current church life and ministry (ecclesial practice) according to the life-act of God (Trinitarian practice) for the sake of the world

---

1. See William Stacy Johnson, *The Mystery of God: Karl Barth and the Postmodern Foundations of Theology* (Louisville: Westminster John Knox, 1997).

2. A few theologians have broken ground and prepared the way for further interdisciplinary and ecumenical dialogue from a Barthian perspective. For the relationship between Barth's dogmatic theology and psychology, see Deborah van Deusen Hunsinger, *Theology and Pastoral Counseling: A New Interdisciplinary Approach* (Grand Rapids: Eerdmans, 1995); see also Daniel J. Price, *Karl Barth's Anthropology in Light of Modern Thought* (Grand Rapids: Eerdmans, 2002). For a series of essays bringing Barth into dialogue with Martin Luther King, Jr., Rene Girard, Carl Henry, and others, see George Hunsinger, *Disruptive Grace: Studies in the Theology of Karl Barth* (Grand Rapids: Eerdmans, 2000).

3. George Hunsinger has established a creative dialogue among Lutheran, Reformed, and Catholic theologians, in part by unmasking some of the inadequacies in Barth's understanding of the sacraments along the lines of his emphasis on the *koinonia* relationship. See George Hunsinger, *The Eucharist and Ecumenism: Let Us Keep the Feast* (Cambridge: Cambridge University Press, 2008). *Koinonia* seems to implicitly connect, for example, with the dialogue between Eastern Orthodox ecclesiology, as represented by John Zizioulas's *Being in Communion,* and Roman Catholic ecclesiology, as represented by the work of Joseph Cardinal Ratzinger, presented in Miroslav Volf's *After Our Likeness: The Church as the Image of the Trinity* (Grand Rapids: Eerdmans, 1998).

(societal practice). This practical theology emerges from and returns to the life of the church. However, it does not serve the church as an end in itself; rather, it serves the church so that the church may faithfully participate in the humanization of the world according to the humanity of God in Jesus Christ. Hence, this practical theology is a missional discipline. Ray Anderson writes: "The focus of practical theology is not simply the internal workings of the church (although it includes them) but the praxis of the church as it interacts with the praxis of the world. As such, there is a necessary critical and prophetic aspect to practical theology's reflective activity, the boundaries of which are defined by the boundaries of God's continuing mission."[4]

Neo-Barthian practical theology critically reflects on and interprets ecclesial practice. From a Reformed perspective, the Christian does not exist separate from the church. As Calvin says in the *Institutes,* the church is our mother. Just as a child does not survive apart from his mother (or primary caregiver), so we cannot live spiritually severed from the church. "Away from her bosom one cannot hope for any forgiveness of sins or any salvation . . . it is always fatally dangerous to be separated from the Church."[5] Thus neo-Barthian practical theology — or, more accurately, the neo-Barthian practical theologian — seeks to serve the church even when criticizing it. The neo-Barthian practical theologian recognizes herself as a member of the body of Christ, as one whose life is determined by multidimensional *koinonia.* For these reasons, a neo-Barthian practical theology grants ecclesial practice special priority.

In this regard, my approach to practical theology differs from that of a number of contemporary practical theologians, such as Gerben Heitink.[6] In attempting to avoid the clerical paradigm and the segregation of the church from civic life, Heitink speaks of Christian praxis, or, more generally, religious praxis, rather than ecclesial praxis.[7] Of course, ecclesial praxis falls within religious praxis; but

---

4. Ray S. Anderson, *The Shape of Practical Theology: Empowering Ministry with Theological Praxis* (Downers Grove: InterVarsity Press, 2001), p. 32.

5. John Calvin, *Institutes of the Christian Religion,* ed. John T. McNeill, trans. Ford Lewis Battles (Philadelphia: Westminster Press, 1960), 4.1.4.

6. Gerben Heitink, an emeritus professor of practical theology at the Free University of Amsterdam, is a leading voice in the International Association of Practical Theology. He is the author of *Practical Theology: History, Theory, Action Domains,* trans. Reinder Bruinsma (Grand Rapids: Eerdmans, 1999).

7. In my use of the phrase "clerical paradigm," I am referring to the tendency to di-

general religious language, by contrast to ecclesial language, potentially ignores the locus of God's self-revelation. From a Barthian perspective, one cannot speak theologically about God or humanity without speaking about Christ, and one cannot speak about Christ without speaking about Christ's body, through whom Christ chooses to be present to the world.

That said, it is important to recognize that a neo-Barthian practical theology does not assume that the church's action is superior to other forms of action. In fact, reflection on societal practice in light of Trinitarian practice may lead us to conclude that certain societal practices correspond more closely to Jesus Christ, the Word and work of God, than certain ecclesial practices. In other words, a neo-Barthian practical theologian remembers that all things coexist with and coinhere in Jesus Christ. The world is united to Christ, and Christ is at work in the world even if this work is not recognized as his. Therefore, theories emerging outside the church can witness to Jesus Christ as the true human. Practices outside the church can conform to Christ's likeness. If so, they have the status of secular parables of the truth, as I delineate in the Epilogue. Similarly, because the church exists in and for the world, some practices are not strictly ecclesial. They can also be considered societal, as is the case with small groups.

Neo-Barthian practical theology critically reflects on and interprets societal practice. For Barth, the church is, on the one hand, the earthly-historical form of Jesus Christ, and on the other, a human society that belongs to the sphere of other human societies — domestic, political, economic, social, academic — that intersect the community of faith in the most diverse ways.[8] The church originates from the risen Christ, yet it resides within the temporal realm. The church and hence practical theologians exist in genuine attachment to the world. The histories of the church and the cosmos are united yet differentiated, the former being responsible to the latter. As Barth writes, "[T]he true community of Jesus Christ is the society in which it is given to men to know and practice their solidarity with the world"

---

rect theological education exclusively toward the formation of pastors. One of the unfortunate results of this has been the reduction of the ministry of the church to the ministry of the pastor.

8. Karl Barth, *Church Dogmatics,* ed. G. W. Bromiley and T. F. Torrance, trans. G. W. Bromiley (Edinburgh: T. & T. Clark, 1958), IV/2, p. 284 (hereafter, volume, part, and page references to this work appear in parentheses in the text).

(*CD* IV/3.2, p. 773). As a ministry of the church, practical theology "stands in definite relations to the world around it, and what it does it does in these relations or not at all; it must speak to the people of its time and place, neither past or over them. It must genuinely know them" (*CD* IV/3.2, p. 850).

Neo-Barthian practical theology critically reflects on and interprets Trinitarian practice. This distinguishes it from models rooted in the modernist premise that God in Godself cannot be known by humanity. In these other models, knowledge of God comes from analysis of the created order. The proper object of theological study is not God but rather human experience, especially religious consciousness and practices, and the development of the Christian tradition throughout church history. In that paradigm, practical theology studies human religious experience in a particular sociocultural context in hopes of transforming both domains. Again, Heitink typifies this approach. In his model the practical theologian interprets the relationship between tradition and the contemporary problem. From this emerges a number of presuppositions, which he tests empirically. He then uses the knowledge gained through the interaction of hermeneutics and empirical testing to improve strategies in a particular domain of action — personal, ecclesial, or societal.

In contrast, Trinitarian practice is the foremost object of practical theology since, for Barth, God can actually be known by means of God's self-disclosure.[9] The incarnation reveals the essence of God as the self-giving, -loving, and -knowing Trinity. Not only is God known through Jesus Christ, but also the true essence of humanity is known objectively *in* — and only in — the revelation of Jesus Christ, true God and true human. An adequate understanding of persons must be grounded in an interpretation of Jesus Christ. All theology is Christology; "all ecclesiology [and anthropology] is grounded, critically limited, but also positively determined by Christology" (*CD* IV/3.2, p. 786). Hence a proper understanding of societal action and ecclesial action and its objectives depends on our apprehension of divine action. As

---

9. See George Hunsinger, *How to Read Karl Barth: The Shape of His Theology* (New York: Oxford University Press, 1991), pp. 35-39, 76-151, for an analysis of Barth's revelational and soteriological objectivism. Hunsinger writes: "Barth was convinced that the knowledge of God as confessed by faith is objective in the sense that its basis lies not in human subjectivity but in God" (p. 35).

Duncan Forrester writes, "A theology of practice must first ask questions about God's activity and consider the practice of other agents within the horizon of the divine practice and as actual or potential participation in God's activity."[10]

To be more specific, a neo-Barthian practical theology reflects on God's present action and its relationship to ecclesial action and societal action. The goal is not simply new understanding or meaning-making. Rather, the goal of practical theology from a neo-Barthian perspective is to assist the church (ecclesial action) in participating in God's communion-creating work (Trinitarian action) for the sake of the reconciliation of the world (societal action). Though inextricable from orthodoxy, orthopraxy is the goal of the church, and facilitation of orthopraxy is the goal of its practical theology. Ray Anderson again: "Theology is properly conceived as a performative discipline in which the criterion of authenticity is deemed to be orthopraxy, or authentic transformatory action, rather than orthodoxy (right belief)."[11]

Orthopraxy has been the broad goal of this book. I have utilized the four tasks of practical theology as a hermeneutical circle to guide my interpretation of Trinitarian practice, ecclesial practice, and societal practice in hopes of encouraging the church, through small groups, to practice multidimensional *koinonia*. Each chapter, accordingly, utilizes one or more of the four tasks of practical theology to illuminate one or more dimensions of the threefold objective of a neo-Barthian practical theology — ecclesial practice, Trinitarian practice, and societal practice (see Table 7 on p. 188). Because the four tasks interpenetrate one another, I have moved back and forth between them. The same is true of the threefold objective of practical theology: ecclesial practice, Trinitarian practice, and societal practice are distinct but often united in actuality. For this reason, some chapters have considered two or more forms of practice together.

---

10. Duncan Forrester, *Truthful Action: Explorations in Practical Theology* (Edinburgh: T. & T. Clark, 2000), p. 9. Similarly, Andrew Purves declares that pastoral theology is first a theology of the pastoring God, before it is a theology of what the church or minister does. See Andrew Purves, "The Trinitarian Basis for all Practical Theology," *International Journal of Practical Theology* 2, no. 2 (1998): 224-39.

11. Anderson, *The Shape of Practical Theology*, p. 48.

Four Tasks of Practical Theology

I began this book with the interpretive task of practical theology, partly to demonstrate that the four operations (i.e., tasks or movements) in practical theology do not proceed in a strict linear way. Practical theological reflection can begin with any of the four tasks. Though the tasks can be differentiated conceptually, in actual practice we move in and out of them with significant fluidity. So the interpretive task sets forth a broad sociological framework for understanding the role of small groups in the United States today. Drawing heavily on Anthony Giddens's theory of modernization, I have argued that late-modern people experience a profoundly destabilizing crisis of community. As a result of the dynamics of modernity, we are displaced from local communities; our intimate relationships take on a new and fragile form (the pure relationship); we must construct a coherent life narrative in the face of competing expert advice and the end of tradition; and our ontological security is threatened by new risks and nearly constant transition. All of this impacts the religious orientation of people living in late modernity. Broadly speaking, some retreat into fundamentalism, while others become cosmopolitan. In terms of Christian practice, today more people believe in God without belonging to local communities of faith than ever before. Life on every level — communal, interpersonal, intrapersonal, and transpersonal (or religious) — has changed so much that Giddens refers to our era as a wild ride on an out-of-control train.

After interpreting societal practice broadly, I then moved into the descriptive part of this practical theological journey. I closely examined Robert Wuthnow's national study of the small-group movement in the United States from the mid-1990s. I supplemented this with the findings of other sociologists, such as Ann Marie Minnick and Robert Putnam. I returned to the interpretive task by explaining this sociological research of small groups in light of the late-modern crisis of community. In general, small groups foster a personal rather than ecclesial connection to God. They contain the same structural weaknesses as the pure relationship: that is, people form loose commitments to their groups. Generally speaking, small groups are homogeneous and insular. Identity formation in these groups may lack accountability, so that authenticity becomes the only standard for one's actions. In short, small groups generally embody the crisis of community. They mirror more than mitigate the challenges of life in late modernity.

Table 7: Tasks and objects of practical theology

Chapter	Task of Practical Theology	Object of Practical Theology
1	Interpretive	Societal practice (crisis of community in late modernity)
2	Descriptive-empirical and interpretive	Societal practice and ecclesial practice (small groups in the United States)
3	Descriptive-empirical and interpretive	Ecclesial practice (well-developed small groups)
4	Normative	Trinitarian practice *(koinonia)* and ecclesial practice (the identity and mission of the church as *koinonia*)
5	Normative in conversation with findings from descriptive-empirical task	Ecclesial practice (small groups practicing *koinonia*)
6	Normative in conversation with findings from interpretive task	Ecclesial practice (the healing ministry of the church and small groups)
7	Pragmatic in conversation with descriptive-empirical and normative tasks	Ecclesial practice (strategies for implementing small groups)

Next, I utilized the descriptive-empirical task and the interpretive task to illumine a subset of small groups: well-developed groups in six congregations. Because Wuthnow's research does not target these kinds of groups, I carried out my own empirical research. I compared my findings to Wuthnow's and then considered my findings in light of the crisis of community. I argue that, though these well-developed groups are not a panacea for the church in late modernity, they do overcome some of the ambiguities inherent in the groups studied by Wuthnow. Specifically, the spirituality embodied in these well-developed small groups supports participants' connection to and involvement in local congregations. Even more, they are a significant venue for the congregation's ministry of care. Second, while well-developed small groups may be homogeneous, they are not insular: they propel their members to witness in word and deed outside the congregation. Third, well-developed small groups provide external support for the inherently insecure "pure relationship." Group members travel together through the murky waters created by the transformation of intimacy. Groups also foster communal trust relationships rather than merely dyadic trust relations (in contrast to the pure relationship). Fourth, some of these well-developed groups provide space for healing of shame, loss, and trauma. They thereby strengthen ontological security. In a community of mutual trust and support, small-group members integrate their suffering into a meaningful personal life narrative. Fifth, well-developed small groups help people commune with God through prayer and meditation on Scripture. Consequently, group members practice their faith more regularly outside the group. They pray with spouses, friends, and coworkers. They seek to witness to God's grace in their daily speech and action, and they engage in common mission projects in fulfillment of their group covenant. Therefore, I have concluded that well-developed small groups, while not without their own weaknesses, help people navigate through the crisis of community. They do not completely overcome the crisis, but neither do they simply propagate it.

Examining well-developed small groups is a necessary but not sufficient means for answering the driving question of this book. Therefore, after carrying out the descriptive-empirical and interpretive tasks of practical theology, I plunged into the normative task. To understand the role of small groups in the ministry of the church, I first identified what I mean by "church." Building on Karl Barth's ecclesiology, I defined the church as having its origin and *telos* in the *koinonia* of the Trinity. On the basis of Trinitarian practice, I defined the church as multidimensional *koinonia*. The church exists in a series of interlocking *koinonia* relationships, relationships of the greatest possible intimacy and integrity: that is, *koinonia* with Christ, *koinonia* among church members, and *koinonia* with the world. All of these *koinonia* relationships originate and flow from the very being of God.

Christ's work of reconciliation establishes humanity in multidimensional *koinonia*. The *koinonia*-creating work of Christ has been completed in the past (in the cross and resurrection), and it will be fully manifest in the future. In the present tense, the church is called to witness to this *koinonia;* therefore, the church is distinct from other communities even as it exists in solidarity with them. The church lives in but is not determined by chronological time. Rather, it is determined by christological time, which, among other things, means that the church will be no more: its existence is temporal. In the here and now, however, the church has a critical role to play in the divine economy of reconciliation. It is called to participate in God's work of reconciliation and the creation of communion. This work has the potential to transform the crisis of community. In particular, the *koinonia*-creating work of Christ in the power of the Spirit through the church reconfigures intimacy in late modernity. In the context of *koinonia,* intimacy becomes a thoroughly communal and fully mutual gift. It is not so much chosen or created as it is received and lived into.

After defining the church as multidimensional *koinonia,* and after bringing it into dialogue with the crisis of community, I have proceeded to unpack how the church lives in light of its objective reality. Following Barth, I have noted that the church lives out multidimensional *koinonia* in three modes. The various *koinonia* relationships cannot be separated from each other, but they can be differentiated. Thus I have focused on the church's practice of *koinonia* with Christ in the mode of gathering, *koinonia* among its members in the mode of upbuilding, and *koinonia* with the world in the mode of sending. I have explored how small groups, on the one hand, might contribute to the church's *koinonia* in each of these modes and, on the other hand, might be challenged to practice multidimensional *koinonia.* In other words, I have proposed normative guidelines for small-group ministries by bringing the research of well-developed small groups into dialogue with this ecclesiology. In this regard, the normative and descriptive-empirical tasks influenced each other. Some of those guidelines included the following:

- Small-group membership should reflect the grace through which we enter *koinonia.*
- Some small groups should be organized to reflect the ecumenical nature of the church.
- Small groups should become a primary site for learning to live the way of the cross.
- Overall, small-group ministries should reflect the unity and diversity of *koinonia.*
- Small groups should accept and work through conflict as a way of honoring the radical particularity of each member of Christ's body.
- Small groups should practice confession, forgiveness, and mutual forbearance.
- Small groups should be marked by mutual service.

- Small groups should be connected intentionally to the worship life of congregations.
- Small-group ministries should be dynamic and exemplary, always being reformed so that they more faithfully reflect life in *koinonia*.
- Small groups should nurture generosity, openness, and compassion among their members.
- Small groups should contribute indirectly, if not directly, to the church's solidarity with the world.

As the third component of the normative task, I have explored the role of small groups in strengthening ontological security. I have defined ontological security psychologically, sociologically, and theologically. From the perspective of object-relations theory, ontological security is established in the earliest years of life with respect to our primary caregiver. As we experience the pleasures of touch and mirroring and the routine meeting of our most basic needs, we become ontologically secure. We trust ourselves and others. Trust becomes an embodied reality, a part of our personal identity that enables us to maintain the balance between belonging and autonomy in relationships throughout our lives. From a sociological perspective, however, ontological security is undermined in late modernity. Persistent doubt and risk, an atmosphere of chronic crisis, the lack of trust in tradition and authority of any kind, and the fragility of the pure relationship — all these dynamics erode our basic sense of well-being in the world. From a theological perspective, we must differentiate actual (objective) ontological security from existential (subjective) ontological security. Objectively, we are secure in multidimensional *koinonia;* in Christ our being is sustained. Subjectively, we may experience the threat of annihilation, for the effects of our ontological security — our union with Christ — are not yet fully manifest in our lives.

As a result of creating a multidisciplinary dialogue among these three distinct but related understandings of ontological security, I have projected a vision for how *koinonia* can transform and heal ontological insecurity so that, with Julian of Norwich, we trust that "all will be well." In this regard, the interpretive task carried out in chapter 1 has influenced the normative task and vice versa. I suggested that, in the context of *koinonia,* we encounter the face of God in Jesus Christ, the face that never goes away. Jesus heals our ontological insecurity by becoming our true mirror, our source of psychological and spiritual sustenance, and the one who gives us a new identity. Through its ministry of Word and sacrament, the church participates in Christ's healing ministry. Small groups expand on this healing potential. As I suggested, small-group members are uniquely positioned to participate in the healing of ontological insecurity in the following ways:

- By pointing each other to the face of God in Jesus Christ
- By mirroring delight and acceptance to one another
- By being present to each other in the midst of sorrow and despair
- By providing continuity of routine

Finally, on the last leg of this practical theological journey, I have carried out the pragmatic operation of practical theology. I have proposed strategies for practicing *koinonia* in small groups: (1) how to construct small-group mission statements that encourage *koinonia;* (2) how to train small-group leaders to practice *koinonia;* (3) how to practice *koinonia* in the congregation by creatively linking small groups to other congregational ministries; and (4) how to assess small groups' growth in practicing *koinonia.* My hope remains that congregations will creatively nuance these rules of art in light of their own situations and that somehow, by the grace and mystery of God, fractured persons, families, and communities may be mended and made whole and empowered for mission through the ministry of small groups.

Toward a Neo-Barthian Practical Theology

Karl Barth's work draws both sharp criticism and loyal praise from many quarters in theological education. With the exception of a few people,[1] practical theologians by and large have veered away from Barth as a source for their constructive work. While the reasons for this are likely diverse and varied, one criticism stands out among the rest: that Barth's theology leaves little room for human agency. Don Browning claims that Barth saw no role "for human understanding, action, or practice in the construal of God's self-disclosure. In this view, theology is practical only by applying God's revelation as directly and purely as possible to the concrete situations of life."[2] More pejoratively, Thomas Groome claims that Barth's theology "robs us of our historical agency and reduces human history to basketweaving."[3] This reading of Barth assumes that Barth prevents the possibility of inter-

---

1. See Ray S. Anderson, *The Shape of Practical Theology: Empowering Ministry with Theological Praxis* (Downers Grove, IL: InterVarsity Press, 2001); Deborah van Deusen Hunsinger, *Pastoral Counseling: A New Interdisciplinary Approach* (Grand Rapids: Eerdmans, 1995); James E. Loder, *Logic of the Spirit: Human Development in Theological Perspective* (San Francisco: Jossey-Bass, 1998); Andrew Purves, *Reconstructing Pastoral Theology: A Christological Foundation* (Louisville: Westminster John Knox, 2004).

2. Don S. Browning, *Fundamental Practical Theology* (Minneapolis: Fortress Press, 1991), p. 5.

3. Thomas Groome, "Theology on Our Feet," in *Formation and Reflection: The Promise of Practical Theology*, ed. Lewis Mudge and James Poling (Minneapolis: Augsburg Fortress, 2009), pp. 55-78.

disciplinary and ecumenical dialogue and reduces practical theology to applied dogmatics.[4]

By contrast, I have drawn on a very different reading of Barth in this book, one with a clear role for human action in the divine economy of salvation, one that allows for multidisciplinary thinking, and one that cannot avoid public discourse. Perhaps this is because I have emphasized Barth's later works — *Church Dogmatics* III and IV — while Browning refers predominantly to Barth's earliest work, the *Commentary on Romans*. Perhaps the difference lies in my reading of Barth through particular constructive theologians such as George Hunsinger. It is likely that some of the differences lie in the fact that I have not strictly followed Barth's definition of practical theology.[5] Rather, I have built on aspects of his overall methodology, at times extending his argument and at other times going beyond it. In this sense I have been working from what I call a "neo-Barthian practical theology."

As I have defined it in the conclusion, this neo-Barthian practical theology critically reflects on and interprets three forms of action (or practice): Trinitarian action, ecclesial action, and societal action. It does so with a particular *telos* in mind: to form and reform ecclesial action so that it participates in Trinitarian action for the sake of the reconciliation of societal action to God. In other words, neo-Barthian practical theology orders these three forms of action in a very specific way. This ordering shapes the whole of a neo-Barthian practical theology. James Loder writes:

> In practical theology, the core of the discipline is not its operations, procedures, practices, roles, congregations, and the like. Rather, its core problematic resides in why these must be studied; why these are

4. Browning, *Fundamental Practical Theology*, pp. 5, 7, 45.

5. Barth does not present a sustained definition of practical theology in his writings. His references to it are few and scattered. In *CD* I/1, he claims that practical theology deals with the aim or goal of the overall theological enterprise. It focuses on whether or not the church's words and deeds correspond to Christ (Karl Barth, *Church Dogmatics*, trans. G. T. Thomson [Edinburgh: T. & T. Clark, 1936], I/1, p. 3). In *CD* IV/3.2, he declares that practical theology deals with what is "normative for the practice of [the church's] ministry in every branch" (*Church Dogmatics*, ed. G. W. Bromiley and T. F. Torrance, trans. G. W. Bromiley [Edinburgh: T. & T. Clark, 1962], p. 880). It "must aim to give meaningful directions to the community in the world" (*CD* IV/3.2, p. 881). (Hereafter, volume, part, and page references to the *CD* appear in parentheses in the text and notes.)

a problem. There are countless superficial responses to such a question, but the fundamental problematic implied in this question, and what drives this discipline forward and generates its issues, is that such phenomena or events combine two incongruent, qualitatively distinct realities, the Divine and the human, in apparently congruent forms of action.[6]

In light of this premise, in this epilogue I will consider the following: how a neo-Barthian practical theology relates divine action and human action in ecclesial practice; how a neo-Barthian practical theology relates interpretations of divine action and human action in ecclesial practice and societal practice; and how a neo-Barthian practical theology uses empirical research methods to describe and interpret divine action and human action.

Divine and Human Action in Ecclesial Practice

Neo-Barthian practical theology often begins with questions arising from everyday experience, especially ecclesial practices. If the questions are significant enough to constitute a crisis, then the community of faith critically reflects on the following: (a) its current and past practices (i.e., ecclesial practice); (b) practices within other communities (i.e., societal practice); (c) interpretations of these practices using both theological and nontheological (i.e., often social-scientific) theories; and (d) the practice of God (i.e., Trinitarian practice). This is precisely what I have done throughout this book. I have examined the small-group movement in the United States, as well as well-developed small-group ministries in six congregations; I have interpreted these groups using sociological and psychological theories; and I have explored the practice of God in and through the church on the basis of Karl Barth's theology. I have placed all of this in conversation in order to develop guidelines and strategies for implementing small groups that practice multidimensional *koinonia*.

At the center of this conversation has been an assumption about the peculiarity of ecclesial practice. From a neo-Barthian perspective,

6. James E. Loder, "Normativity and Context in Practical Theology," in *Practical Theology: International Perspectives*, ed. Friedrich Schweitzer and Johannes van der Ven (New York: Peter Lang, 1999), p. 374n2.

ecclesial practice embodies the confluence of two disjunctive forms of action, that is, divine and human. To understand how these actions are brought together, we begin with Jesus Christ, God's Word of revelation and work of reconciliation.

Divine action and human action commune perfectly in the incarnation of the second person of the Trinity, Jesus Christ, in an asymmetrical, bipolar relational unity. As Hunsinger explains, Barth posits the relationship between Jesus' divinity and humanity as a *koinonia* relationship ordered according to the Chalcedonian pattern.[7] In attempting to explain how Jesus Christ could be both God and human, the Council of Chalcedon (451 CE) concluded that the divine and human natures of Jesus Christ are related "without separation or division (inseparable unity)," "without confusion or change (indissoluble differentiation)," and "with asymmetrical ordering (indestructible order)." In the very being of Jesus Christ, divine nature and human nature are united, differentiated, and ordered asymmetrically. Two other Christological patterns further explain this *koinonia* relationship: the anhypostasis/enhypostasis formula and the pattern of correspondence.[8] According to the patristic anhypostasis/enhypostasis formula, Jesus' human nature has no existence apart from the Word of God, but it does have a real existence in the Word of God. Jesus of Nazareth does not exist except in union with the eternal Son. Jesus' life is contingent on participation in the life of the Word. According to the second related pattern, Jesus' humanity corresponds perfectly to his divinity. In his life history, Jesus lives in perfect correspondence to God the Father. His speech and action mimetically reflect the *koinonia* of the Trinity. He is the image of the invisible God. Jesus Christ lives in a perfect *koinonia* of divine and human action. He loves God in gratitude, obedience, humility, long-suffering, and self-giving. Jesus is united to the Father through the power of the Holy Spirit. He does not exist separate from the Father. Jesus is differentiated from the Father; yet he depends on the Father, who is present to him via the Spirit, for all his needs.

By virtue of his life of *koinonia* (i.e., the communion of divine action and human action), Jesus Christ reconciles all humanity to God.

7. George Hunsinger, *How to Read Karl Barth* (Oxford: Oxford University Press, 1991), pp. 185-88; see also Hunsinger, *Disruptive Grace: Studies in the Theology of Karl Barth* (Grand Rapids: Eerdmans, 2000), pp. 133-34.

8. Kimlyn Bender, "The Living Congregation of the Living Lord Jesus Christ," PhD diss., Princeton Theological Seminary, 2002.

By means of the Holy Spirit, humanity is united to Christ. We exist with Christ. We indwell Christ. At the same time, humanity is distinct from Christ. Neither now nor in eternity do humans become divine. Rather, humanity participates in divine life. Humanity has no being except as it is upheld by God. In other words, the relationship between Jesus Christ and humanity also follows the Chalcedonian pattern. As Hunsinger describes it, the patterns governing divine and human action in the history of Jesus Christ also govern, in an analogous way, all divine-human relations.[9] However, divine action and human action do not yet appear to exist in *koinonia*. Only in the *eschaton* will divine action and human action commune in fullness and perfection. In the time between Jesus' cross and resurrection and the fullness of time, the Holy Spirit awakens people to this reality, gathers them together in one body, builds them up, and sends them into the world as witnesses to Jesus Christ. Objectively speaking, the church is united to Christ, differentiated from Christ, and contingent on Christ. Notice the Chalcedonian pattern: the church and Jesus exist in an inseparable unity, an indissoluble differentiation, and an asymmetrical ordering.

As God awakens the church to its objective status in Christ, God calls the church to become who it is, a *koinonia* of divine and human action. That is, divine action and human action commune in the earthly-historical form of Jesus Christ, the church, in the present tense of reconciliation. By a miracle of grace, the church, the communion of saints and the communion of sinners, lives at the intersection and interpenetration of divine and human action. Barth writes: "[T]he true church truly is and arises and continues and lives in the twofold sense that God is at work and that there is a human work which He occasions and fashions" (*CD* IV/2, p. 616). It is crucial to remember that, while the church is the earthly-historical form of Jesus Christ, it is not a surrogate for Christ. Its life-act does not halt the work of Christ through the Spirit in the world. Divine action is sovereign and free. While the church has no ontological status outside of Christ, Christ is not bound solely to the church. His mission continues outside the church. "[The church's] sending is not a repetition, extension or continuation. His own sending does not cease as He sends it. . . . Its sending is simply ordered on its own lower level in relation to His" (*CD* IV/3.2, p. 768).

The *koinonia* of divine and human action in the church follows the

9. Hunsinger, *How to Read Karl Barth,* p. 186.

same patterns as the *koinonia* of the incarnation — correspondence and coinherence (anhypostasis/enhypostasis). Through ecclesial practices the church corresponds to Christ and participates in Christ. As the Son corresponds to the Father, so the church is called to correspond to Christ. It is called to witness to Christ in word and deed. In witness, the church mirrors John the Baptist in Matthias Grunewald's famous portrait of the crucifixion. John points toward the crucified Christ, directing the gaze of all away from himself, decreasing so that Christ can increase. Further, as the Son indwells the Father, so the church indwells the Son; and through the Son the church is united to the Father by means of the Holy Spirit. The church participates in the life of God. It participates in Jesus' ongoing ministry of communion-creating reconciliation in the world. The church is dialectically included in Christ. Its identity is dialectical: "I Not-I But-Christ."[10] In a limited sense, therefore, the church mediates divine action when it lives out its *koinonia*.[11] Consider the following statements from Barth:

- Jesus Christ is "the One who is primarily and properly at work in every human work" (*CD* IV/2, p. 633). He works in and through the church.
- "He that hears us, hears me." The church is "the environment of the man Jesus . . . the centre and medium of communication between Jesus and the world" (*CD* IV/2, p. 658).
- The church "surrounds" Jesus in his prophetic work in the world (*CD* II/2, p. 239).
- The celebration of the Lord's Supper "is His [Christ's] own action; the work of His real presence. Here and now He Himself is for them — His offered body and His shed blood — the communion of saints thanking and confessing Him in this action" (*CD* IV/2, p. 658).

The church's correspondence to Christ and participation in Christ, that is, its witness and mediation, are qualitatively distinct from Christ's correspondence to and mediation of God. Herein lie the indissoluble differentiation and indestructible ordering of the *koinonia* of the

10. James E. Loder, *The Logic of the Spirit: Human Development in Theological Perspective* (San Francisco: Jossey-Bass, 1998), p. 120.

11. For a fuller argument about mediation as a form of ecclesial action, see George Hunsinger, *Disruptive Grace;* see also John Yocum, *Ecclesial Mediation in Karl Barth* (Aldershot, UK: Ashgate, 2004).

incarnation and the *koinonia* between Christ and the church. Christ's correspondence to the Father is perfect unto death. Christ's mediatorial work saves and liberates all humanity. In stark contrast, ecclesial practices are always tainted by sin. They do not save or liberate humanity. At best, they provide a means through which persons can encounter the living Christ and receive his gifts of faith, hope, and love. Nevertheless, through the work of the Spirit they can become a means of grace and thus no small thing in God's work of reconciliation unto *koinonia*.

To summarize: Barth posits room for human action in the divine economy of salvation. While this action is dependent on divine action, it is free. It also is noble in that it participates in the very life of God. And it is ecclesial. Divine action and human action come together in and often in spite of the church. When divine action and human action come together in ecclesial practice, they take two basic forms: witness and participation (or mediation). For this reason, we can say that witness and participation are two broad normative guidelines for the church's life and action in a neo-Barthian practical theology. All the church says and does should either witness to or participate in the ministry of the triune God for the sake of the world. Therefore, throughout this book I have spoken of the ministry of small groups and the ministry of the church in terms of witness and participation. This language makes it clear that the triune God is the preeminent and qualitatively distinct minister to the church and through the church to the world. The church and its members are ministers as their action corresponds to and mediates the *koinonia*-creating reconciliation of Christ. Their ministry is real and effective, though it is contingent on Trinitarian practice.

Interdisciplinary Interpretation of Divine and Human Action

Just as contemporary practical theologians reject Barth as a dialogue partner on the basis of a particular interpretation of his construal of divine and human action, they also assume that Barth's methodology allows no room for interdisciplinary dialogue. There is an assumption that Barth's rejection of natural theology necessitates a rejection of other forms of knowledge.[12] In contrast, a neo-Barthian practical theology assumes that Barth's clarity about the distinctiveness of theology

12. See Browning, *Fundamental Practical Theology,* p. 45.

actually provides solid ground for interdisciplinary dialogue, even if Barth himself did not engage in such dialogue or construct a method for doing so.

To begin with, Barth's rejection of natural theology asserts that knowledge of God cannot be derived solely from orders of creation, human experience, or religious consciousness. Rather, knowledge of God is a gift granted to humanity in and through Jesus Christ. However, this does not mean that Barth rejected the idea that truth, even truth about God, could be discovered outside the church. As George Hunsinger explains, two general rules of Barth's later theology are the coexistence and coinherence of Christ and all reality. Nothing is to be conceived as existing except together with Christ, and nothing is to be conceived that does not coinhere with Jesus Christ, and vice versa. All humanity participates in the humanity of Jesus Christ by virtue of the incarnation. Since Jesus exists in and with the Father by means of the Spirit, all humanity coexists with the triune God. God and humanity, indeed God and all creation, are dialectically included in one another. Therefore, truth — even theological truth — can be found in sources outside the church. "Barth believes that, despite the human mind's being fallen and corrupted from its integrity, truth is still to be found and admired in writers ignorant of or hostile toward the Gospel."[13] As I have noted above, this means that societal practice may be more faithful to the gospel than ecclesial practice. If so, it has the status of a "secular parable of the truth," a witness to the Light.

> Secular parables will be recognized by the fact that they drive the community "more truly and profoundly than ever before to Scripture." ... They will not contradict but illumine, will not denigrate but accentuate, the biblical word, opening it up for the community in a new way and for a particular situation. They will always encourage the community in the execution of its sometimes dispiriting task.[14]

Barth conceptualizes secular parables, the church's ministry of Word and sacrament, Scripture, and Jesus Christ in a series of four concentric spheres. Jesus Christ, the Word and work of God, stands at the center of these spheres. Scripture witnesses to Jesus Christ. In its ministry of Word and sacrament, the church witnesses to Jesus Christ. And

13. Hunsinger, *How to Read Karl Barth,* p. 234.
14. Hunsinger, *How to Read Karl Barth,* p. 255.

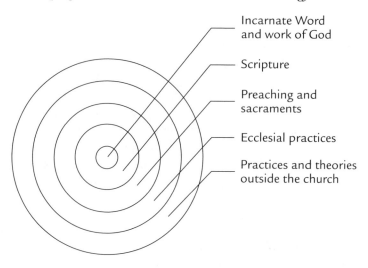

Incarnate Word and work of God

Scripture

Preaching and sacraments

Ecclesial practices

Practices and theories outside the church

through secular parables, the world witnesses to Jesus Christ. All these forms of witness depend on divine action. Only on the basis of the grace of God in and through the work of the Spirit can Scripture, the preached Word, baptism, the Eucharist, or any other practice point to Jesus Christ. Following Barth's depiction of the church's ministries of speech and action (see *CD* IV/3.2, pp. 865-901), I would add another sphere that includes ecclesial practices other than Word and sacrament (see diagram above). By adding this sphere, I am maintaining a distinction between sacraments, which from a Reformed perspective are ordinances of God, and other ecclesial practices that have not been instituted by God in the same sense. Ecclesial practices may function similarly to other means of grace by the Word and Spirit of God, but they are not promised as such by God.

Barth's description of secular parables of the truth opens up the possibility of interdisciplinary dialogue from a Barthian perspective. Insights from other disciplines can witness to Jesus Christ. They can critique theology, not on the basis of external validity claims but rather on the basis of their faithfulness to God's revelation of true humanity in Jesus Christ.[15] At the same time, such a critique would not mean

15. Here a neo-Barthian practical theology would be distinct from Don Browning's proposal for practical theology in which five validity claims adjudicate the dialogue between theology and nontheological resources. See Don S. Browning and Terry Cooper, *Religious Thought and Modern Psychologies,* 2nd ed. (Minneapolis: Augsburg Fortress, 2004).

that theology relinquishes its particular subject matter (God) and methods of study (critical reflection on God's self-revelation). Elsewhere Barth writes: "The 'place' of theology . . . will be determined by the impetus which it receives from within its own domain and from its own *object*. Its object — the philanthropic God Himself — is the law which must be the continual starting point of theology."[16] Theology does not begin with alien philosophical, psychological, or anthropological presuppositions; nor should it be "forced into any alien scheme" (*CD* IV/3.2, p. 839). It focuses on God's chosen means of self-revelation — the living Word of God present in the power of the Holy Spirit and the biblical witness as interpreted throughout church history and heard anew in the present. Barth says:

> Theology can be only theologically defined. Theology is science seeking the knowledge of the Word of God spoken in God's work — science learning in the school of Holy Scripture, which witnesses to the Word of God; science laboring in the quest for truth, which is inescapably required of the community that is called by the Word of God. . . . [I]t depends actually upon God's living Word, on God's chosen eyewitnesses, and on the existence of God's people in the world.[17]

In this regard, a neo-Barthian practical theology diverges from other models. Consider Gerben Heitink's model: "All branches of theology borrow their methodology from other fields of inquiry."[18] If this is the case, practical theology potentially loses its distinctively theological center. Neo-Barthian practical theology seeks to maintain a theological identity in at least two ways: (1) by studying divine action as witnessed to in Scripture, interpreted throughout the Christian tradition, and at work today in and in spite of the church; and (2) by granting priority to divine action over human action in ecclesial practice. In other words, neo-Barthian practical theology seeks to conform ecclesial practice to Trinitarian practice on the basis of Jesus Christ, God's Word of revelation and communion-creating work of reconciliation.

Even if the insights of other disciplines do not witness to Jesus

16. Karl Barth, *Evangelical Theology: An Introduction* (Grand Rapids: Eerdmans, 1963), p. 16.

17. Barth, *Evangelical Theology*, p. 50.

18. Gerben Heitink, *Practical Theology: History, Theory, Action Domains* (Grand Rapids: Eerdmans, 1999), p. 102.

Christ and thereby function as secular parables of the truth, they still may be valuable, even necessary, dialogue partners in a neo-Barthian practical theology. Since the object of a neo-Barthian practical theology is divine and human action within three forms of practice — Trinitarian, ecclesial, and societal — it must be interdisciplinary, incorporating insights from those disciplines that study and interpret human action (theology and nontheological sciences) and those that study and interpret divine action (theology). Though its task is not that of anthropology, sociology, psychology, or any other natural science, a neo-Barthian practical theology can (and often does) discover common cause with these other disciplines. It may accompany them from within its domain without forfeiting its central purpose to assist the church in carrying out its mission. Barth insists that the church cannot be light for any other reality demanding to be recognized or supported. It may accompany other causes, which may deserve the church's zealous attention, but it cannot make these causes its own cause. It cannot add another purpose alongside its ministry of attesting Christ. It cannot serve two different lords. It must not squander its time and energy (*CD* IV/3.2, pp. 837-38).

Having justified the appropriateness and even necessity of interdisciplinary dialogue in a neo-Barthian practical theology, we are left with the question of how exactly to relate interpretations of divine action and human action in ecclesial practice. How do theology and other sciences relate to each other as they interpret ecclesial practice?

As delineated above, Barth orders divine action and human action according to the parameters of the Chalcedonian pattern. Divine action and human action in ecclesial practice conform to divine action and human action in the life of Jesus Christ. This same Chalcedonian pattern has been transposed by two contemporary practical theologians, James Loder and Deborah van Deusen Hunsinger, as a model for interdisciplinary dialogue.[19] In this model, theology and psychology (or any other discipline) are related "without separation or division (inseparable unity)," "without confusion or change (indissoluble differentiation)," and with an "asymmetrical ordering (indestructible order)." It is important to note that in interdisciplinary dialogue, the Chalcedonian pattern does not describe an ontological union as it does in the *koinonia* relationships. When applied to the incarnation or to ecclesial

19. Loder, *Logic of the Spirit;* van Deusen Hunsinger, *Pastoral Counseling.*

practice, the Chalcedonian pattern describes the contours of the *koinonia* of divine and human action. When utilized to relate theological and nontheological concepts or practices, it functions as a pattern (not an actual ontological union) that describes the relevance of particular concepts and thought forms to one another.

To explain further: "without separation" (inseparable unity) means that psychological, sociological, and theological interpretations are relevant to any practice, situation, or context being interpreted. The neo-Barthian practical theology in this book demonstrates the inseparable unity of psychology, sociology, and theology. All three disciplines contribute to our understanding of the role of small groups in supporting the mission of the church in North America today. This book also demonstrates how psychological, sociological, and theological realities interpenetrate and reciprocally influence one another. We have seen how the crisis of community (a sociological reality) creates anxiety and destabilizes ontological security (a psychological reality) just as it points toward the larger reality of *koinonia* (a theological reality). By indwelling the distinct but related perspectives of psychology, sociology, and theology, I have constructed a multidisciplinary definition of ontological security and guidelines for the healing ministry of the church and its small groups.

"Without confusion" (indissoluble differentiation) indicates that different disciplinary interpretations of an ecclesial practice are "logically diverse; they have different aims, subject matters, methods, and linguistic conventions."[20] The language and concepts of psychology, sociology, and theology must maintain their own integrity. Reductionist interpretations are eschewed. Theology is not translated into psychology or sociology — or vice versa. Again, consider ontological security as defined in this book. Sociology, psychology, and theology contributed uniquely to our understanding of ontological security without being subsumed by each other. *Koinonia* was not conceived as being synonymous with or interchangeable with ontological security defined psychosocially. "Without confusion" also means that each discipline's normative criteria are generated internally, that is, within their respective disciplines, so that, as van Deusen Hunsinger explains, theology cannot interfere with the proper functioning of psychology or sociology. Theology cannot tell us, for instance, whether small-group

20. Van Deusen Hunsinger, *Pastoral Counseling*, p. 6.

practice is a functional or dysfunctional psychosocial antidote to the crisis of community. Conversely, sociology and psychology cannot determine normative criteria for *koinonia*. Theology alone can do that.

"Asymmetry" means that logical precedence is given to theology because it is a more comprehensive discipline. While the social sciences interpret the penultimate realm, theology alone addresses the ultimate questions of human existence. It alone has as its object the triune God. Therefore, I have argued throughout this book that empirical research on small groups cannot tell us what small groups *should* do. Empirical research alone does not answer the question, How can small groups participate in and witness to the work of Jesus Christ in our world? Asymmetry also means that social-scientific concepts can function as analogies for theological concepts. They are both similar and dissimilar to theological concepts. They point to and illuminate larger theological realities, because their ultimate meaning lies in a theological context.[21] Ontological security defined from the perspective of object-relations theory functioned as an analogy for *koinonia* in chapter 6. The significance of the mother's face as depicted in object-relations theory pointed us toward the significance of the face of God in Jesus Christ. Viewing the bond between mother and child in the earliest months of life illuminates the love of God, who is both mother and father to us. Because the relationship is analogous, our mother's face is both similar and dissimilar to God's face. In the best of circumstances, both convey delight, joy, and acceptance. Yet our mother's face goes away; God's does not. The face of God in Jesus Christ provides for us all that our mother's face never could. This is what it means to suggest that the face of God in Jesus provides the ultimate context for understanding the significance of the mother's face in early childhood.

---

21. Van Deusen Hunsinger demonstrates the use of the Chalcedonian pattern by relating the theological concepts of sin and salvation and the psychological concepts of neurosis and healing. The "inseparable unity" of sin and neurosis exists in the fact that freedom from sin, i.e., salvation, ultimately includes freedom from neurosis, i.e., healing. The "indissoluble differentiation" between the two sets of concepts is maintained by delineating the differences between the plight of the sinner and that of the victim. The "indestructible ordering" of the concepts means that the healing of neurosis has penultimate significance while salvation from sin has ultimate significance. Viewed from the perspective of faith, healing points toward the greater and qualitatively distinct actuality of salvation, which in its ultimate form — that is, in the *eschaton* — includes physical and psychological healing (*Pastoral Counseling*, pp. 65-69).

Asymmetry does not mean that theology has ontological superiority over any other disciplines. Theology is a human, finite, and frequently flawed endeavor. At its best, it witnesses to Jesus Christ, the Word and work of God. Like other ecclesial practices, it exists in one of the outer spheres that potentially point to Christ. As human reflection on and response to the Word and Spirit of God, theology (or, more accurately, the theologian) is put to death and resurrected, again and again, by Jesus Christ. Barth writes: "As a human concern for truth, it recognizes its solidarity with other such concerns now grouped under the name of science. It protests against the idea of an ontological exaltation above them. . . . It remembers that it is only a science and therefore that it is secular even as it works in its own relatively special way and in the highest of spheres" (*CD* I/1, p. 11).

In summary, social-scientific concepts influence a neo-Barthian practical theology in numerous ways. At the simplest level, insights from social science help translate theological norms into pragmatic guidelines for ecclesial and societal practices, as demonstrated in my use of Giddens's theory of modernization and Wuthnow's empirical research of small groups. Second, social-scientific concepts may be analogies for theological concepts. The social sciences may prompt deeper comprehension of theological analogues, as demonstrated in my use of object-relations theory and aspects of modernization theory to define ontological security. Third, concepts and theories from the social sciences may function as secular parables of truth by interpreting reality in a more faithful way than the church (and its academic theologians) at a given moment in time.[22] In such instances, social sciences admonish the church — and hence practical theologians — to return to the resources of the Christian tradition and uncover what has been lost, repressed, or never fully developed. Fourth, social-scientific research methods can assist us in constructing thick, nuanced descriptions of practices, situations, and contexts, as I will demonstrate in the next section.

---

22. Though a full argument is beyond the scope of this book, I have hinted in chap. 6 and in this conclusion that object-relations theory may function as a secular parable of *koinonia*. For a full explication of object-relations theory in conversation with Karl Barth's theological anthropology, see Daniel J. Price, *Karl Barth's Anthropology in Light of Modern Thought* (Grand Rapids: Eerdmans, 2002).

Empirical Research in a Neo-Barthian Practical Theology

A neo-Barthian practical theology critically reflects on and interprets three forms of action (or, practice) — societal action, ecclesial action, and Trinitarian action — with the goal of reforming current church life and ministry (ecclesial practice) according to the life-act of God (Trinitarian practice) for the sake of the world (societal practice). The four operations of practical theology — descriptive-empirical, interpretive, normative, and pragmatic — moved us toward that goal in this book. The empirical-descriptive task focused primarily (but not exclusively) on investigating ecclesial action, specifically the practice of small groups. Yet it also sought to discern *signs of* divine action and societal action in these small groups. What I am suggesting is that signs of Trinitarian practice and signs of the crisis of community can be discerned through empirical research. To claim that a neo-Barthian practical theology seeks to discern divine action partially through empirical investigation might sound contradictory or logically incoherent. Is it possible to be committed to both Barthian theological methods and empirical research methods? Yes — if the researcher maintains distinctions between divine action and *signs of* divine action; if the researcher chooses empirical methods that uphold the humanity of those under investigation; and if the researcher proceeds in prayerful humility.

Signs of Divine Action

Trinitarian practice, that is, divine action, can be discerned at the descriptive-empirical moment of practical theology, because (1) God has chosen to reveal Godself to humanity, and (2) God's work is simultaneously "historically complete, completely contemporaneous, and completely future" (*CD* II/1, p. 262). The incarnation of the second person of the Trinity is the self-revelation of God. "Nothing essential of God's identity ever needs to be sought elsewhere, Barth argues, than in Jesus Christ, God's definitive, final, and binding act of self-revelation."[23] God's being *ad extra,* in relation to humanity, is no different than God's being *ad intra,* within the Trinity. On the basis of the

---

23. Hunsinger, *How to Read Karl Barth,* p. 37.

former, we can, by faith, make positive assertions about the latter.[24] In other words, "God is who He is in His works" (*CD* II/1, p. 260). The work of God in Christ, summarized by the one word "reconciliation," is the revelation of God's being. Jesus Christ is the Word and work of God, the Word of revelation who works reconciliation for the purpose of establishing *koinonia* between God and humankind, among humans irrespective of sociological descriptors, and between humankind and all creation. Thus the origin and *telos* of human existence and of the church's vocation is multidimensional *koinonia*.

In the here and now, the body of Christ experiences, albeit imperfectly, reconciliation and the concomitant creation of *koinonia* as the Holy Spirit awakens it to faith, quickens it to love, and empowers it to hope — or, to put it differently, as the church fulfills its vocation. While not fully manifest or realized in daily life, Jesus Christ through the Holy Spirit gives the church faith, which opens our eyes to this objective, ontological reality of life in multidimensional *koinonia*. Barth writes: "Faith does not realise anything new. It does not invent anything. It simply finds that which is already there for the believer and also for the unbeliever. It is simply man's active decision for it, his acceptance of it, his active participation in it" (*CD* IV/2, p. 742). Eyes of faith see not only the work of God in the past, in the life, death, and burial of Jesus Christ, but also the work of God in Christ in the present. For the living God encounters humanity anew daily.

Because *koinonia* is not yet fully realized in the existential moment of salvation, that is, in the present, we only see indicators or signs of *koinonia*, analogues of this ontological reality in our life together. Barth writes: "What [the church] is, its mystery, its spiritual character, is not without manifestations and analogies in its generally visible form. But it is not unequivocally represented in any such generally visible manifestations and analogies" (*CD* IV/1, p. 657). It shines forth "in the power of the Holy Spirit" and in spite of its members' sin and brokenness. "This takes place only as we can see and read the dark letters of an electric sign when the current is passed through it" (*CD* IV/2, p. 619). In other words, *koinonia*, not as a fully realized actuality but rather as an in-breaking, transforming actuality, can be discerned in, through, and in spite of the church.

Consequently, my empirical investigation intentionally sought to

24. Hunsinger, *How to Read Karl Barth*, pp. 35-39, 76-151.

discern signs of *koinonia* in small-group ministries. I looked for evidence of *koinonia* with Christ in the practice of confession, *koinonia* among group members in the practice of self-giving love, and *koinonia* with the world in witnessing to and practicing solidarity with others outside the group. With regard to the operations of practical theology, the normative moment influenced the descriptive-empirical moment. This points again to the fact that the four tasks of practical theology interpenetrate each other. The movement from one task to another is circular rather than linear or stage-like.

Prayerfully Upholding the Humanity of the Other

It is possible to be committed to aspects of Barth's theological method and certain empirical methods if the empirical methods prayerfully uphold the humanity of those under investigation. For Barth, all theological work begins, continues, and ends in prayer.[25] It requires an entreaty that the theologian's "blind eyes and deaf ears may be opened, that he may be permitted to do and hear God's work and word . . . that God's work and word may not be withdrawn, but may, instead, be disclosed to the eyes and ears of this man."[26] In the empirical operation, the practical theologian prays to see signs of God's hidden work in the lives of those who have willingly opened themselves to her inquiring gaze. So that she might serve the church, the practical theologian invokes the Holy Spirit:

> The eye of God between me and each eye,
> The purpose of God between me and each purpose,
> The hand of God between me and each hand,
> The desire of God between me and each desire.[27]

In this context of prayer, the neo-Barthian practical theologian constructs a research design that respects the dignity and otherness of those under investigation. The empirical operation of this practical theological project has relied primarily on qualitative-research design

---

25. Barth, *Evangelical Theology*, pp. 159-70.

26. Barth, *Evangelical Theology*, p. 169.

27. Saint Patrick, *The Eye of God*, quoted in Deborah van Deusen Hunsinger, *Pray Without Ceasing: Revitalizing Pastoral Care* (Grand Rapids: Eerdmans, 2006), pp. 10-12.

strategies (as I have delineated in Appendix A).[28] By definition, qualitative research permits open, nondirected, and thus potentially truer-to-life input. Michael Patton observes: "Qualitative data describe. They take us, as readers, into the time and place of the observation so that we know what it was like to have been there. They capture and communicate someone else's experience of the world in his or her own words."[29] The researcher takes an active role in qualitative inquiry. She physically and psychologically immerses herself in the lived world of the observed. "The inquirer gets close to the people under study through physical proximity for a period of time *as well as* through development of closeness in the social sense of shared experience, empathy, and confidentiality."[30]

Qualitative research potentially places the researcher and those researched in an I-thou relationship that changes both parties. In this case, that method has allowed small-group members to remain indissolubly "subject." For Barth, true humanity is cohumanity, and cohumanity involves mutual seeing, mutual speech and hearing, rendering mutual assistance, and doing it all with gratitude. "To take the Thou seriously is to be concerned for the Thou in self-expression and self-declaration" (*CD* III/2, p. 254). Therefore, from a Barthian perspective, the researcher and the researched exist in a relationship in which both subjects are simultaneously open and closed to each

---

28. In recent decades, qualitative research has been adapted by a variety of academic disciplines, yielding a vast array of qualitative research strategies. Michael Patton lists sixteen qualitative strategies, each emerging from particular disciplines and theoretical commitments (*Qualitative Research and Evaluation Methods*, 3rd ed. [Thousand Oaks, CA: Sage Publications, 2002]). While Patton argues that research strategies should be adapted to a project's core questions in a pragmatic way, others argue that strategies of inquiry be chosen in light of their underlying philosophical biases. See John Creswell, *Research Design: Qualitative, Quantitative, and Mixed Methods Approaches*, 2nd ed. (Thousand Oaks, CA: Sage Publications, 2003). The argument of Patton and Creswell can be seen as analogous to Don Browning's contention that each school of psychology projects its own "horizon of meaning" or "vision of ultimacy." Browning argues that practical theologians dialogue with these theories, comparing their inherent visions of ultimacy, perceptions of human needs and tendencies, etc., with those set forth by the Christian tradition. While such dialogue between the philosophical underpinnings of sixteen traditions of inquiry and Barth's theology is far beyond the scope of this project, it is possible to suggest that qualitative research (as a paradigm) has the potential to uphold the humanity of those researched and thereby cohere with Barth's theological anthropology.

29. Patton, *Qualitative Research*, p. 45.

30. Patton, *Qualitative Research*, p. 48.

other.[31] Though the experiences and subjective meanings of small-group members can be known, they remain, at another level, inaccessible to the researcher. The other is a mystery that needs to be respected, and the other sets limits on the researcher. The other places a claim on the researcher, a claim for full and accurate representation, a claim for humanization, a claim for advocacy. When the researcher is a theologian and the researched is the community of faith, the claim is even more pronounced. There is no neutral research: the researcher must always be concerned with upholding and promoting the humanity of the other. Barth writes:

> [The being of the other] poses questions which must be answered. And there are answers for which it asks. I am in encounter with the other who is in the same way as I am. I am under the conditions imposed by this encounter. . . . [T]here is no line of retreat to a place where I exist neutrally for him, where I do not affect him, where I do not owe him anything, where I with my being and positing do not have to take account of his. (*CD* III/2, pp. 246-47)

Consequently, to speak about another as if he is merely an object — instead of speaking to and with him — is a violation. It deforms both the researcher and the researched, moving them from an I-Thou cohumanity to an I-it form of inhumanity. In contrast to an I-it relationship, I-Thou relationality places a demand on both me and Thee. As Barth says, "Everything that happens or does not happen in the life of this people directly concerns the theologian; whether it happens in one way or another, well or ill, it becomes inexorably his concern."[32]

Given this conviction and my own vocation as theologian and pastor, I could not carry out the research as neutrally as a social scientist might. As I discovered, the small-group members did not expect me to do so either. For example, during an observation, I was called on to offer my opinion in a youth small group. Amanda told the group that many new questions were emerging from changes in her religious beliefs. She was comforted when a friend at school encouraged her to "live your questions." Another group member, Jenny, was alarmed by this advice: she suggested instead that the Bible clearly prescribes par-

31. See Ray S. Anderson, *On Being Human: Essays in Theological Anthropology* (Pasadena, CA: Fuller Seminary Press, 1982).
32. Barth, *Evangelical Theology,* p. 81.

ticular beliefs and ethical behaviors. The rest of the group chimed in along similar lines. Finally, the group leader turned to me and asked, "You're a pastor. What do you think?" I was actually being requested to join their deliberations, which no doubt was a consequence of the rapport established already among us. I self-consciously took the opportunity to not only offer input on the role of doubt in the Christian faith but also to affirm the basic humanity of a vibrant young woman.

Conclusion

In this brief excursus, I have presented a neo-Barthian practical theology. I have not defined practical theology as Barth defines it. I have gone beyond Barth, while maintaining certain Barthian commitments, such as the uniqueness of theology, the comprehensiveness of theology, the *telos* of theology as service to the church, and the dependence of theology on the work of the Holy Spirit. To understand the relationship between divine action and human action in ecclesial practice on the one hand, and societal practice on the other, I have drawn on Barth's implicit theology of *koinonia*. *Koinonia* describes the nature of the relationship between divine action and human action: they exist in intimacy and integrity, with human action contingent on and responsive to divine action. *Koinonia* also describes the formal contours of the relationship between interpretations of divine action and interpretations of human action from theology and nontheological resources. Theology and nontheological resources exist in unity, differentiation, and order. Yet, because all things coexist with and coinhere in Jesus Christ, practices and theories arising outside the church may faithfully witness to the reality of *koinonia*. In these instances, God uses societal practice to admonish ecclesial practice toward faithful living. For this reason, the neo-Barthian practical theologian is open to wisdom from many sources, knowing that God is the one who redeems both theology and its nontheological dialogue partners.

Empirical Research Methodology

Given the sociological and theological ambiguities of small groups, their overwhelming presence within congregations, and the inability of prior research to answer the normative question — that is, What should be happening in small groups? — I carried out empirical research of well-developed small-group ministries in six congregations. I explored the understanding of group members and leaders of their connections within their groups, with the congregation, with other communities, and with God. The purpose of this investigation was summative evaluation. "Summative evaluations . . . render an overall judgment about the effectiveness of a program, policy, or product for the purpose of saying that the evaluand (thing being evaluated) is or is not effective and, therefore, should or should not be continued, and has or does not have the potential of being generalizable to other situations."[1]

In general, my research design was action-oriented and exploratory. It was action-oriented in that it sought to discern the nature of three types of action: divine action (Trinitarian practice), ecclesial action (small-group practice), and societal action (sociological dynamics of late modernity). It was exploratory in the limits of its investigation (i.e., well-developed small groups in six congregations) and in its potential to refine and pose new research questions. In regard to the latter, questions emerging within the empirical research included: What can

---

1. Michael Patton, *Qualitative Research and Evaluation Methods,* 3rd ed. (Thousand Oaks, CA: Sage Publications, 2002), p. 213.

small groups accomplish? Which ecclesial practices are clustered in small groups? Which ecclesial practices are best left to other aspects of congregational-ministry design? Perhaps most interestingly, indications of a distinct niche of congregations — mainline evangelicals — emerged in my research (see Appendix B).

More specifically, my empirical research was guided by previous small-group research (e.g., Robert Wuthnow's national small-group study, as well as case studies presented by Robert Putnam and Anne Marie Minnick) and the interpretive categories that emerged from my analysis of it: connection to God, connections within the group, and connection to the self. Building on these categories, my core research questions included the following: How do members of well-developed small groups in congregations understand and experience connection with God? Connection with their small group(s)? Connection to other communities, such as religious bodies, places of employment, and neighborhoods? Parallel to Minnick's research, the connection to self emerged in this investigation as an important function of small groups related to community formation.

I defined "well-developed small-group ministries" as those fulfilling three of Wuthnow's and Putnam's suggestions for reforming small groups: those with explicit mission statements, leadership training, and intentional organization within a congregation's ministry design. In order to identify small-group ministries that fit these criteria, I used "purposeful sampling," in which "cases for study (e.g., people, organizations, communities, cultures, events, critical incidences) are selected because they are 'information rich' and illuminative, that is, they offer useful manifestations of the phenomenon of interest."[2] I limited my sample to small groups within Presbyterian Church (USA) congregations and Reformed Church in America (RCA) congregations. I expected to discover an affinity between the practices of these groups and Wuthnow's guidelines, given his current affiliation with a Presbyterian congregation. Groups embedded in other theological traditions — Eastern Orthodoxy or Roman Catholicism, for example — likely would conceptualize and practice community in other ways. Second, I wanted to explore whether or not core principles of Reformed ecclesiology (e.g., the primacy of the church over the individual and the church's transformational stance with regard to culture) filter down into the

2. Patton, *Qualitative Research,* p. 40.

practice of PCUSA and RCA small groups. Third, from an empirical standpoint, studying congregations within the same tradition limited the number of dependent variables. Finally, in order to test provisionally for "generalizability," I included in my sample certain distinctions. The six small-group ministries have divergent levels of training, organizational structure, and mission-development strategies. The congregations exhibit a wide range of active membership (from 250 to 1200 members), and they are situated in different socioeconomic contexts (ranging from an upper-middle-class suburban community to an urban, predominantly blue-collar community).

The strategy of inquiry was mixed methods. I obtained quantitative data from Robert Wuthnow's 1991 small groups survey, the 1998 National Congregations Study, and a miniature survey administered to representatives from each congregation's small-group ministry (see below for a copy of the survey). The survey elicited demographic information about individual small-group participants as well as the groups qua groups. It acquired group members' and leaders' assessment of group diversity — racial, gender, socioeconomic, and age. The survey also inquired about group activities, which contributed to my definition of small groups as a "cluster of practices."[3] Moreover, the survey supplemented qualitative data regarding group members' and leaders' perceptions of how group participation has shaped various dimensions of their faith, for example, their personal piety, interpersonal relationships, congregational participation, and witness. In order to facilitate comparison with Wuthnow's extensive research of general small groups, the survey included three questions (questions 20-22) from his survey.[4] I adapted one of these (question 20) to include three other practices significant to the Reformed faith: confession of sin, celebration of communion, and discussion of Reformed theology.

My exploratory research depended heavily on qualitative-design strategies, which gather descriptive data through interviews, observations, and written documents. Not only does qualitative-research design honor the humanity of the observed; it also permits analysis of the processes of human interaction, which — especially in the case of small groups — shape social reality more than content. It also openly ac-

---

3. See Robert Wuthnow, *Sharing the Journey: Support Groups and America's New Quest for Community* (New York: The Free Press, 1994), esp. chap. 3, pp. 33, 35.

4. See Wuthnow, *Sharing the Journey*.

knowledges the unavoidable influence of the researcher on his or her observations and interpretations. The researcher's prior experience and theoretical constructs color even observation and description. My personal and professional involvement with small groups undoubtedly influenced my observations and even my prior interpretation of small groups as ambiguous. Nevertheless, I strove to take a stance of "empathic neutrality," for instance, by bracketing theological judgment of group content and asking instead, "What is the meaning of this idea about God for the group? How does it function in the lives of group members?"[5]

In each congregation, I conducted two or three focus-group interviews and anywhere from three to eight individual interviews. One focus group consisted of small-group leaders, and the others consisted of small-group members. Focus-group interviews enabled me to observe relational patterns among group participants. As noted by Krueger and Casey, interviewees in focus groups generally influence one another, encourage self-disclosure, and provide an internal corrective to any extreme views, which would potentially skew data analysis.[6] (See Appendix B for the focus-group interview guides.) I interviewed small-group members who were unable to attend the focus groups due to scheduling conflicts. I interviewed pastors and staff regarding the history, leadership training, and community formation of small groups in their respective congregations. This design enabled multilevel analysis, that is, among the three types of interviewees (staff, group leaders, and group members) within the same congregation and among the six congregations.[7]

In order to compare and contrast well-developed groups with groups in general, I included in the interviews a series of questions about the shape of community, that is, questions about the depth of personal sharing in the group, the presence or absence of diversity, and the suppression-versus-acknowledgment of disagreement and conflict. In the first set of interviews, I discovered, as did Wuthnow, that group members and leaders use the word "accountability" to describe rela-

---

5. Patton writes: "Empathy . . . describes a stance toward the people one encounters — it communicates understanding, interest, and caring. Neutrality suggests a stance toward their thoughts, emotions and behaviors — it means being nonjudgmental" (*Qualitative Research,* p. 53).

6. Richard A. Krueger and Mary Anne Casey, *Focus Groups: A Practical Guide for Applied Research,* 3rd ed. (Thousand Oaks, CA: Sage Publications, 2000), p. 8.

7. Krueger and Casey describe this as "double layer design" (*Focus Groups,* p. 32).

tionships among participants. Therefore, subsequent interviews added the questions, "How does the group hold its members accountable? For what things/issues are you accountable to each other?"

Finally, I supplemented the focus-group and individual interviews with document analysis and (minimal) participant observation. The participant observation included attendance at four small groups, a half-day leadership-training seminar, and a two-day church leadership workshop. I collected the following documents: small-group training materials, such as curricula, email documents, and handouts for leaders; printed promotions of small groups in church bulletins and newsletters; books written by their respective pastors; and copies of small-group Bible studies.

Appendix A

Interview Guide for Small-Group Leaders

Introduction

In our time together, I'd like us to focus our discussion on three topics: (1) the purpose of your small group(s); (2) the preparation needed to become a small-group leader at _name of church_ ; and (3) the kinds of relationships formed in your group(s). I'd like to begin with some brief introductions.

1. Could you tell me your name and what group(s) you are leading right now?
2. Let's say that I'm a newcomer to your group this week. Walk me through your group meeting. Describe what happens in the group and how much time the group spends on each activity.

Integration of Small-Group Mission

Now that I know the variety of small groups you are leading, it would be helpful to know about the purpose, or mission, of each of these groups.

1. If you could sum it up in a few sentences, what would you say is the purpose of your group(s)?
2. Some of the purposes you mentioned are . . . . How do you know if the group is fulfilling these purposes? [Probe: For example, how do you know if group members are growing spiritually?]
3. What do you think are the reasons for people to join small groups here at _name of church_ ?

Leadership Training

I'd like now to shift our conversation to talk about the specifics of the training you received to become a small-group leader at your church.

1. What topics were covered in your training?
2. What skills did you learn in your training?
3. What parts of the training were most beneficial to you?
4. What do you wish you had received more training in?

Multidimensional Community in Small Groups

1. Communion with God:
   a. How do group members "connect" with God?
   b. What kinds of images or phrases does your group use to talk about God?
   c. What do you hope people learn about God in your small group?
2. Community within the group:
   a. What kinds of personal things do group members share with each other in the group?
   b. What kinds of differences exist among group members?
   c. What causes disagreement or conflict in your group?
   d. What happens in the group when people disagree?
   e. Groups are never perfect. What do you wish was different about the relationships within your group?
3. Connection to other communities:
   a. Does your group do anything together outside of your regular meeting time? If so, what?
   b. Does your group discuss "problems" or "issues" in society?
   c. How do you think being in the group changes the way people live out their daily lives?

Conclusion

We've covered a lot in our short time together. Your input has helped me better understand small-group leadership here at *name of church* . Is there anything that you'd like me to know that I haven't asked about or that you didn't get a chance to share?

Interview Guide for Small-Group Members

Introduction

In our time together, I'd like us to focus our discussion on how your small group has influenced your relationships with God, with others in the group, and with those outside of the group. I'd like to begin with some brief introductions.

1. Could you tell me your name, what group(s) you participate in right now, and how long you've been a member of this group (or groups)?
2. Suppose that I'm a newcomer to your group this week. Walk me through your group meeting. Describe what happens in the group and how much time the group spends on each activity.
3. What do you consider to be the purpose of your group(s)?

Community within the Group

1. What kinds of personal things do group members share with each other in the group?
2. What kinds of differences exist among group members? Differences in religious beliefs? Political perspectives? Differences in age, race, socioeconomic status?
3. What, if anything, causes disagreement or conflict in your group?
4. What happens in the group when people disagree?
5. How do you feel about relationships among group members?
6. Groups are never perfect. What do you wish was different about the relationships within your group?
7. How has the group helped you personally?

Connection with God

1. How does your group "connect" with God?
2. What kinds of images or phrases does your group use to talk about God?
3. How has being in this small group affected your understanding of God? Your relationship with God?

Community Outside the Group

Many people talk about how being in the group has influenced their relationships outside the group. For example, some people say being in the group has helped their relationships at home or at work. Some say that they've become involved in other church activities. Still others say that they've become involved in their neighborhoods, in volunteering, in working for social justice.

1. How has the group affected your relationships with people outside of the group?
2. PROBE: As a result of being in this group, have you done any of the following?
   a. become involved in volunteer work in your community
   b. become more active in church programs
   c. worked with the group to help people outside the group
   d. become more interested in social and political issues
   e. changed your attitude on social or political issues
   f. become more interested in peace and justice
   g. donated money to a charitable organization
   h. increased the amount of money you give to your church

Conclusion

We've covered a lot in our short time together. Your input has helped me better understand small groups here at ___*name of church*___. Is there anything that you'd like me to know that I haven't asked about or that you didn't get a chance to share?

Appendix A

Small-Group Participants' Survey

Q-1: Name: _____

Q-2: Gender: ☐ MALE
☐ FEMALE

Q-3: Date of birth: _____

Q-4: Race: _____

Q-5: Occupation: _____

Q-6: Highest level of education completed:
☐ High School
☐ Some college
☐ College degree
☐ Graduate Degree
☐ Doctoral degree
☐ Other

Q-7: Phone: _____

Q-8: Email: _____

Q-9: Name of your congregation: _____
_____

Q-10: Which of the following small groups do you currently participate in? (check all that apply)

☐ Youth group   ☐ Bible study
☐ Singles group   ☐ Couples' group
☐ Men's group   ☐ Women's group
☐ Recovery group   ☐ 12-step group
☐ Self-help group   ☐ Prayer group
☐ Sunday school class
☐ Fellowship group
☐ Accountability group
☐ Political-action group
☐ Mission group/Ministry team
☐ Community outreach group

Q-11: How many small groups have you previously participated in?

_____

Q-12: How long (in years), if at all, have you been a small-group leader? _____

Q-13: How often, on average, does your group meet?
    ☐ Weekly
    ☐ Every two weeks
    ☐ Once/month
    ☐ Less than once/month
    ☐ Other _____

Q-14: How long does an average meeting of the group last?
    ☐ 1 hour
    ☐ 1.5 hours
    ☐ 2 hours
    ☐ More than 2 hours

Q-15: How many people usually attend the group? _____

Q-16: Are group participants:
    ☐ Mostly your age
    ☐ Mostly younger than you
    ☐ Mostly older than you
    ☐ Of all different ages
    ☐ Don't know

Q-17: Are group participants:
    ☐ All white
    ☐ Mostly white
    ☐ About even
    ☐ Mostly nonwhite
    ☐ All nonwhite

Q-18: Are group participants:
    ☐ All women
    ☐ Mostly women
    ☐ About even
    ☐ Mostly men
    ☐ All men

Q-19: Are group participants:

    ☐ About the same economic status as you

    ☐ Mostly wealthier than you

    ☐ Mostly less wealthy than you

    ☐ Of all different statuses

    ☐ Don't know

Q-20: Does your group do any of the following?

a.	Study or discuss the Bible	YES	NO
b.	Pray together	YES	NO
c.	Discuss religious topics	YES	NO
d.	Eat together	YES	NO
e.	Sing together	YES	NO
f.	Share their problems	YES	NO
g.	Work on projects	YES	NO
h.	Discuss social/political issues	YES	NO
i.	Do things for the community	YES	NO
j	Have parties	YES	NO
k.	Provide emotional support	YES	NO
l.	Follow a 12-step program	YES	NO
m.	Focus on addictions	YES	NO
n.	Practice speaking in tongues	YES	NO
o.	Focus on a specific need/problem	YES	NO
p.	Hold members accountable	YES	NO
q.	Celebrate communion	YES	NO
r.	Discuss Reformed theology	YES	NO
s.	Confess sin to one another	YES	NO

Q-21: *As a result of being in this group,* which of these, if any, have you experienced?

a.	answers to prayers	YES	NO
b.	healing of relationships	YES	NO
c.	new love toward others	YES	NO

d. feeling closer to God	YES	NO
e. less time spent with people outside your group	YES	NO
f. conflict with people in your group	YES	NO
g. more understanding of persons with different religious beliefs	YES	NO
h. more open and honest with yourself	YES	NO
i. more open and honest with others	YES	NO
j. feeling better about yourself	YES	NO
k. Bible has become more meaningful to you	YES	NO
l. receive God's forgiveness	YES	NO
m. better able to forgive others	YES	NO
n. better able to forgive yourself	YES	NO
o. has helped you share your faith with others outside the group	YES	NO
p. has helped you serve people outside the group	YES	NO
q. has given you a new understanding of Reformed theology	YES	NO

Q-22: As a result of being in this group, have you done any of the following?

a. become involved in volunteer work in your community	YES	NO
b. become more active in church programs	YES	NO
c. worked with the group to help people in need outside the group	YES	NO
d. worked with the group to help someone in need inside the group	YES	NO
e. become more interested in social and political issues	YES	NO
f. changed your attitude on any social or political issues	YES	NO

g. become more interested in peace or
social justice   YES   NO

h. donated money to another charitable
organization   YES   NO

i. increased the amount of money you give
to your church   YES   NO

j. worked with your congregation to help
people in need outside the church   YES   NO

Q-23: Would you participate in a follow-up phone
interview (45 minutes)?   YES   NO

Q-24: Would you like to receive a written summary
of this research?   YES   NO

APPENDIX B

Mainline Evangelicals in the Reformed Tradition

Of the six congregations studied for this project, four belong to the Presbyterian Church (USA), and two belong to the Reformed Church in America (RCA). These six congregations do not fit neatly into any of the common sociological categories used to depict congregations: fundamentalist, evangelical, mainline, liberal, independent, and so forth. Rather, it suggests the possible existence of another niche of congregations: mainline evangelicals. These congregations are embedded within a mainline denomination yet simultaneously differentiated from it by the subidentity "evangelical." In fact, these six congregations might best be described as "Reformed mainline evangelicals."

Niche congregations emerge in response to a changing religious ecology. In recent decades, mainline Protestant congregations have declined, while evangelical congregations have multiplied. Nancy Ammerman, professor of sociology of religion at Boston University, explains these changes from the perspective of institutional ecology:

> [N]ew life forms are constantly emerging, as old ones fade from the scene. As the resources of the environment change, some species find they already have the adaptive mechanisms needed for survival. Others evolve new ways of gathering resources, and still others whose habitat needs are not met by the new environment must move or face extinction.[1]

---

1. Nancy Ammerman, *Congregation and Community* (New Brunswick, NJ: Rutgers University Press, 1997), p. 346.

227

Robert Wuthnow's study of Presbyterianism demonstrates the impact of this changing religious ecology on PCUSA congregations. PCUSA congregations increasingly self-identify as "evangelical," "liberal," or "moderate." While North American Presbyterianism has been restructured throughout its existence — for example, New Side "revivalists" versus Old Side "ecclesiasticals" in the nineteenth century and modernists versus fundamentalists in the early twentieth century — Presbyterian congregations have increasingly identified over against each other as either liberal or conservative (evangelical) since the 1960s.[2] While this may be true, Ammerman points out that congregations *and* their members cannot easily be sorted into two polarized, vitriolic camps — liberal (or mainline) versus evangelical. In fact, the six congregations studied for this project suggest that "mainline" and "evangelical" may be combined to form a new identity distinct from both strict mainliners and strict evangelicals. Consider the following observations:

(1) Pastors at all four Presbyterian congregations distinguished themselves from "non-mainline evangelicals," including Southern Baptists and Pentecostals. They also interpret evangelicalism as somewhat ambiguous. Pastors at the two Reformed Church of America congregations identify themselves somewhat differently due to the overall more conservative stance of their denomination as well as the unique demographics tied to geography. They distinguish themselves, on the one hand, from Northeastern liberal RCA congregations and, on the other hand, from West Coast conservative RCA congregations. However, pastors in all six congregations acknowledge dissatisfaction with, if not dissent from, denominational structures and hierarchy.

(2) Like evangelicals in general, members and leaders in all six congregations affiliate with "special-interest groups," especially congregational renewal groups. Church members and leaders from all six congregations participate in similar three-day retreat programs — Walk to Emmaus, Tres Dias, Great Banquet — aimed at equipping laity for theologically grounded leadership in their respective congregations. Two of the Presbyterian congregations affiliate with "struggle groups," such as Presbyterians for Renewal.

2. See Robert Wuthnow, *The Restructuring of American Mainline Religion* (Princeton: Princeton University Press, 1988); see also Wuthnow, "The Restructuring of American Presbyterianism: Turmoil in One Denomination," in *The Presbyterian Predicament: Six Perspectives,* ed. Milton J. Coalter, John M. Mulder, and Louis B. Weeks (Louisville: Westminster John Knox, 1990).

(3) The evangelical bent of all six congregations predisposes them to develop small groups. Wuthnow's research demonstrates that members of more conservative denominations or congregations are more likely to participate in small groups than those of liberal denominations. Of the members of church-based small groups, 41 percent self-identify as conservative, 39 percent as moderate, and 18 percent as liberal.[3] Similarly, George Barna's *State of the Church 2002* report revealed that twice as many evangelicals participate in small groups as do mainline Protestants.[4]

(4) Pastors in all six congregations referred to weaknesses of evangelical thought and certain incompatibilities with the Reformed tradition. On the basis of my interviews with them, my reading of Karl Barth's ecclesiology, and an unpublished lecture presented by George Hunsinger at Princeton Theological Seminary, I was able to discern a tentative theological description of "Reformed mainline evangelicals" emerging. In contrast to evangelicals at large, this niche (if it exists) seems to emphasize more social action (if only slightly), more theological rigor, and more ecclesial connectionalism than is true of independent evangelicals. These six congregations tend to reject the doctrines of scriptural inerrancy and premillennialism, which are common among evangelicals. More than liberal Presbyterian and Reformed churches, they emphasize the importance of sanctification, personal conversion to Christ, and the authority of Scripture. Perhaps Reformed mainline evangelicals would embrace the following theological commitments: (1) confession and conversion as two dynamics of Christian awakening, with priority given to confession; (2) evangelism and social action as two sides of mission; (3) differentiation among the incarnate Word of God, the written Word of God, and the preached Word of God, whereby the written Word of God is the rule of faith and life, which shapes the preached Word and is itself reformed by the incarnate Word; and, (4) the precedence and priority of the *ecclesia* over the individual believer.

Certainly, further research is needed to support the existence of "Reformed mainline evangelical" and, more broadly, "mainline evangeli-

---

3. Robert Wuthnow, *I Come Away Stronger: How Small Groups Are Shaping American Religion* (Grand Rapids: Eerdmans, 1994), p. 376.

4. George Barna, *The State of the Church 2002* (Ventura, CA: Issachar Resources, 2002), p. 31.

cal" congregations as a significant slice of North American Protestantism. The identity and mission of these six congregations and their small-group practice, however, do pose a number of questions for further investigation: Are mainline evangelical congregations formed in response to the changing religious ecology? To what degree does the practice of this niche embody aspects of the Reformed and evangelical traditions? What practices and theological commitments distinguish mainline evangelicals not only from other congregations in their respective denominations but also from nondenominational evangelicals? Do small groups within this niche serve purposes distinct from those embedded in either mainline Protestants or evangelical congregations?

Bibliography

Ammerman, Nancy T. *Congregation and Community.* New Brunswick, NJ: Rutgers University Press, 1997.

Anderson, Ray S. *On Being Human: Essays in Theological Anthropology.* Pasadena, CA: Fuller Seminary Press, 1982.

———. *The Shape of Practical Theology: Empowering Ministry with Theological Praxis.* Downers Grove, IL: InterVarsity Press, 2001.

Arnold, Jeff. *The Big Book on Small Groups.* Rev. ed. Downers Grove, IL: InterVarsity Press, 2004.

Augsburger, David. *Caring Enough to Confront.* 3rd ed. Ventura, CA: Regal Books, 2009.

Augustine, Saint. *Confessions.* Translated by R. S. Pine-Coffin. London and New York: Penguin Books, 1961.

Ballard, Paul, and John Pritchard. *Practical Theology in Action: Christian Thinking in the Service of Church and Society.* London: SPCK, 1996.

Barna, George. *The State of the Church 2002.* Ventura, CA: Issachar Resources, 2002.

Barth, Karl. *Church Dogmatics.* 4 volumes in 13 parts. Edited by G. W. Bromiley and T. F. Torrance. Translated by G. W. Bromiley. Edinburgh: T. & T. Clark, 1956-1975.

———. "The Church: The Living Congregation of the Living Lord Jesus Christ." In *Barth: God Here and Now.* Translated by Paul M. van Buren. London and New York: Routledge, 2003.

———. *Evangelical Theology: An Introduction.* Grand Rapids: Eerdmans, 1963.

Bass, Dorothy, and Miroslav Volf. *Practicing Theology: Beliefs and Practices in Christian Life.* Grand Rapids: Eerdmans, 2002.

Bellah, Robert N., Richard Madsen, William M. Sullivan, Ann Swidler, and Steven M. Tipton. *Habits of the Heart: Individualism and Commitment in American Life.* Updated ed. Berkeley: University of California Press, 1996.

Bibliography

Bender, Kimlyn. "The Living Congregation of the Living Lord Jesus Christ: Karl Barth's Christological Ecclesiology." PhD diss., Princeton Theological Seminary, 2002.

Berry, Wendell. *The Unsettling of America: Culture and Agriculture.* 2nd ed. Berkeley: University of California Press, 1986.

————. *Fidelity: Five Stories.* New York and San Francisco: Pantheon, 1992.

————. *Sex, Economy, Freedom and Community: Eight Essays.* New York and San Francisco: Pantheon, 1993.

————. *Jayber Crow.* Washington, DC: Counterpoint, 2000.

Billings, J. Todd. "The Problem with Mere Christianity." *Christianity Today* (February 2007): 46-47.

Blackaby, Henry. *Experiencing God: Knowing and Doing God's Will.* Nashville: Lifeway Press, 1990.

Bonhoeffer, Dietrich. *Life Together.* San Francisco: Harper and Row, 1954.

Book of Order: Constitution of the Presbyterian Church (USA), Part II. Louisville: Presbyterian Church (USA), 2007.

Branson, Mark Lau. *Memories, Hopes, Conversations: Appreciative Inquiry and Congregational Change.* Herndon, VA: Alban Institute, 2004.

Browning, Don S. *From Culture Wars to Common Ground: Religion and the American Family Debate.* Louisville: Westminster John Knox, 1997.

————. *A Fundamental Practical Theology: Descriptive and Strategic Proposals.* Minneapolis: Fortress Press, 1991.

————. *Marriage and Modernization: How Globalization Threatens Marriage and What to Do About It.* Grand Rapids: Eerdmans, 2003.

————, ed. *Practical Theology: International Perspectives.* New York: Peter Lang, 1999.

Browning, Don S., and Terry Cooper. *Religious Thought and Modern Psychologies: A Critical Conversation in the Theology of Culture.* 2nd ed. Minneapolis: Fortress Press, 2004.

Buechner, Frederick. *Telling Secrets: A Memoir.* New York: HarperCollins, 1991.

Butin, Phil. "Two Early Reformed Catechisms, the Threefold Office, and the Shape of Karl Barth's Ecclesiology." *Scottish Journal of Theology* 44 (1991): 195-214.

Calvin, John. *Institutes of the Christian Religion.* Edited by John T. McNeill. Translated by Ford Lewis Battles. Philadelphia: Westminster Press, 1960.

Chaves, Mark. *Congregations in America.* Cambridge, MA: Harvard University Press, 2004.

————. *National Congregations Study: Data File and Codebook.* Tucson: University of Arizona, Department of Sociology, 1998.

Colledge, Edmund, James Walsh, and Jean Leclercq. *Julian of Norwich: Showings.* Classics of Western Spirituality. Mahwah, NJ: Paulist Press, 1978.

Collins, Jim. *Good to Great: Why Some Companies Make the Leap . . . and Others Don't.* San Francisco: Harper Business, 2001.

Constitutions, Bylaws and Continuing Resolutions of the Evangelical Lutheran Church in America. Minneapolis: Augsburg Fortress Press, 2008.

Bibliography

Creswell, John W. *Research Design: Qualitative, Quantitative, and Mixed Methods Approaches.* 2nd ed. Thousand Oaks, CA: Sage Publications, 2003.

Dean, Kenda Creasy. *Practicing Passion: Youth and the Quest for a Passionate Church.* Grand Rapids: Eerdmans, 2004.

Donahue, Bill, and Russ Robinson. *Walking the Tightrope: Meeting the Challenges Every Small Group Faces.* Grand Rapids: Zondervan, 2003.

Dykstra, Craig. "Reconceiving Practice." In *Shifting Boundaries: Contextual Approaches to the Structure of Theological Education,* edited by Barbara Wheeler and Edward Farley, pp. 35-66. Louisville: Westminster John Knox Press, 1991.

Emerson, Michael, and Christian Smith. *Divided by Faith: Evangelical Religion and the Problem of Race in America.* New York and Oxford: Oxford University Press, 2000.

Esbjornson, Carl D. "Does Community Have a Value? — A Reply." In *Rooted in the Land: Essays on Community and Place,* edited by William Vitek and Wes Jackson, pp. 85-94. New Haven and London: Yale University Press, 1996.

Forrester, Duncan. *Truthful Action: Explorations in Practical Theology.* Edinburgh: T. & T. Clark, 2000.

Fortune, Marie. "Confidentiality and Mandatory Reporting: A Clergy Dilemma?" http://www.faithtrustinstitute.org/downloads/confidentiality_and_mandatory _reporting.pdf (accessed August 3, 2005).

Gerkin, Charles. *An Introduction to Pastoral Care.* Nashville: Abingdon, 1997.

Giddens, Anthony. *The Constitution of Society.* Berkeley: University of California Press, 1986.

———. *Modernity and Self-Identity: Self and Society in the Late Modern Age.* Stanford: Stanford University Press, 1991.

———. *The Consequences of Modernity.* Stanford: Stanford University Press, 1992.

———. *The Transformation of Intimacy: Sexuality, Love and Eroticism in Modern Societies.* Stanford: Stanford University Press, 1992.

———. *Runaway World: How Globalization Is Reshaping Our Lives.* New York: Routledge, 1999.

Gorman, Julie. *Community That Is Christian.* 2nd ed. Grand Rapids: Baker Books, 2002.

Greenberg, Jay R., and Stephen A. Mitchell. *Object Relations in Psychoanalytic Theory.* Cambridge, MA: Harvard University Press, 1983.

Groome, Thomas. "Theology on Our Feet." In *Formation and Reflection: The Promise of Practical Theology,* edited by Lewis Mudge and James Poling, pp. 55-78. Minneapolis: Augsburg Fortress, 2000.

Guntrip, Harry. *Psychoanalytic Theory, Therapy and the Self.* New York: Basic Books, 1971.

Heitink, Gerben. *Practical Theology: History, Theory, Action Domains.* Grand Rapids: Eerdmans, 1999.

Hunsinger, Deborah van Deusen. "Practicing *Koinonia.*" *Theology Today* 66, no. 3 (October 2009): 346-67.

————. *Theology and Pastoral Counseling: A New Interdisciplinary Approach.* Grand Rapids: Eerdmans, 1995.

————. *Pray Without Ceasing: Revitalizing Pastoral Care.* Grand Rapids: Eerdmans, 2006.

Hunsinger, George. *Disruptive Grace: Studies in the Theology of Karl Barth.* Grand Rapids: Eerdmans, 2000.

————. *The Eucharist and Ecumenism: Let Us Keep the Feast.* Cambridge: Cambridge University Press, 2008.

————. *How to Read Karl Barth: The Shape of His Theology.* New York: Oxford University Press, 1991.

————. "A Tale of Two Simultaneities." In *Conversing with Barth,* edited by John McDowell and Mike Highton, pp. 68-89. Aldershot, UK: Ashgate, 2004.

Johnson, William Stacy. *The Mystery of God: Karl Barth and the Postmodern Foundations of Theology.* Louisville: Westminster John Knox, 1997.

Kaspersen, Lars Bo. *Anthony Giddens: An Introduction to a Social Theorist.* Translated by Steven Sampson. Oxford: Blackwell Publishers, 2000.

Katz, Alfred H., and Eugene I. Bender, eds. *The Strength in Us: Self-Help Groups in the Modern World.* New York: Franklin Watts, 1976.

Kierkegaard, Søren. *The Concept of Anxiety.* Edited and translated by Reidar Thomte and Albert B. Anderson. Princeton: Princeton University Press, 1980.

Kirkpatrick, Thomas. *Small Groups in the Church: A Handbook for Creating Community.* Herndon, VA: Alban Institute, 2005.

Krueger, Richard A., and Mary Anne Casey. *Focus Groups: A Practical Guide for Applied Research.* 3rd ed. Thousand Oaks, CA: Sage Publications, 2000.

Laing, R. D. *The Divided Self: An Existential Study in Sanity and Madness.* Baltimore: Penguin, 1965.

Lake, Frank. *Clinical Theology.* London: Darton, Longman, and Todd, 1966.

Latini, Theresa F. "Grief-Work in Light of the Cross: Illustrating Transformational Interdisciplinarity." *Journal of Psychology and Theology* 36, no. 2 (Summer 2009): 87-95.

————. "Nonviolent Communication: A Humanizing Educational and Ecclesial Practice." *Journal of Education and Christian Belief* 13, no. 1 (2009): 19-31.

————. "Nonviolent Communication and the Image of God." *Perspectives: A Journal of Reformed Thought* (May 2007): 10-17.

Lawrence, Brother. *The Practice of the Presence of God.* New Kensington, PA: Whitaker House, 1982.

Loder, James E. "Educational Ministry in the Logic of the Spirit." Unpublished manuscript.

————. *Logic of the Spirit: Human Development in Theological Perspective.* San Francisco: Jossey-Bass, 1998.

————. "Normativity and Context in Practical Theology." In *Practical Theology: International Perspectives,* edited by Friedrich Schweitzer and Johannes van der Ven, pp. 359-82. New York: Peter Lang, 1999.

————. *Religious Pathology and Christian Faith.* Philadelphia: Westminster Press, 1966.

Bibliography

—————. *The Transforming Moment: Understanding Convictional Experiences.* San Francisco: Harper and Row, 1981.

Loder, James E., and Jim Neidhardt. *The Knight's Move: Relational Logic of the Spirit in Theology and Science.* Colorado Springs, CO: Helmers and Howard, 1992.

McDonald, Glenn. *The Disciple-Making Church: From Dry Bones to Spiritual Vitality.* Grand Haven, MI: Faith Walk Publishers, 2004.

McIntyre, Alasdair. *After Virtue: A Study in Moral Theory.* Nortre Dame, IN: University of Notre Dame Press, 1984.

McKinney, William, and Wade Clark Roof. *American Mainline Religion: Its Changing Shape and Future.* New Brunswick, NJ: Rutgers University Press, 1987.

Meyer, Richard. *One Anothering.* Philadelphia: Innisfree Press, 1999.

Miller, Keith. *Hunger for Healing: The Twelve Steps as a Classic Model for Christian Spiritual Growth.* San Francisco: Harper, 1991.

Minnick, Anne Marie. *Twelve Step Programs: A Contemporary American Quest for Meaning and Spiritual Renewal.* Westport, CT: Praeger, 1997.

Morris, Bill. *Complete Handbook for Recovery Ministry in the Church: A Practical Guide to Establishing Recovery Support Groups within Your Church.* Nashville: Oliver Nelson, 1993.

Murphy, Nancey, and George F. R. Ellis. *On the Moral Nature of the Universe: Theology, Cosmology, and Ethics.* Minneapolis: Fortress Press, 1996.

Napier, Rodney W., and Matty K. Gershenfeld. *Groups: Theory and Experience.* 4th ed. Boston: Houghton Mifflin, 1992.

Nelson, James B. *Thirst: God and the Alcoholic Experience.* Louisville: Westminster John Knox, 2004.

Osmer, Richard R. *Confirmation: Presbyterian Practices in Ecumenical Perspective.* Louisville: Geneva Press, 1996.

—————. *The Teaching Ministry of Congregations.* Louisville: Westminster John Knox, 2005.

—————. *Practical Theology: An Introduction.* Grand Rapids: Eerdmans, 2008.

Osmer, Richard R., and Friedrich Schweitzer. *Religious Education Between Modernization and Globalization.* Grand Rapids: Eerdmans, 2004.

Ott, E. Stanley. *Small Group Life: A Guide for Members and Leaders.* Pittsburgh: Vital Faith Resources, 1994.

—————. *Transform Your Church with Ministry Teams.* Grand Rapids: Eerdmans, 2005.

—————. *Twelve Dynamic Shifts for Transforming Your Church.* Grand Rapids: Eerdmans, 2002.

—————. *The Vibrant Church.* Ventura, CA: Regal, 1989.

Patton, Michael. *Qualitative Research & Evaluation Methods.* 3rd ed. Thousand Oaks, CA: Sage Publications, 2002.

Poling, James N., and Donald E. Miller. *Foundations for a Practical Theology of Ministry.* Nashville: Abingdon Press, 1985.

Price, Daniel J. *Karl Barth's Anthropology in Light of Modern Thought.* Grand Rapids: Eerdmans, 2002.

Purves, Andrew. *Reconstructing Pastoral Theology: A Christological Foundation.* Louisville: Westminster John Knox, 2004.

———. "The Trinitarian Basis for Practical Theology." *International Journal of Practical Theology* 2, no. 2 (1998): 224-39.

Putnam, Robert. *Bowling Alone: The Collapse and Revival of American Community.* New York: Simon and Schuster, 2000.

Putnam, Robert, and Lewis Feldstein. *Better Together: Restoring the American Community.* New York, London, Toronto, Sydney: Simon and Schuster, 2003.

Root, Andrew. *Revisiting Relational Youth Ministry: From a Strategy of Influence to a Theology of Incarnation.* Downers Grove, IL: InterVarsity Press, 2007.

Rosenberg, Marshall. *Nonviolent Communication: A Language for Life.* Encinitas, CA: Puddle Dancer Press, 2003.

Sartre, Jean Paul. *Being and Nothingness: An Essay on Phenomenological Ontology.* 2nd ed. New York: Routledge, 2003.

Schleiermacher, Friedrich. *Brief Outline of Theology as a Field of Study.* Translated by Terrence Tice. Lewiston, NY: The Edwin Mellen Press, 1990.

Selby, Saul. *Twelve Step Christianity: The Christian Roots and Application of the Twelve Steps.* Center City, MN: Hazelden, 2000.

Smith, Christian, with Michael Emerson. *American Evangelicalism: Embittered and Thriving.* Chicago: University of Chicago Press, 1998.

Smith, Christian, and Melinda Lundquist Denton. *Soul Searching: The Religious and Spiritual Lives of American Teenagers.* Reprint ed. New York: Oxford University Press, 2009.

Tall, Deborah. "Dwelling: Making Peace with Space and Place." In *Rooted in the Land: Essays on Community and Place,* edited by William Vitek and Wes Jackson, pp. 104-12. New Haven and London: Yale University Press, 1996.

Taylor, Charles. *Sources of the Self: The Making of Modern Identity.* Cambridge, MA: Harvard University Press, 1989.

Thompson, David L. *Holiness for Hurting People: Discipleship as Recovery.* Indianapolis: Wesleyan Publishing House, 1998.

Van der Ven, Johannes. *Practical Theology: An Empirical Approach.* Kampen, Netherlands: Kok Pharos, 1993.

Volf, Miroslav. *After Our Likeness: The Church as the Image of the Trinity.* Grand Rapids: Eerdmans, 1998.

Warren, Rick. *Better Together: What on Earth Are We Here For?* Lake Forest, CA: Purpose Driven Publishing, 2004.

———. *Better Together: 40 Days of Community.* Lake Forest, CA: Purpose Driven Publishing, 2004.

Winnicott, Clare, Ray Shepherd, and Madeleine Davis, eds. *Deprivation and Delinquency: D. W. Winnicott.* London: Tavistock, 1984.

Winnicott, D. W. *Collected Papers: Through Paediatrics to Psycho-Analysis.* New York: Basic Books, 1958.

———. *Home Is Where We Start From: Essays by a Psychoanalyst.* New York: W. W. Norton, 1986.

————. *Maturational Processes and the Facilitating Environment: Studies in the Theory of Emotional Development.* London: Hogarth Press, 1965.

————. *Playing and Reality.* London: Tavistock/Routledge, 1971.

Wuthnow, Robert. *The Restructuring of American Mainline Religion.* Princeton: Princeton University Press, 1988.

————. "The Restructuring of American Presbyterianism: Turmoil in One Denomination." In *The Presbyterian Predicament: Six Perspectives,* edited by Milton J. Coalter, John M. Mulder, Louis B. Weeks, pp. 27-48. Louisville: Westminster John Knox Press, 1990.

————. *I Come Away Stronger: How Small Groups Are Shaping American Religion.* Grand Rapids: Eerdmans, 1994.

————. *Sharing the Journey: Support Groups and America's New Quest for Community.* New York: The Free Press, 1994.

Yocum, John. *Ecclesial Mediation in Karl Barth.* Aldershot, UK: Ashgate, 2004.

Zizioulas, John D. *Being as Communion.* Crestwood, NY: St. Vladimir's Theological Seminary Press, 1993.

Index